Einstein taking the oath of American citizenship in the Federal District Court in Trenton, New Jersey, in 1940 with Helen Dukas, his secretary (left), and his stepdaughter, Margot Einstein. (National Archives.)

THE MUSES FLEE HITLER

Cultural Transfer and Adaptation 1930-1945

Edited by
JARRELL C. JACKMAN
and
CARLA M. BORDEN

Smithsonian Institution Press
Washington, D.C.
1983

Library of Congress Cataloging in Publication Data
Main entry under title:
The Muses flee Hitler.
  Bibliography: p.
  Includes index.
  Supt. of Docs. no.: SI 1.2:M97/5
  1. Germans—Foreign countries—History—20th century—Congresses.
  2. Germany—Emigration and immigration—History—1933–1945—Congresses.
  3. Refugees, Political—Germany—History—20th century—Congresses.
  4. Acculturation—Congresses. I. Jackman, Jarrell C. II. Borden, Carla M.
DD68.M85 1983   304.8′0943   82-600357
ISBN 0-87474-554-3
ISBN 0-87474-555-1 (pbk.)

This book is dedicated to Renée Jackman

and Herbert and Yetta Borden

Contents

Foreword

On the eve of World War I, Sir Edward Grey,* a great hero of mine, wrote: "The lamps are going out all over Europe; we shall not see them lit again in our lifetime." Twenty years later, his image would be tragically apropos again, and I would reflect on it as a seventeen-year-old preparing a speech for school on the rise of the Nazi movement and the danger it posed to us in this country. It seems strange now to think back to those days, when I and my roommate, whose great-grandfather had been a refugee from Germany in 1848, were almost alone in our class in feeling deep concern about the impending crisis abroad.

In this volume, an inquiry into the extraordinary transfer and adaptation of artists and intellectuals from Hitler's Europe to various regions of the world, particularly the United States, the essayists and editors are asking where the "lamps" turned on again and under what conditions. What did this diaspora of savants mean to the receiving countries? How were the fruits of their intellects affected by being planted in new soil? How did they succeed or fail in establishing new niches for themselves in new geographical and human environments? How would the world later profit fom the rescue and nurturing of such talent?

*later Viscount Grey of Fallodon

Albert Einstein—whose name remains the one we most identify with the 1930–45 exodus from Europe and whose one hundredth birthday inspired "The Muses Flee Hitler"—exemplified the minds that could not be controlled, repressed, or destroyed by forces of tyranny then unleashed. As Erik Erikson observed, Einstein was the victorious child who never lost his sense of wonder. The intellectual dowry he brought to Princeton continued to grow in the new environment; the whole world became his beneficiary, his role in the development of the atomic bomb notwithstanding.

It is the function of the intelligentsia to see further than others, further backward in time and into the future, and to help others form a world view based partly on what their intellectual radar, so to speak, has picked up. The American world view is still evolving, but our appreciation of the value of intellectual perceptions from art to science and the development of our social consciousness were dramatically influenced by those who came here in the 1930s and 1940s. Thomas Jefferson helped set our republic on the path of cosmopolitan openness to new ideas and techniques in the eighteenth century. He was building, at the same time, the "native" institutions that could embody and transmit them to later generations. I can imagine his delight at the company he might have kept at the White House or Monticello if his public career had been pursued in the twentieth century.

However, we must not confuse Jefferson's open-mindedness and hospitality with the American norm, then or later, or assume that the rest of the world would follow in his footsteps. As is persuasively documented in these pages, not all refugees were admitted here or greeted warmly. Some countries shut their doors altogether. Others that accepted refugees from Nazism were less receptive than the United States, for a variety of reasons, and not comparably influenced. What fertilization and enrichment we can claim as a result of this migration, and what we offered those urgently in need of asylum, cannot offset the scope of upheaval, persecution, and mass destruction perpetrated by the Third Reich that triggered the movement of people and ideas.

As new forms of brutality and tyranny darken more lamps in the world, the United States continues to be challenged by Emma Lazarus's words at the base of the Statue of Liberty. Refugees including Mexicans, Vietnamese, Cubans, Koreans, Israelis, Ethiopians, Chinese, and Haitians have arrived here since the 1940s, with their knowledge and skills, because of immigration policy that grew out of the World

10

S. DILLON RIPLEY

War II experience. We should be mindful that newcomers need not be Einsteins to make a contribution, that cultural migration and adaptation today can be better understood by the history of earlier "waves." And, as we talk of great men and women, of "the muses," let us remember the others from whose ranks they came.

S. DILLON RIPLEY
Secretary
Smithsonian Institution

Acknowledgments

First and foremost, we wish to express our gratitude to those whose interest and financial support enabled us to plan "The Muses Flee Hitler" colloquia and see this volume through to publication: the Rockefeller Foundation, the Joseph H. Hazen Foundation, and the Smithsonian Institution's Educational Outreach Project. We are also particularly thankful for the generosity of the Embassy of the Federal Republic of Germany, through Dr. Haide Russell, cultural counselor.

Projects of this scope hinge upon contributions in imagination, energy, and expertise from numerous individuals working in concert. With the program under the overall direction of Carla Borden, Cynthia Jaffee McCabe, and Nathan Reingold, the following brought noteworthy dedication and much pleasure to the enterprise:

THE OFFICE OF SMITHSONIAN SYMPOSIA AND SEMINARS: Wilton S. Dillon, director, master catalyst and metteur-en-scène; Barrick W. Groom, consultant, invaluable sounding board and font of felicitous ideas; Helen F. Leavitt, assistant; and Ilo-Mai Lipping, whose presence and abilities were an extraordinary boon to us all.

THE JOSEPH HENRY PAPERS: Arthur P. Molella, then associate editor, ever a source of vigor and humor; and Beverly Jo Lepley, research

13

assistant, who managed many administrative matters with great care and skill.

Carol Parsons of the Hirshhorn Museum and Sculpture Garden and Sarah Lowe, volunteer; the Office of Special Events, especially Susan Werner; Carole Rader Taylor, then of the Office of Membership and Development; and the late Janet B. Stratton, designer and friend. In addition, the experts in the fields covered who let us pick their brains, organizations such as the Leo Baeck Institute that opened their doors and archives to essayists wishing to conduct research, the journalists who publicized the program, and the audience whose concern and knowledge allowed for such rich dialogue—all have earned our genuine appreciation.

Our gratitude also goes to Michele Jackman for her unfailing support and perseverance, to Harold Kirker for his sage advice, to Adrienne Ash for the endless hours spent tracking down photographs, and to Carol Pfeil for typing the manuscript with great meticulousness and good humor. From the Smithsonian Institution Press, Bradley Rymph and Stephen Kraft demonstrated exceptional patience and diligence, as well as creativity and taste, in bringing this book to its final form.

14

Introduction

JARRELL C. JACKMAN

In 1980 the Smithsonian Institution, as part of its observance of the one hundredth birthday of Albert Einstein, convened two colloquia on the mass exodus of intellectuals from Europe during the Nazi period. Organized by Nathan Reingold, editor of the Joseph Henry Papers, and Cynthia Jaffee McCabe, curator at the Hirshhorn Museum, in cooperation with the Office of Smithsonian Symposia and Seminars, the colloquia provided an opportunity for scholars from different disciplines to present papers and exchange ideas on subjects ranging from the origins of Nazism to the émigrés' flight from Europe and their reception in and influence on their host countries. Most of the papers delivered appear in this volume, which follows closely the format of the two colloquia (see Appendix); those essays not included will at least be referred to in the following remarks.

Since the end of World War II, an enormous amount of published and unpublished primary material has been collected in libraries and archives in this country and Europe, and lists of names of thousands of refugee artists and scientists have been compiled by American and German research foundations and institutions. A great number of scholarly works on the migration have also been written, though most of these writings have been published in German by German academics specializing in *Exilforschung*. Of those works published   15 in English, the two most important have been Laura Fermi's *Illustrious Immigrants* (1968; revised edition, 1971) and *The Intellectual Migration: Europe and America, 1933–1960* (1969), edited by Donald Fleming and Bernard Bailyn. Incorporating new research and archival material unavailable ten years ago, this volume complements those two earlier efforts while going one step further to examine the migration to other countries besides the United States.

No one would deny that a significant transfer of knowledge and talent resulted from the refugees' flight from Germany, Austria, Italy, Hungary, and other European countries during the Nazi period. What is less often appreciated is the fact that this transfer could succeed only if the host country was willing to allow it to do so and offered a suitable environment to nurture the refugees' skills and experience. The essays in this volume sadly illustrate that nowhere were unlimited numbers of fleeing intellectuals accepted, regardless of how gifted they each might have been. Furthermore, because some countries were more foreign to the émigrés than others, and some groups of émigrés less adaptable than others, host countries did not always benefit from the refugee talent, though they at least served as temporary havens until the war was over.

At the first colloquium, held in February 1980, the emphasis was on the origins of Nazism, the resultant persecution of the Jewish and non-Jewish intellectual class of Europe (mainly from Germany and Austria), its movement to the United States, and the reaction and adjustment of exiles and Americans to one another. Professor Alan Beyerchen began the colloquium by tracing Nazi racial attitudes and anti-intellectualism back to nineteenth-century German Romantics, who, he argued, had since the time of Napoleon perceived reason as a product of the French Enlightenment—not of the German spirit. He further identified signs of anti-Semitism in earlier *völkisch* ideas that would be embraced by Adolf Hitler and his followers. Fortunately, Beyerchen concluded, instead of incarcerating intellectuals the Nazis initially chose to drive them out of the country—in order to keep the German people free from racial and political contamination. Only later, when expulsion of the non-Aryans and political undesirables was no longer possible, did the Nazis resort to the "final solution."

16

In his comments as a panelist at the colloquium, Professor Fritz Ringer provided another perspective by attempting to explain the origins of Nazism as an outgrowth of the German Idealist tradition:

One of the advantages . . . of emphasizing the idealist rather than the romantic element is that it allows me to stress the discontinuity as well as the continuity between earlier and later versions of this tradition.

At first, Ringer felt, the idealist tradition represented an insurgent intellectual elite, "challenging the dominance of an aristocracy of birth" and "championing the claims of intellect—of merit." What led the neurotic potential to come to the surface, he went on, was

the very rapid, traumatic transformation of Germany from an early industrial society to a high or late industrial society, in which the notables of the educated upper middle class were displaced abruptly by the masses . . . and by the economic bourgeoisie; where politics changed from the politics of the notables to the politics of the masses and political machines, and where politics also changed—or so it seemed to the intellectuals—from the politics of principle to the politics of interest.

This situation, he added, provoked two kinds of reactions. On the one hand, there were those who wanted to discover what was essential in the idealist intellectual tradition so that it could be transplanted and adapted to a "more modern, more democratic environment." However, from the end of the nineteenth century into the Weimar period, the majority of Germans assumed a more negative position, becoming "hypernationalist," "racialist," and "right-wing." Jews who thus became associated with the democratic, universalist outlook found themselves increasingly in opposition to the dominant German tradition and, according to Ringer, were the ones who ended up in America, where their ideas found a more fertile environment.

As soon as Hitler was installed as chancellor in 1933, many Jews and non-Jews began emigrating, but as Professor Herbert Strauss indicated in his essay, not all the Nazi policies against Jews and political undesirables were perceived as uniform, with the result that other "intended victims" did not attempt to leave at once. Professor Strauss estimated that of the more than one million Jews persecuted by Nazi policies in Germany, Austria, and Czechoslovakia, at least five hundred thousand were eventually able to emigrate. To this number must be added those who fled from countries overrun by the Nazis and Italian Fascists. Among these refugees, whose successful escapes prevented their becoming victims of extermination camps, were some of the finest minds of the twentieth century.

Unfortunately, as Professor Roger Daniels's essay poignantly revealed, the United States, while accepting more refugees than any other country, did not swing its doors open to unlimited immigration—at a time when it was most needed. Dismayed by this fact, Professor Daniels argued at the colloquium that American immigration policy was inexcusable and no better than that of other countries, a point of view the reader may or may not agree with after reading of the courses of action taken by the nations discussed in this volume. By the turn of the nineteenth century, there were already many voices speaking out against the stream of European immigrants flooding America. Then at the end of World War I, in a mood of isolationism, Congress passed legislation restricting immigration. Professor Daniels demonstrated that it was not until after World War II—too late for the thousands who sought refuge but could not find a host country to receive them in the 1930s and 1940s—that legislation was enacted to assist refugees.

Since the American government was derelict in coming to the rescue of the European refugees, a number of private relief agencies were formed. One of them, the Emergency Rescue Committee, sent young Varian Fry to Marseilles to bring out the best and most talented among those stranded in the south of France. Fritz Ringer's reaction to the selection process described in Cynthia McCabe's essay was most compelling:

From among crowds of young intellectuals and artists gathered somewhere in Western Europe, somebody [Varian Fry] was sent to rescue the top two percent, or five percent, or whatever; the object was to pick the best ones. One gets the awful picture of somebody saying: "Bring me your folder of art, and if I think it's good, we can save your life."

There was something very distasteful about surviving under these circumstances, a fact reflected on by Bertolt Brecht, when he wrote the following poem in southern California:

I know of course: it's simply luck
That I've survived so many friends. But last night in a dream
I heard those friends say of me: "Survival of the fittest"
And I hated myself.

18

Of those who did make it to America, the despair expressed by Brecht was not uncommon—especially among the émigré writers. For the most part, this volume celebrates the adaptability of the émigrés and their contributions to American culture, but this should not disguise the immense suffering so many of them had to endure. They had departed their European homelands unsure if they would ever be able to return. Once here it was all too easy to become frustrated by the changes in their everyday lives. Often exile brought out what was most petty and futile in them: there was a great deal of backbiting, jealousy, and outright anger vented against Americans and fellow émigrés as they attempted to adapt to new lives in this country. The two largest exile communities developed in New York and Los Angeles, the latter attracting thousands of refugees, a number of whom were able to find jobs as writers and musicians in the Hollywood studios. Because these cities were decidedly different from their homelands, the émigrés often clung to their exile groups, even if they did not always get along with one another.

As Professor Helmut Pfanner pointed out at the Muses I colloquium, one of the cruelest aspects of exile in America was the loss of language. Previous generations of immigrants also had had to face the hostility of the native population to their arrival and the difficulties of learning English. But the linguistic plight of the refugees who spoke German was complicated by the strong anti-German feelings in the country during the Nazi period, feelings that became even more intense when America entered the war. At a cafe in Hollywood in 1942, for example, the émigrés Alfred Döblin and Ludwig Marcuse were told by the angry proprietor to stop speaking German or get out.

After overcoming the day-to-day problems of exile, certain preconditions, some of which are outlined by Professor H. Stuart Hughes in his essay, still had to exist if the émigré intellectual was to exert influence on his new environment. Employed along with a number of refugee social scientists at the newly formed Office of Strategic Services (OSS) in Washington, D.C., during World War II, Hughes engaged in conversations with refugees that he surmises would not have been possible in an academic setting. Hughes remembered discussions with émigrés "in the informal, frequently chaotic, and benignly tolerant atmosphere" of the OSS from which he and other young American scholars emerged "deprovincialized" and "less hypnotized by facts." But on the whole, the interaction between European and American social scientists was incomplete, Hughes concluded, in part because of a Teutonic unwillingness to open up to the American experience.

In his talk on "German Gestaltists in Behaviorist America," Professor Michael Sokal emphasized that one of the important factors in the initial reaction to émigré Gestaltists such as Kurt Lewin and Wolfgang Köhler was personality. Lewin was a gregarious, affable fellow immediately popular among students and colleagues in this country, while Köhler was more proper and stiff, putting off some American psychologists, especially Edwin G. Boring at Harvard. Still, as Sokal went on to say, the ideas of both Lewin and Köhler as well as a number of other German Gestaltists were well received. Sokal also demonstrated that the transatlantic transmission of Gestalt psychology had begun long before the Nazi era, with the first contacts made between Germans and Americans as early as 1910. Hitler's rise to power only hastened and completed the migration of Gestalt psychology to America. The same pattern of earlier exchanges setting the stage for acceptance of the exiles and their ideas was evident in other fields examined at the colloquium.

In the arts, the American response to the refugees was generally favorable, although the writers had a rather difficult time finding an audience for their works. Focusing on Thomas Mann and Hannah Arendt in his essay, Professor Alfred Kazin contrasted their "instinctive sense of history" with the American belief that "the future is as real as the present," which he felt explained why neither of them ever was really at home in exile. But Kazin added that it was not necessary for them to feel so, Mann because he was already a recognized international literary figure and Arendt because she was able to begin writing in English while still drawing upon her German philosophical training.

Most of the writers who ended up in Hollywood working as scriptwriters also felt alienated from their home in exile, but in his talk on the German presence in Hollywood, Professor Hans-Bernhard Moeller mentioned that many of them made lasting contributions to screenwriting. With a huge number of their unused scripts still buried in studio archives, he concluded that the full picture of their Hollywood experience awaits further research.

While the refugee writers' influence on America was rather limited, the émigré contribution to music, architecture, and art was well-nigh pervasive. The sheer numbers of composers, musicians, and musicologists who sought refuge in this country are almost overwhelming. Already under a strong European musical influence dating back to the nineteenth century, when Europeans began making concert tours to this country, America in the 1930s and 1940s became the home of the musical greats of the twentieth century, from Arturo Toscanini to Béla Bartók, Arnold Schoenberg, and Igor Stravinsky. It can even be argued that the arrival of the émigrés led to a further Europeanization of American music, a point alluded to in Professor Boris Schwarz's paper when he said, "The recently arrived [émigré] conductors showed little interest in furthering the cause of modern American music, to the distress of indigenous composers." A glance at the programs of orchestras around the United States today suggests that European composers still dominate American concert halls. Yet, even if the European presence hindered the development of native talent, this must be weighed against the upgrading of the performance of music that resulted from the migration.

One might also say that the arrival of Bauhaus architects Walter Gropius, Ludwig Mies van der Rohe, and Marcel Breuer led to the Europeanization of the American architectural landscape, while Bauhaus artists including Herbert Bayer and Josef Albers succeeded in transmitting their theories of art to the New World as well. Founded under Walter Gropius in Weimar after World War I, the Bauhaus, with its coterie of architects and artists, became a clearinghouse for modern art in Europe and a catalyst for the international style in architecture. According to Wolf von Eckardt, then architecture critic of the *Washington Post*, it also revolutionized the way art was taught by insisting that the individual "forget anything. . .ever learned before and any preconceived notions of what art is."

As Professor Christian Otto revealed in his essay on Mies and the American skyscraper, this country, with its love of the machine and technology, was an ideal place to implement Mies's architectural ideas. The Bauhaus architects' desire to free architectural style from the past and to erect buildings that reflected the needs of modern society seemed to belong in America, a country whose founding was in itself an act of escape from the past. Carrying antihistorical notions to the New World, the Bauhaus began afresh in Chicago under László Moholy-Nagy and Mies, at Harvard under Gropius, and at Black Mountain College in North Carolina under Albers.

The émigré artist Hans Hofmann, discussed at the colloquium by Cynthia Goodman, was another key figure in the migration. He became one of the most respected and popular teachers of art in America, helping to impart a full range of modernist ideas on painting to New York. In addition, he gave a series of lectures in 1938 and

1939 (attended by Arshile Gorky, Willem de Kooning, Jackson Pollock, Clement Greenberg, and Harold Rosenberg) that contributed to the development of abstract expressionism in this country.

What happened, through all of this, to the native-born talent? Certainly many young students were enriched and enlightened by the encounter with artists and architects from Europe. At the same time, a long tradition of American realism in painting was supplanted by European ideas and artists, while Frank Lloyd Wright felt neglected and expressed bitterness toward the dominance of the International Style in architecture. Recently, however, there has been a recrudescence of American realism in the work of painters such as Richard Estes, and American architecture seems to be returning to a stylistic eclecticism.

The preceding comments suggest how the presence of a whole generation of Nazi refugees in this country affected and altered American culture. In analyzing the interaction between refugee scientists and their American counterparts, it is important to note that by the 1930s American universities had already advanced far enough in almost every scientific discipline to rival the great European centers of learning. One major, perhaps *the* major, force behind that advancement both before and during Hitler's regime was the Rockefeller Foundation, which subsidized research through fellowships for Europeans and Americans and through the purchase of scientific instruments.

At the Muses I colloquium, Dr. Nathan Reingold and Professors Gerald Holton and P. Thomas Carroll described the processes by which European mathematicians, physicists, and chemists were able to resume their careers in this country. While many of them secured academic positions, they did not always have a painless and easy time of it. American mathematicians in some cases resisted the placement of émigrés because they believed that this would limit opportunities for their young colleagues. And anti-Semitism reared its ugly head all too often against mathematicians and chemists, compounding the hardship of adjusting to an academic life in which teaching was given greater prominence than research. Still, Professor Holton's paper on physicists in America, which focused mainly on Albert Einstein, demonstrated that America was prepared for the brain drain. From previous visits to the United States in the 1920s, Einstein had found to his liking that Americans were an optimistic and future-oriented people. When he finally decided to move permanently to the New World, his choice, Holton related, was based

22

not just on sentiment: for a person such as Einstein, and for émigré chemists and mathematicians, America quite simply had become the logical place to continue their work.

This same kind of logic did not apply to the rest of the world, as the Muses II colloquium revealed. Who would have guessed that Canada would be one of the countries to receive the fewest refugees or that Shanghai and Argentina would shelter so many more of them? That Britain, whose record of accepting refugees compares favorably with any other country, according to Professor Bernard Wasserstein, would, when the war broke out, in a mood of hysteria intern many innocent refugees and ship them to Canada and Australia? That Switzerland, as Professor Helmut Pfanner recounted, would escort certain Jewish émigrés who had entered the country illegally from Germany or Austria back to the frontier, whence they would probably be sent to concentration camps? It must be added, however, that thousands of refugee intellectuals did find permanent homes in Britain and Switzerland and enhance the cultural and scientific life of both countries. Less surprising was Professor David Pike's story of the German leftists who sought asylum in the Soviet Union only to suffer the same fate as millions of Russians who were either executed or shipped off to Siberia during the Stalin years.

While the Muses II colloquium did not attempt to deal with every nation throughout the world, a fair sample of the émigré experience in a number of countries was presented to provide a worldwide perspective of the intellectual migration during the 1930s and 1940s. One of the more depressing cases during the refugee crisis of the 1930s was that of Canada, which literally closed its doors to Jewish refugees. In several papers at both colloquia, the anti-Semitism the émigrés faced was cited as a nagging problem in many countries, but in Canada, as described by Professors Irving Abella and Harold Troper, it dominated the attitudes of men in high places, including Prime Minister Mackenzie King, and clearly affected the fate of thousands of refugees who were not permitted entry by the government. And as Paula Draper explained in her essay, the treatment of those refugees interned in Canada during the war was also distressing, though these émigrés remained undaunted, setting up their own schools in the camps and later, after their release, going on to successful careers in Canada.

23

The situation in Australia for the interned refugees was also trying, with the sheer distance of that faraway land taking its toll on some homesick émigrés. Professor Guy Stern's preliminary study nevertheless indicated that the European "muses" had a permanent and enriching influence on both Australia and New Zealand.

Such was hardly the case for most of Latin America. Dr. Judith Elkin's essay presented a vivid picture of the limited opportunities for refugee intellectuals in Cuba, Mexico, and Colombia, among other countries. Still mostly agrarian and not advanced enough to take advantage of the refugee talent, these countries either closed their borders or insisted that the refugees take up farming. A few academics did have an impact on the university systems in Cuba and Panama, but for the most part, unstable governments, unfriendly welcomes, and a meddling United States fearful of spies among the refugees severely limited the amount of intellectuals entering the circum-Caribbean during the whole period of the emigration.

In Brazil as well, the number of refugee intellectuals was very small, but those who were admitted were treated reasonably well, according to Professor Robert Levine. The two most famous refugees to seek asylum in Brazil were the French writer Georges Bernanos and the Austrian author Stefan Zweig, whose years in exile were discussed at the Muses II colloquium by Jean-Jacques Lafaye. Both men were impressed by Brazil as a boundless land of the future, but, as Lafaye concluded, neither ever really adjusted to Brazilian society. Zweig committed suicide there in 1942, and Bernanos moved on after the war to Tunisia, before returning to France where he died of "exhaustion."

The record of Latin America during the refugee crisis would have been even more dismal had it not been for the large number of Jewish and non-Jewish émigrés accepted in Argentina, a country that has had a long history of contact with Germany. In fact, as Professor Ronald Newton explained, Argentina became the home of the largest number of Jewish refugees on a per capita basis of any country except Palestine. Even so, the émigrés' impact on Argentine culture was rather minimal when compared, for example, with the refugees' contributions to the United States.

Similarly, the interaction between the large refugee population that found asylum in Shanghai and their Chinese hosts was negligible. Most of the émigrés were merely biding their time, waiting for Nazism to run its course—though in the meantime, as Renata Berg-Pan recounted, an active theater life and school system kept their intellectual and cultural traditions alive. In contrast, the small contingent of some one hundred émigré professors hired to teach at the University of Istanbul helped usher in modern European academic education in Turkey. Their presence and influence had been made possible by Kemal Atatürk's efforts to forge a new society out of the decay of the Ottoman Empire following World War I. In his talk on the German refugee scholars hired to teach in Istanbul and Ankara, Professor Mark Epstein said that in the 1930s and 1940s they held a majority of the chairs in the humanities as well as in the natural and social sciences. Epstein concluded that, though most of the professors eventually re-immigrated to the United States or returned to Austria or Germany, they had nevertheless helped to lay the foundations of Western-style life in Turkey.

My own interest in the intellectuals' flight from Nazism dates from 1965 when, after having read *The Caucasian Chalk Circle,* I discovered the play had been written by Bertolt Brecht during his Hollywood years just a few miles away from the campus of the University of California at Los Angeles, where I was then studying as an undergraduate. From that time to the present, a great deal of my life has been spent researching and writing about the history of the émigrés in southern California. I have agonized and fretted over the meaning of that history, searching all the while for the thread that ties it together. As a participant in the Muses I colloquium, I continued my search: I listened as my colleagues shed light on the political, social, cultural, and institutional factors that influenced the reception of the émigrés in the United States. I remember also discussions on "national character" and on the different attitudes of German and American scholars toward "specialization." But what I came away with was a strong feeling that the intellectual migration must above all else be perceived at its most personal level—that of the individual.

Because so many fled, there is the natural tendency to view the émigrés in terms of numbers and to make large generalizations. Yet when I think about the migration, what comes to mind are specific individuals and events: I think of the émigré opera singer Lotte Lehmann boldly telling Hermann Goering that she wanted nothing to do with Hitler's Germany, of Einstein at the moment he decided to immigrate to the United States, of the interned refugees in Canada 25 and Australia who refused to give up hope; I think of Professor Hughes meeting Herbert Marcuse and other refugee social scientists at the OSS, of the Jewish intellectuals forced to take up farming in the Dominican Republic, of Bernanos and Zweig stranded in Brazil, of the bitter Marxist Brecht writing screenplays for Hollywood. History cannot be reduced to biography, but we should never forget that the artists, architects, authors, and scientists who are the subjects of this volume were made of flesh and blood—were each individuals whose lives were permanently altered by historical events that proved to be beyond their control. It is, in the end, the courage they demonstrated in the face of Hitler's terror, as much as their status as intellectuals, that makes their story so profound.

BACKGROUND AND MIGRATION

Anti-Intellectualism and the Cultural Decapitation of Germany under the Nazis

ALAN BEYERCHEN

I Nothing captures the imagination better than a spectacle, and no political leaders in modern times have been more aware of this than the National Socialists, who came to power in Germany at the end of January 1933. The Nazis were masters at staging events that seized attention and stamped indelible impressions upon the minds of all who participated and observed: the mass arrests and ruthless suppression of political opposition that followed the fiery destruction of the Reichstag building in February 1933; the united march of hundreds of thousands of S.A. brownshirts, Stahlhelm veterans, Reichswehr soldiers, and S.S. blackshirts through the German capital in March 1933; and the awesome orchestration of crowds and symbols during the Nuremberg party rallies. The shattering brutality and sacrilege of *Kristallnacht* in November 1938 evoke yet another image of the Third Reich. All these were overshadowed by the ultimate spectacles of *Blitzkrieg*, the titanic struggle on the Eastern Front, and the implementation of the Final Solution, which are now etched into our collective consciousness.

For those who value cultural and intellectual achievement, one of the most appalling spectacles of the Third Reich was the way in which the Nazis drove from Germany scholars, scientists, artists, writers, composers, architects—creative persons in every field. It is

29

hardly necessary here to call the roll of the great and famous names or to attempt to fix with precision the startlingly high number of gifted refugees. By the end of the first two months following Adolf Hitler's arrival in power, hundreds of prominent literary and artistic figures were in exile. Many of these had enjoyed international recognition during the Weimar years and had been affiliated in some way with leftist or left-liberal portions of the political spectrum. The implementation of the Civil Service Law of April 7, 1933, also immediately forced well over a thousand scholars from their academic positions as either "politically unreliable" or "non-Aryan" undesirables. The process of defining "non-Aryan" was to take some time yet, with firm categories resulting finally from the Nuremberg Laws of 1935, but the introduction of the "Aryan paragraph" robbed many persons of Jewish or partially Jewish heritage of their livelihoods as early as 1933.[1]

Since these events took place in the midst of the Great Depression, it was remarkable that most of those expelled from their positions and cut off from their public in Germany were able to find refuge abroad. This fact was due, as is well known, more to the Herculean efforts of the private relief agencies that sprang up to meet the emergency than to governmental initiative in the adopted countries.[2]

Among the Germans who stayed behind were some who tried to help by signing petitions, pleading with Nazi officials, or sending information abroad concerning people in need of aid. One of these was Max von Laue, a Nobel-Prize-winning physicist who lived in Berlin. In a letter to his friend Albert Einstein, von Laue confided the frustration and humiliation experienced by patriots who opposed the assault on the cultural greatness of their country:

With great joy I have heard of the efforts to aid German refugees in England, Holland and America. Unfortunately the joy is not quite free of shame. A few years ago aid committees were created for Armenians and other half-wild peoples when they were politically repressed. And now one has to help us in the same way; that is bitter.[3]

The shameful expulsion of scholars was probably the greatest single factor in the physicist's decision to continue opposing the policies of the Nazis while refusing to abandon his homeland to them.[4]

Like von Laue, most observers were distressed by the scenes of cultural destruction, barbarism, and wastefulness they witnessed as the Nazis imposed their will on Germany. On May 10, 1933, an unforgettable scene occurred when students at the University of Berlin and elsewhere hurled into bonfires creative works written by

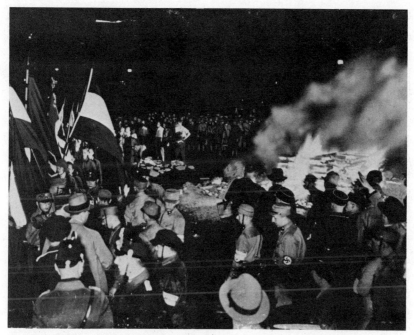

The Nazi book burnings staged on May 10, 1933, symbolized the auto-da-fé of a century of German culture. (Ullstein.)

authors ranging from Heine, Marx, and Bernstein to Preuss and Rathenau; from Einstein, Freud, and Kafka to Kaiser, Kraus, Remarque, and Hesse; from Thomas and Heinrich Mann to Barlach, Broch, Hofmannsthal, Zuckmayer, Werfel, Brecht, von Ossietzky, and Tucholsky. All of this was done in the name of "Action Against the Un-German Spirit," but it has been described more accurately as the "auto-da-fé of a century of German culture."[5] The book burnings and the expulsions demonstrated a disdain for the achievements of reason that seemed to many contemporary observers to be truly alien to the German spirit. This, however, was not really the case.

II   There had long existed a deep and popular strain of anti-intellectualism in Germany. This strain was not an absolute rejection of all products of the mind but rather constituted opposition to and contempt for the Enlightenment belief that man could use rational processes to comprehend nature. It was rooted in the romantic back-   31 lash against the Age of Reason and posited an antagonism between objective, mechanistic universalism and subjective, organic nationalism. The fact that the universalism of the Enlightment became popularly associated with the French occupation armies of Napoleon fed the notion that internationalism was merely a way of keeping the Germans weak, divided, and at the mercy of the Great Powers.

Romantic thinkers and popularizers such as Johann Gottlieb Fichte, Friedrich Schleiermacher, and Adam Müller deprecated the rational conception of a human society based on individual liberty, arguing ironically that it would lead only to uniformity and sterility. In contrast, they praised an intuitive, idealized image of a national community based on personalities formed by tradition and language. The entire cultural and physical milieu, from children's stories and folk songs to the landscape itself, contributed to the personal history of each member of a collective, living entity—the *Volk*. The political expression of the *Volk*, namely the state, was not the Lockean design of citizens joining together voluntarily. It was, in the words of the distinguished twentieth-century historian Koppel Pinson,

a living organism, a *macroanthropos*, a living individuality which was not merely a sum of individuals bound together by a rational contract but organically related by blood, by descent, by tradition, and by history.[6]

Clearly, according to the proponents of the organic world view, only a person born into this community could belong to it. All others belonged to their own communities, to which they were tied by their own traditions and lineage. It was also apparent to them that the members of a community should preserve their unique heritage and remain true to it in their own highest interests.

The works of the early nineteenth-century romanticists still contained many traces of classical humanism and a pre-nationalist attention to all mankind. However, with the rise of urbanization and industrialization in Germany from the 1830s on, adherents to the romantic view of reality began to sound ever more bitter and fearful in their writings. The utilitarian form of rationalism inherent in industrialization was particularly scorned as a form of sophism in which ideas were regarded as little more than tools with which to make money or build machines. While progressive German political leaders and entrepreneurs began looking to either France or England as a model for Germany's future, others were appalled at the coming industrial transformation.

32

Some of the opponents of change began to identify three major antagonists who, for them, embodied the evils of rationalism: the Jews, the liberals, and the Marxist socialists. All of these were linked together in one or another form of conspiracy to destroy the purity of the German *Volk*. George Mosse and Fritz Stern have given us particularly able studies of the ideas of these admonishers, whom Stern has aptly termed "cultural pessimists." In the cultural pessimist scheme of things, the Jews were a restless, homeless breed scattered among the settled nations of the world. As such, they were the only truly international group, and those who advocated internationalism—Jews and non-Jews alike—were not only weakening Germany but also espousing the cause of the Jews. Since their emancipation by Napoleon in accordance with Enlightenment precepts, the Jews were steadily becoming more influential in German affairs. In particular, they made common cause with the liberals to secularize public life, expropriate landed estates from pure-blooded Germans, and finance industrialization. They were the natural inhabitants, declared writers like Wilhelm Heinrich Riehl and Paul de Lagarde, of the ugly, godless, urban centers beginning to consume ever more of the German landscape.[7]

The liberals were, in the eyes of the cultural pessimists, willing allies of the Jews and nothing less than traitorous representatives of the French Revolution or of British industrialization. Like the Jews, they were homeless, constituting for de Lagarde a "Gray International" in league with secularizers and industrializers in other lands.[8] The liberals were the mainstay of utilitarian science, technology, and commerce, which the cultural critic Julius Langbehn felt were dogmatic, rationalistic enterprises threatening the intuitive vitality of the *Volk*.[9] They were out to inhibit creative action and tear down the natural hierarchical political order by means of interest groups, parliamentary debate, and majoritarianism.

The socialists at least understood the need for community, but the Marxist anticipation of a materialistic leveling of society was anathema to the cultural pessimists. The proletariat was a creation of the industrialization wrought by the Jews and liberals, and, of course, it inhabited the cities. The only hope for the German workers was that they drop their banner of internationalism, abandon Jewish leaders, and realize their national roots. As Moeller van den Bruck, cultural pessimistic author of *Das dritte Reich*, demanded, socialism would have to abandon class and refound itself on the basis of race.[10]

The "blood and soil" ideology of the cultural pessimists was cha-   33 otic and garbled, as befitted an alternative to rationalism. However, it provided powerful images that were often expressed in the biological vocabulary of the nineteenth century and that would later be appropriated by the Nazis. The references to the Jews as vermin, parasites, or bacilli were particularly venomous and left a lasting impression upon a population exposed to the Social Darwinist concept of survival of the fittest.[11] Not only were Germans and Jews different, but they were locked in a mortal struggle. Modernity in the form of rationalism, individualism, urbanization, and industrialization was a creation of the Jews and their allies. If belief in the efficacy of reason constituted intellectualism, then anti-intellectualism was a patriotic duty.

The cultural pessimists did much to popularize this negative view, and some of their books, such as Langbehn's *Rembrandt als Erzieher*, were best sellers. More pervasive, however, was a second line of development in resonance with the first, derived largely from the positive emphasis on the racial destiny of the *Volk* espoused by the composer Richard Wagner. As a young man, Wagner had been enamored of the "French ideas" of reason and liberalism, but he abandoned individualist values as un-German during the revolution of 1848. By the end of the 1850s, he was praising as truly German concepts the dynamic will to action, the role of a "man of Providence" as a voice of the collective will, and the need for racial purification of the *Volk*.[12] Wagner's racial optimism complemented the fears of the cultural pessimists and were even more widely disseminated.

All of the cultural pessimists as well as the racial optimists demanded a rejuvenation of the spirit and culture of the *Volk*. By the turn of the century, this was a concern also of the traditional, educated elite, particularly the academic professoriate, which regarded itself as the custodian of German culture. As Fritz Ringer has shown in his study of these "German mandarins," they believed implicitly in the distinctiveness and superiority of Germany's cultural traditions and achievements and contrasted them with the mere materialist civilization of French and especially of the Anglo-Saxon lands. The "orthodox" majority particularly disdained utilitarian rationalism as un-idealist and foreign and harbored romantic, conservative ideas that were simply milder versions of the cultural pessimists' views.[13] Their great fear, in effect, was that men of thought would be reduced to mere technicians of the mind with no higher social status than that of other modern "experts."

A "modernist" minority believed just as firmly in a unique German cultural heritage but was at least willing to accept that the trends of industrialization and increased mass participation in politics could not be reversed. As Ringer writes,

They hoped to guide the social and political forces that had been released by the industrial revolution, to take the sting out of democracy, to wean the Social Democratic workers from the radicalism and internationalism of Marxist orthodoxy, and to inculcate in the masses a certain minimum of respect for the cultural traditions and national ideals of the mandarin heritage.[14]

Both groups were fully committed to the "national cause" during the prewar and World War I periods, but tension grew over issues linked to war aims and peace[15] and led to an unmendable breach after 1918 over the extent to which accommodation of the Weimar regime was necessary or desirable. By and large the most sophisticated, cosmopolitan, and internationally recognized among the scholars, the modernists were willing to work with the Republic in hopes of perpetuating the authority of the educated elite among its leaders. However, the vast majority of the professoriate remained doggedly orthodox and obstructionist, with no desire to identify with internationalism or with the government. Its members were willing to serve the German state but not parliamentary democracy. Those few academicians who genuinely espoused the internationalist cause, such as Albert Einstein or Emil Gumbel, were anathema to the overwhelming majority of the mandarins.[16]

We, thus, come to the striking and paradoxical observation that a sizable proportion of the German-educated elite projected a form of anti-intellectualism, that is, a contempt for faith in the efficacy of reason, and displayed a reluctance to perceive their own position in other than romantic, culturally restricted terms.

Another paradox was reflected in nonacademic literature and the arts. The dazzling achievement of Weimar culture was, as Peter Gay has argued, "the creation of outsiders, propelled by history into the inside, for a short, dizzying, fragile moment."[17] The internationalists, who firmly believed in reason, were temporarily in the limelight; the contemporary glare and their achievements after leaving Germany still keep us from seeing what an isolated group they actually were.

Historians usually dwell upon the representatives of this Weimar avant-garde, but Georg Kaiser, Alfred Döblin, and Bertolt Brecht were hardly the most popular representatives of German culture in Germany. Walter Laqueur has argued that the *Zeitgeist* was represented more appropriately by Ernst Jünger and Hermann Loens than by Heinrich Mann and Franz Werfel, by films about the Napoleonic Wars than about Dr. Caligari, and by the Hugenberg nationalist press than by the *Weltbühne*.[18] Writers like Loens and Jünger or films like *Stosstrupp 1917* were not projecting images of reason to their audiences, but a glorification of force and relentless will.

The predominant culture, in other words, was divorced from the legend of Weimar. It was overwhelmingly and firmly nationalist-right. Even most Weimar figures were not committed to interest-group politics and parliamentary compromise, for that would have been too materialistic. And practically no one on the left really favored fulfilling the Versailles Treaty, for that would have meant supporting French colonialism and British imperialism. The ambivalence of the Weimar figures came to symbolize for many Germans the weaknesses of international intellectualism. The most determined and alienated critics of the Weimar Republic could be found actively joining the Nazis, while many others disdainfully looked forward to Hitler's arrival in power.

III By late 1922 the National Socialists had already emerged as dominant among the racist groups on the extreme right of the political spectrum. These groups were the direct heirs of Wagner and of the anti-Semitic, anti-liberal, anti-Marxist cultural pessimists. They articulated the cultural-political desires of most Germans—a rejuvenation of the spirit of the *Volk* and a rejection of the advocates of international cooperation—at a time when unity and strength were needed for the good of Germany. Since even assimilated Jews had never been fully accepted as Germans, many Germans were susceptible to the assertion that Jews were, by definition, alien and an internationalist element causing divisiveness and debilitating weakness. The fact that many of the prominent Weimar cultural figures and political leaders, especially among the socialists, *were* Jewish only served to confirm prejudices.[19]

In opposition to enlightened, rational, universal intellectualism, the Nazis praised romantic, irrational, racist willfulness. They were especially adamant in denouncing any idea of intellectual endeavor for its own sake. Since all healthy creation stemmed from the spirit of the *Volk* and its blood and soil, "pure art" or the pursuit of "pure

36

science" was inherently sick and poisonous. In response to a plea from the conservative music conductor Wilhelm Furtwängler to consider only the quality of art in carrying out the great Nazi revolution, Joseph Goebbels responded definitively:

There must be no art in the absolute sense as known by liberal democracy. The attempt to serve it would result in the people no longer having any inner relationship to art and in the artist himself isolating and cutting himself off from the driving forces of the time in the vacuum of the *l'art pour l'art* point of view. Art must be good; but beyond this it must be responsible, professional, popular *(volksnah)* and aggressive.[20]

Or, again, as Hitler is alleged to have said to some of his followers in private:

Science is a social phenomenon, and like every other social phenomenon is limited by the benefit or injury it confers on the community.
    The slogan of objective science has been coined by the professoriate simply in order to escape from the very necessary supervision by the power of the State.[21]

Yet such statements did not mean that the Nazis had no appreciation of art or science. They clearly understood the significance of both for their own purposes. In his speech on art in September 1935, Hitler said flatly:

I am . . . convinced that art, since it forms the most uncorrupted, the most immediate reflection of the people's soul, exercises unconsciously by far the greatest direct influence upon the masses of people, but always subject to one condition: that it draws a true picture of that life and of the inborn capacities of a people and does not distort them.[22]

Indeed, for the Nazis, art and science were to be instruments used against modernity itself. This does not mean that they thought they could turn the clock back. Urbanization and industrialization had produced irreversible changes, and the Nazis did not intend to return to a premodern world; instead, they wanted to go forward to a postmodern one. They wanted not simply to destroy, but to supersede.[23]

Within this context, it can be said that the purpose of art and science in the Nazi scheme of things was to provide bulwarks for a form of cultural autarky. Within the closed world of the Nazi empire, products of the mind were now to be directed against all the accomplishments of the Enlightenment designed to give men individual rights and to make them think for themselves. Essentially, such products would have only limited, specified functions—to educate

37

the *Volk* in its own nature, to exhort the *Volk* to action, and to serve the needs of the *Volk* in its struggle for existence.

In other words, artists and writers would generate images, architects would erect structures, and composers would create scores that would each reduce the significance of the individual in his own eyes and integrate his perceptions into the homogeneous framework of the *Volk*. Scientists would develop processes needed for economic self-sufficiency or devices useful in warfare. Isolated from international influences, a truly Germanic art would flourish, an Aryan science would replace objective research, and enormous structures in Berlin and Linz would rise to demonstrate the massed power of a unified and purified race.

Only those persons who derived their creative power from the *Volk* itself would be acceptable providers of these services. Thus, from the Nazi viewpoint, losing the talents of intellectuals who fled to lands where they were more welcome was no great cause for concern. As Hitler was reputed to have said to a leading scientist when the latter protested against the damage being wrought by the expulsions in 1933:

Our national policies will not be revoked or modified, even for scientists. If the dismissal of Jewish scientists means the annihilation of contemporary German science, then we shall do without science for a few years.[24]

IV With such an extremist attitude emanating from their leadership, it is quite obvious that the Nazis were capable of driving out thousands of intellectuals and cultural figures. Yet, given the Nazi penchant for ruthless exploitation, the question arises why these people should have been allowed to go at all. Even men and women of allegedly dubious *völkisch* value could be put to use somehow, and, by detaining them in Germany, the problem of their making contributions in science and culture elsewhere would be eliminated. Why not prevent the intellectuals from emigrating, confine them, and exploit their abilities?

There was, after all, a contemporary example of just such a process. The Soviet Union under Stalin faced reluctant cooperation from various quarters and was not above brutal measures, imposition of ideological rigor, and the politicization of art and science. However, instead of forcing capable persons to leave, the Soviets restrained them and forced them to work for the regime. A case in point was that of Peter Kapitza, a brilliant physicist who had been working in Cambridge with Ernest Rutherford. In 1934, on a visit to his homeland, he was simply detained permanently and put to work on projects for the state.[25]

Obviously wholesale, or even selective, confinement and exploitation of intellectuals prior to the onset of war was not the Nazi tactic. The expulsions staged by Goebbels and Hitler were a spectacular display of contempt for the achievements of reason and perhaps a case of the Nazis being too busy with other things and too inept and uncaring to worry about confining intellectuals before they fled.

Another angle to consider, however, is that confinement had long been viewed in the history of criminal reform as an advancement over corporal and capital punishment. Although the Nazis initiated a reversal of this trend and began to view confinement not in lieu of but as a prelude to corporal punishment and death,[26] the basic justifications for confinement were all unappealing to them.

One classic purpose of confinement has been to segregate offenders in order to protect society. Since the eighteenth century, however, the rationale behind such segregation in Western civilization had assumed an enlightened value structure, namely that all reasonable men wish to join society as productive members and all members of society are reasonable enough to accept them. The ultimate goal has been to include all men in a universal, rational world order.

In contrast, the Nazi mentality held that only a small segment of humankind belonged among the chosen citizenry and that if the "undesirables" were to be segregated from the rest of society, no prison or internment camp seemed large enough to contain them all. The sheer magnitude of the numbers seemed an impassable obstacle until the early victories of the Second World War deluded the Nazis into believing that the Germans *could* oversee the population of all of Europe and perhaps the rest of the world.

Another problem with segregation for the Nazis was that it conflicted with the second major justification for confinement, rehabilitation. Those in the acceptable racial category, who might be salvaged, could only be brought into the fold by immersion in, not divorce from, the community. Only through hard work and communal experiences like S.A. camps, party rallies, or military training could their feelings for the blood and soil of the *Volk* be rejuvenated.

Rehabilitation, however, had its drawbacks. It would be a priori

39

impossible for persons of an alien community to be educated or worked to the point where they would be considered acceptable. Furthermore, those who were racially acceptable but espoused such evils as internationalism or pacifism could not be argued into rehabilitation; they would have to be subjected to communal experiences among the members of the *Volk*, whom in the process they might infect with their ideas.

The third purpose of confinement also related to hard work. The Soviets, for example, imposed forced labor in order to generate products of value. Intellectuals, however, made notoriously poor physical laborers. In addition, the products of racially inimical or racially infected minds were by definition inferior and worse than useless— they were potentially poisonous and should not be encouraged even in captivity.

That left only a fourth justification for confinement, which was punishment to deter unwanted behavior and ideas on the part of others. To the Nazis, it seemed more efficient to deter by expulsion than by confinement. Once undesirable artists, scientists, and the like had been removed, intellectual autarky would be achieved and cultural insulation from foreign ideas would make deterrence by confinement superfluous.

Thus, there were no compelling grounds on which to detain undesirable intellectuals. Inherently distasteful to the Nazis was the prospect that those confined would still be in Germany and would still be able, by private example, to serve as an inspiration to others. Much more consistent with Nazi sensibilities was the plan to eliminate intellectual or cultural figures entirely, although liquidation would be liable to create martyrs at home and a backlash abroad (particularly since, until the Saar plebiscite in early 1935, Hitler had no desire to jeopardize the return of this territory home into the Reich by exacerbating unfavorable foreign reaction).

From the Nazi point of view, the most appealing way to deal with the Weimar and Jewish intellectuals was not to confine them, but to ostracize them. Because the worst fate imaginable to an adherent of *völkisch* ideas was to be cut off from the spirit of the German people and the land, exile was a much more profound and painful punishment than confinement. It may seem strange for the Nazis to claim that Jews and leftists were untrue to the German spirit and then to exact the kind of a retribution that would most hurt someone who indeed *did* love Germany. But it was precisely this sort of irrationalism that made the Nazis so effective.

40

By labeling an intellectual un-German, the Nazis were meting out a punishment they feared greatly themselves. But at the same time, they were sure to get what they wanted: they cut creative persons off from their public so that they either fell into silence and isolation or went into exile. By leaving, moreover, a person proved—at least to Nazi satisfaction—that he or she was not loyal enough to stay, and left friends, family, and estate open to reprisals. In addition, persons who emigrated usually had been dismissed from their positions, and their absence from Germany made it easier to replace them with dedicated or opportunistic Nazis.

These are some of the considerations that caused those who left their homeland to do so very reluctantly, often with the expectation that the Nazi government would not last. Emil Gumbel later recalled that he had been a "fool" to have accepted a post in Paris in the belief that the Nazis would soon be overthrown and the old order reestablished.[27] Franz Neumann explained that he spent the first three years of exile in England, "in order to be close to Germany and not to lose contact with her. . . . But," he wrote, "Nazism did not simply change the political system of Germany; it changed Germany."[28]

This last remark betrays a misunderstanding of the situation perhaps as serious as the chapter heading "Germany Goes Berserk" in Pinson's excellent textbook on modern German history. Hitler did not transform the Germans overnight from a cultured people into barbarians. On the contrary, the roots of anti-intellectualism—in the sense of a fundamental opposition to faith in the efficacy of reason—ran broad and deep in German society. The social and cultural divisiveness of the Weimar period had created a yearning for unity as intense as the longing for unification generated by political divisiveness in the years prior to Bismarck's Reich.

Hitler was undeniably seeking what many Germans wanted—a purging of "internationalists," who were seen as weakening the country at a time when strength was imperative to undo the Versailles Treaty and to cope with the Depression. The spectacle of the muses fleeing Hitler can perhaps best be understood as the manifestation of a demand for cultural homogeneity so strong that, in order to obtain it, the population was willing to forfeit creativity and excellence, even to pay the price of the intellectual decapitation of Germany.

41

Notes

1. The best figures to date are still provided in Edward Y. Hartshorne, Jr., *The German Universities and National Socialism* (London, 1937). Analyses of the Civil Service law (*Gesetz zur Wiederherstellung des Berufsbeamtentums*) of Apr. 7 and its supplements and successors are provided by Raul Hilberg, *The Destruction of the European Jews* (Chicago, 1961) and Hans Mommsen, *Beamtentum im Dritten Reich* (Stuttgart, 1966).

2. See Norman Bentwich, *The Rescue and Achievement of Refugee Scholars: The Story of Displaced Scholars and Scientists, 1933–1952* (The Hague, 1953); Stephen Duggan and Betty Drury, *The Rescue of Science and Learning: The Story of the Emergency Committee in Aid of Displaced Scholars* (New York, 1948); and David S. Wyman, *Paper Walls: America and the Refugee Crisis, 1938–1941* (Amherst, Mass., 1968).

3. Max von Laue to Albert Einstein (original in German), June 26, 1933, Einstein Archives, Princeton University, Princeton, N.J.

4. See Alan Beyerchen, *Scientists under Hitler: Politics and the Physics Community in the Third Reich* (New Haven, 1977), pp. 64–66.

5. Karl Dietrich Bracher, *The German Dictatorship: The Origins, Structure and Effects of National Socialism*, trans. Jean Steinberg (New York and Washington, D.C., 1970), p. 258. One must keep in mind that the book burnings were conducted in emulation of the nationalist student celebration at the Wartburg in 1817, where antinationalist writings were consigned to the flames in symbolic remembrance of Luther's burning of the papal bull in 1521. See Hans-Wolfgang Strätz, "Die studentische 'Aktion wider den undeutschen Geist' im Frühjahr 1933," *Vierteljahrshefte für Zeitgeschichte* 6 (1968):347–72.

6. Koppel Pinson, *Modern Germany: Its History and Civilization*, 2d. ed. (New York and London, 1966), p. 43.

7. George Mosse, *The Crisis of German Ideology: Intellectual Origins of the Third Reich* (New York, 1964), pp. 19–51; Fritz Stern, *The Politics of Cultural Despair: A Study in the Rise of the Germanic Ideology* (Berkeley and Los Angeles, 1961), pp. 53–70. See Wilhelm Heinrich Riehl, *Die bürgerliche Gesellschaft* (Stuttgart, 1851); and Paul de Lagarde, *Ausgewählte Schriften*, ed. Paul Fischer, 2d. ed. (Munich, 1934), pp. 239, 248.

8. Paul de Lagarde, "Die graue Internationale" (1881), in *Deutsche Schriften*, ed. Karl August Fischer, 4th ed. (Munich, 1940).

9. Stern reminds us of the power of the assault on mechanistic science and positivism mounted contemporaneously with Langbehn's career by indicating some of those who prepared the way for modernity in a number of fields: Henri Bergson, Samuel Butler, Wilhelm Dilthey, Sigmund Freud, William James, and Friedrich Neitzsche. Stern, *Politics of Cultural Despair*, p. 124.

10. Arthur Moeller van den Bruck, "Sozialistische Aussenpolitik," in *Sozialismus und Aussenpolitik*, ed. Hans Schwarz (Breslau, 1933), p. 81.

11. De Lagarde, *Ausgewählte Schriften*, p. 239. See also Alexander Bein, "Der Jüdische Parasit," *Vierteljahrshefte für Zeitgeschichte* 13 (1965): 121–50; and Daniel Gasman, *The Scientific Origins of National Socialism: Social Darwinism in Ernst Haeckel and the German Monist League* (London, 1971).

12. Despite some simplistic analysis and much invective, a useful assessment of the Germanic ideas of Wagner is Peter Viereck, *Meta-politics: The Roots of the Nazi Mind* (New York, 1965), pp. 90–177. See also Jacques Barzun, *Darwin, Marx and Wagner* (Boston, 1941).

13. Fritz K. Ringer, *The Decline of the German Mandarins: The German Academic Community, 1890–1933* (Cambridge, Mass., 1969), pp. 128–43.

14. Ibid., p. 132.

15. See Klaus Schwabe, *Wissenshaft und Kriegsmoral: Die deutschen Hochschullehrer und die politischen Grundfragen des Ersten Weltkriegs* (Göttingen, 1969).

16. On Einstein, see Friedrich Herneck, *Albert Einstein: Ein Leben für Wahrheit, Menschlichkeit und Frieden* (East Berlin, 1963); on Gumbel, see Emil T. Gumbel, *Freie Wissenschaft: Ein Sammelbuch der deutschen Emigration* (Strasbourg, 1938), pp. 267–68.

17. Peter Gay, *Weimar Culture: The Outsider as Insider* (New York and Evanston, 1968), p. xiv.

18. Walter Laqueur, "The Role of the Intelligentsia in the Weimar Republic," *Social Research* 39 (Summer 1972):216–19.

19. Eberhard Jaeckel, *Hitlers Weltanschauung: Entwurf einer Herrschaft* (Tübingen, 1969), p. 69, points out that for Hitler *Jew* and *internationalist* were practically synonymous.

20. Jeremy Noakes and Geoffrey Pridham, eds., *Documents on Nazism 1919–1945* (New York, 1975), p. 343.

21. Hermann Rauschning, *Voice of Destruction* (New York, 1940), p. 223.

22. Nuremberg "Address on Art and Politics," Sept. 11, 1935, in Adolf Hitler, *The Speeches of Adolf Hitler, April 1922–August 1939*, ed. Norman H. Baynes (London, 1942), p. 574.

23. Some of the implications of taking the Nazis seriously on this point have been explored by Leonard Krieger, "Nazism: Highway or Byway?" *Central European History* 11 (March 1978):3–22, especially pp. 16–19.

24. Hartshorne, *German Universities*, p. 112.

25. This example has been examined by Lawrence Badash in "Rutherford, Kapitza and the Kremlin" (Talk presented at the West Coast History of Science Society meeting in Los Angeles, 1975).

43

Anti-Intellectualism and the Cultural Decapitation of Germany

26. See the analysis in chapter 11 of Georg Rusche and Otto Kirchheimer, *Punishment and Social Structure,* International Institute of Social Research (New York, 1939), pp. 177–92.

27. Charles John Wetzel, "The American Rescue of Refugee Scholars and Scientists from Europe, 1933–1945" (Ph.D. diss., University of Wisconsin, 1964), p. 94.

28. Franz Neumann, "The Social Sciences," in Neumann et al., *The Cultural Migration: The European Scholar in America* (Philadelphia, 1953), p. 17.

ALAN BEYERCHEN

The Movement of People in a Time of Crisis

HERBERT A. STRAUSS

This Einstein centennial symposium has taken as its theme the flight of the muses from totalitarian oppression. Our program is dedicated to the transfer of people and ideas. We celebrate achievement, success, and the overcoming of a deep collective and personal catastrophe. We salute the great men and women and the significant migration movement that resulted and brought about a creative response to the challenges of the time.

It is the purpose of the following remarks not to diminish the joy and vicarious pride we feel about this reaffirmation but to place the successes we are commemorating into several contexts that reflect the realities of the period. The archives of the Leo Baeck Institute in New York contain a watercolor by Felix Nussbaum, who was brought to France in October 1940 from his native Baden with sixty-five hundred other southwest German Jews and interned in the camp of Gurs. The painting shows an emaciated group of men and women sitting around a makeshift table of wooden crates, dressed in blankets and rags. Before them, on the table, stands a globe. The group around the table stares at the globe with expressions that seem to convey hopelessness and hope, despair and determination.

I shall try here to relate these two symbolic worlds, the muses fleeing the crude force and the victims, nearly crushed or soon to be crushed by this crude force, assembled around a silent globe. In Walt Whitman's lines from *Leaves of Grass,*

I play marches for conquered and slain persons
....
Battles are lost in the same spirit
in which they are won.

Those who know their Walt Whitman realize that I did not include Whitman's stanza " . . . I also say it is good to fail . . . " No historian contemplating this period could make his peace with this kind of *amor fati.*

II The persecution of persons that the Third Reich considered to be its enemies, or the objects of racial hatred, was, of course, totally irrational and self-destructive—in the words of Professors Helge Pross and Alan Beyerchen, a form of collective suicide. The historian describing even a small part of the events in a factual way has difficulties pointing to any rational functions or functional rationality they may have had, even within their totally nonrational framework.

Correspondingly, the victims of Nazi persecution do not form a group by any definition that history or social science can devise. Their only common characteristic was precisely their being persecuted, just as the common characteristic of the émigrés among them was their emigration. It is possible, however, to group together larger numbers of victims by using either major external determinants that affected their lives or subjective factors that determined their self-understanding.

In February 1933, after the Reichstag had burned down, the Nazi party and police machines unleashed their first great wave of physical terror, arrests, murders, and tortures against their most determined and visible foes. The intellectuals, writers, artists, and political leaders among them who avoided being caught, or who feared that they would become victims of future terror, fled legally or illegally to neighboring countries. They were followed by other "enemies of the regime" who also saw their lives endangered. A few years later the terror expanded into Austria and Czechoslovakia. This group, which formed the political emigration in the narrower sense, and which between 1933 and 1939 may have numbered as many as thirty thou-

46

sand refugees, included many of the intellectuals and artists who had created what is now called Weimar Culture. They represented an important part of the intellectual transfer process, whatever their views of themselves as exiles and of their ultimate return to a democratic Germany may have been. Of those who survived their exile, the persecution of the Vichy police, or Stalin's concentration camps, only a minuscule number returned to their native lands. From exiles, they had turned into immigrants.

The number of political émigrés pales when compared with the number of émigrés persecuted on account of their Jewish ancestry—all the more so if the observation of contemporaries that 80 percent of political refugees were also of Jewish background could be substantiated. Compared with the 1933 German population of about 65 million, the approximately 525,000 Jews (by religion) were a minute minority in their Christian environment. (In Austria, too, the 185,000 Jews constituted such a minority, although their concentration in Vienna, where they accounted for 9 percent of the population, and in some branches of business and the professions may have given them additional visibility.) In addition, under Nazi law and ideology persons were classified as Jews if they had one or two Jewish grandparents, if they had a Jewish spouse, or even if they had left the Jewish religion of their ancestors, joining a church or remaining unaffiliated. If these three last groups are added up, Nazism claimed another 350,000 potential victims. As a result, the total number of persons affected by Nazi persecution of Jews in Germany alone may have been as high as 875,000.

The cultural identity of those 875,000 persons was widely diverse. The process of integrating the Jewish minority in the German states and in German culture had begun in the middle of the eighteenth century in Germany and Austria. During the subsequent 160 to 180 years, generations of Jews had become an indistinguishable component of German and Austrian life: the large number of Christians with some Jewish ancestry attests to this integration. At the other end of the spectrum were the traditionally religious Jews, concentrated especially in the rural areas of south and west Germany, and the nearly 100,000 Jews of foreign, mostly eastern and south-eastern European, nationality and culture. They formed an ethnic core group among German Jewry. In Austria, where Jews were primarily concentrated in the old capital of the *Kaiserreich*, the share of the ethnically identified Jewish population was considerably higher.

III The pattern of emigration was the result of the pattern of persecution to which this group of persons as defined by Nazi laws and measures was exposed. This is a truism but one that, on closer investigation, needs considerable modification.

Whether the innumerable decrees and measures enacted by the Third Reich against the Jews were part of a preexisting master plan ranging from exclusion and despoliation to concentration and extermination is debatable. It has been established that the German anti-Semitic tradition of the nineteenth and twentieth centuries represented a model of ethological fantasies run wild: The idea of removal, of placing space between Jews in culture or politics and the German population, of forcing Jews into emigration, was part of this tradition. The Nazi program of anti-Jewish measures up to the deportation and extermination phase in 1940 can be seen as the realization of German right-wing conservative Christian anti-Semitic ideas. Only the implementation varied from Nazi thuggery to conservative refinement. And, as it unfolded, Nazi persecution of Jewish enemies was not a consistent priority in the policy of the Third Reich; it had to compete with other priorities.

Yet Nazi measures, in all their irrationality, also served some purposes—even the wholesale removal of the intellectual and technical elites. Between 1929 and 1933, about one-half of all university graduates in Germany (estimated at about twenty-five thousand per annum) did not find employment in the fields for which they were trained. This dismal prospect accounts in part for the excessive inroads made by Nazism among students and student parliaments in many German universities and in Austria before 1933 and 1938, respectively. The removal of Jews in law, medicine, government service, and the universities appeared to be an easy pseudosolution for the ills of academic overcrowding and the academic proletariat. Anti-Semitic measures acquired a political function and an economic pseudofunction.

Viewed in the context of Nazi policy priorities, the anti-Semitic measures of the Third Reich may be divided into several tactical periods, not described here. They also took place on several levels. There was central Reich policy as expressed in decrees, laws, or directives. However, there were also countless local or regional terror actions taken against Jews. Some of these were "against the law," as local radicals and party groups committed atrocities, engaged in public attacks and threats, or boycotted Jewish businesses. Conversely, there was passive resistance against such measures as Chris-

48

tians continued to patronize Jewish stores or disregard anti-Semitic crusades. On all levels, conservative officials or Weimar survivors of the Nazi purges in the civil service slowed down or sabotaged Nazi directives.

As a result of this and other factors, Nazi policies against Jews were not perceived as uniform by the intended victims. They rather appeared, and in fact were, polymorphous and discontinuous. For the first few years, they also were polycentric: more than one power center was competitively involved in decision making about Jews.

Time is too short to describe in detail the decisions that accounted for the shifts in Nazi policy, or to elaborate the function of these shifts in the context of Nazi priorities. For our purpose here, these shifts explain the fact that the date at which a person emigrated from Nazi Germany was not an immediate function of his dismissal from a job or position. We cannot understand why so many of the intellectual émigrés did not emigrate from Germany following the Law of April 7, 1933, or the Nuremberg Laws of September 15, 1935, unless we remember that they were faced with a confusing and, in fact, confused reality that they could legitimately interpret in several selective frameworks.

The number of persons who left Germany and Austria as émigrés of the Nazi period cannot be established with absolute precision. No statistical data of any reliability are available for most of the 350,000 German and Austrian persons of Jewish descent but not of the Jewish religion. Of the about 525,000 Jews by religion, as many as 300,000 may have emigrated from Germany, and as many as 125,000 may have fled Austria, but the pattern of emigration was not continuous, precisely as a result of Nazi tactics. Of these 300,000 Jews, about 30,000, however, were caught in the Nazi maze when the German armies overran western Europe in 1940 and occupied Vichy France in November 1942. Many of these 30,000 persons were interned by the French police or the occupying powers, and deported to extermination camps in eastern Europe.

IV If we now turn from the "push" aspects of this migration to its "pull" aspects, it would be pleasant to be able to report that the governments of the time understood the nature of the threat posed by the rise of Nazism in Germany, sympathized with the victims, and helped all those who needed it.

49

The record, however, does not support such a euphoric view. Clio brings in a mixed verdict: many governments either failed to see the threat in time or did not extend a helping hand to Nazi victims in time. In hindsight, many a child-Einstein, a child-Hindemith, or a child-Courant was lost to mankind in this way, and numerous intellectuals perished because governments did too little too late or because the public lacked the imagination to see the indivisibility of human freedom and human rights.

In fact, between 1933 and 1941, as many as 500,000 persons may have been absorbed by countries around the globe as immigrants from Germany, Austria, and Czechoslovakia. Their admission was often achieved, not on account of, but in spite of those politically responsible for the immigration policies of their countries, notwithstanding the many unforgotten men and women in this and in many other countries, in or out of government, who risked their careers, their health, and sometimes their lives to save the victims of persecution.

A summary review shows the following picture: in absolute numbers of German and Austrian immigrants admitted, the United States topped the list with about 132,000 immigrants from Nazi Germany and (after March 1938, Austria), followed by all of Latin America (about 80,000 to 85,000), Great Britain (72,000, including Czechs), Palestine/Israel (about 56,000, including 1,800 illegal immigrants), France (about 30,000 permanent refugees, with many more persons in transit to overseas destinations), Shanghai (about 17,000 from all countries of origin), Czechoslovakia (about 6,500), and other small nations in Europe. Switzerland and Holland each admitted over 30,000 transients. Immigration to South Africa, Canada, and Australia remained limited to a few thousand each.

It should be understood that many of these figures remain tentative: They do not account adequately for the transients who were especially numerous in western Europe between 1933 and 1940; they include persons counted more than once, as residents of countries of intermediate and of final settlement; they exclude persons entering a country on visitors' visas or staying on following the expiration of a residence permit. They also exclude persons who owed their admission to a consul's or other foreign service officer's willingness, for one reason or another, to bypass regulations—as was evidenced in some Latin and Central American republics at the time.

If we list countries on the basis of the period during which immigrants or refugees were admitted, the grouping changes. The first

50

wave extended to the European neighbors of the Third Reich. As a result, France, Czechoslovakia, Switzerland, and Holland were selected as the first refuge by political émigrés in 1933. In 1933, between 72 and 75 percent of all émigrés were estimated to have sought refuge in France, which, like Czechoslovakia, followed humanitarian as well as political impulses in admitting the opposition to Hitler. Switzerland and Holland, like France, insisted throughout that their countries were unable to absorb the refugees as immigrants and promoted their remigration. (They did so especially in response to the flight of thousands of Austrian victims across European frontiers in 1938.) Still, the European neighbors of the Third Reich remained the target for about 25 percent of all émigrés and transients until the outbreak of the war.

In contrast to continental Europe, the United States and Great Britain did not absorb appreciable numbers of refugees from Nazi persecution until 1938—i.e., until after the pogroms of November 9–10, the so-called *Kristallnacht.* South Africa closed its doors to immigrants in late 1936. Brazil and Argentina had closed their doors in the mid-1930s but reopened them for some categories of immigrants after November 1938: in Argentina, Anglophile General Roberto M. Ortiz had been influential in this reversal, much as in France the popular front government of Léon Blum had eased government practices on work and residence permits in the mid-1930s.

Palestine/Israel was the first of the overseas countries to absorb immigrants in sizable numbers beginning in 1934. Its doing so was in part made possible by a special transfer agreement *(Haavarah)* between economic and Zionist interests in Palestine and the German Finance Ministry in 1933 and by an intensive program of retraining young people for agriculture and crafts in Germany and other countries. This movement came to an end in 1936 when Arab unrest led the British Mandatory Administration to close the doors of Palestine to Jewish immigration.

Among the major potential immigration countries closed in the 1930s were the Soviet Union, Canada, and Australia and New Zealand. Records submitted by a German-Jewish agency to the Nazi Secret Police (S.D.) during the war suggest that about one thousand persons in addition to a small number of German and Austrian political refugees were admitted as refugees to the Soviet Union. (There is no way to verify these figures.) The three Commonwealth countries admitted a few thousand refugees from all central European countries, as well as a few hundred civilian internees who had been

51

shipped overseas by Great Britain in 1940 as enemy aliens in spite of their refugee character.

It was the tragedy of the early 1930s that the same factors in world economic conditions that had radicalized German voters and had led to the polarization between Communists and Nazis also brought about the worldwide restriction on the free movement of people. No political entity—with the singular exception of the International Settlement of Shanghai—permitted free immigration. In most countries, especially in Europe, control over immigration had begun in the mid-nineteenth century and was motivated by fear of political subversion. In the Western Hemisphere, in Australia and New Zealand, concern with racial and cultural homogeneity had been taken to absurd lengths in restricting immigration. Since the 1920s all countries had added economic motives to their restrictive ideologies. The record also shows that after 1933 Hitler declared his policy of dumping the impoverished Jews of Germany on the world to test the sincerity of the world's profession of concern and also to stimulate additional anti-Semitism and thus export sympathy for Germany's policies of persecution. There is enough evidence to substantiate the partial success of these tactics. Public opinion led by conservative and right-wing nationalists, supported in many countries by trade union and labor opinion as well, had turned protectionist not only in trade and monetary policies but also in the admission of people in distress. Unemployment and the threat to the middle classes in business or the professions vitiated attempts in most countries to liberalize immigration policies. Foreign offices feared that liberal accommodations of large numbers of refugees might encourage governments such as the ones in Poland or Rumania to follow Hitler's lead and expel large numbers of Jews from their countries.

Even the U.S. Department of State enforced a directive issued by President Herbert Hoover in 1930 in response to the onset of the Depression: it ordered consuls to ask for extensive proof that an immigrant would not become a public charge. For the first five years of the Nazi emergency, immigration to the United States remained minimal; in fact, during the first three years, 1933–35, emigration from the United States exceeded immigration by a combined total of over seventy thousand persons. In 1936 immigration to the United States exceeded emigration from the country by 512 persons. The quota for persons born in Germany was generous enough to have permitted the admission of twenty-five thousand persons a year.

German Jews should thus have benefited from the social, religious, or racial prejudices that had generated American immigration legislation since 1917, but few were admitted until the violent events occurring in Germany and Austria in 1938 changed American, British, and other countries' policies.

V At this point, enough has been said to allow us to focus on the artists' and intellectuals' uprooting and resettlement. The events summarized by the words *cultural migration* or *cultural transfer*—in their successes and their failures—covered a very large number of persons, larger than could be accommodated by the panels of this symposium. Not only intellectuals of worldwide influence but also the middling and younger generations of migrants, whether they were trained partly or fully in foreign lands, also belonged to the story. Universities and public life in several countries offered outstanding careers to such younger men. In addition, behind the great men and women recorded in our histories and to be discussed in this symposium were significant numbers of lesser-known intellectuals and artists who also had to flee for their lives and rebuild their careers. Since 1972, the struggling, privately funded Research Foundation for Jewish Immigration in New York, in cooperation with the government-financed Institute for Contemporary History of the German Federal Republic in Munich (Institut für Zeitgeschichte), has been assembling a biographical data bank about émigrés from Nazi Germany, Austria, and Czechoslovakia. This collection now includes about twenty-five thousand biographical files of people in public life, the professions, in business, religion, literature, the arts, and the sciences. The biographies of about nine thousand men and women selected from this total by group-, sex-, country-, and community-specific criteria are being published in the three-volume *International Biographical Dictionary of Central-European Émigrés 1933–1945 (Handbuch der deutsch-sprachigen Emigration 1933–1945).*[1] The work owes its realization primarily to the Deutsche Forschungsgemeinschaft, in Godesberg, West Germany, and, in its later stages, to a grant from the National Endowment for the Humanities.

Work has not advanced far enough at this stage to say precisely how many of these files belong to the artists and intellectuals that are the subject of this symposium. The apparently large number of such individuals indicates, however, the enormous breadth and depth

53

of the movement. It also suggests the complexity of the events we are about to discuss. And it suggests that the transfer of men and ideas began before Hitler's ascent to power and has paid handsome dividends to postwar central Europe through the retransfer of men and ideas after 1945 in a number of areas of great public significance.

Further, for many émigrés, the usual tight occupational or professional categories of middle-class life or of census takers cannot be applied, because emigration has forced—or allowed—many often middle-aged persons to change their occupations, in some cases with outstanding success in their new fields. Part of the problem lies in the absence of records, especially for persons not affiliated with a cultural institution before or after their emigration. Many did not attain standards of achievement that would have led to their coming to the notice of biographical dictionaries or *New York Times* obituaries—and all of these men and women, whether of the older or the younger generation of immigrants, are part of the cultural transfer process in productive or reproductive ways that must be seen together to account for the whole. A recent German compilation lists over three thousand university employees of all levels and in all departments *(Fakultäten)* as having migrated. (This figure appears higher than those offered by most observers and social agencies in the 1930s.) The maximum percentage of émigré professors and lecturers that had returned to the two Germanys or Austria by 1949 or 1953 lies between 13 and 17 percent; they, too, are a chapter in the history of the cultural transfer that remains to be investigated. However, the vast majority of intellectual émigrés not only resettled but found new and permanent roots as their acculturation proceeded.

A recent compilation of writers among the émigrés lists, in its second edition, approximately twenty-five hundred names. The number of performing or plastic artists—i.e., of full-time artists or teaching artists-in-residence—is not available at this time, but it will probably reach hundreds if not thousands of persons of professional performance levels. American immigration statistics list 1,500 musicians, 3,569 professors and teachers, 1,900 scientists and literary persons, and 702 sculptors or artists among the total number of immigrants for the years 1933–44. While these figures are all-inclusive for immigrants of all kinds from all countries, more refined figures for refugees from Germany and Austria suggest similar proportions: of 7,622 professionals, there were 1,000 educators, 2,352 medical personnel, 811 lawyers, 465 musicians, and 296 plastic artists. It is not possible to project the American figures onto the entire movement of artists and intellectuals. But at least some intimation of the breadth of the intellectual migration may tentatively be gained from such figures.

Under the immigration laws of most countries in the 1930s, no preference was given to professionals. Quite the contrary: unless they were widely recognized, prestigious figures or useful for some national purpose, intellectual émigrés were unwelcome in many countries around the globe, as were physicians, lawyers, or other professionals. Their migration thus reflected the economic or ideological barriers erected at the time to protect national or economic group interests. And, although many of the victims had only a tenuous connection with Judaism, they also faced in many countries prejudice against Jewish professionals or, ironically, on account of their German background, against foreigners.

Where immigration laws provided for special nonquota immigration for academic and religious professionals, as in the United States, the problems shifted from the legal to the economic and social area. Clearly, the transplantation of intellectuals and artists from one national culture to another presented unique difficulties. In *Science as a Vocation* Max Weber had earlier drawn attention to the fact that the modern research scholar had long lost his character as an independent and free intellectual; he had become dependent on the large impersonal institutions housing the archives and libraries that were his means of production.

From a social history point of view, this observation may be expanded: the difference postulated by Karl Mannheim in the 1920s between the salaried and the so-called free-floating intellectuals lay actually in the types of social networks that connected them with other social groups or institutions. The "free" intellectual was linked with his special public—his *Gemeinde*—which recognized and bought his work. He had his political connections, the political publishing houses and political or literary journals—in short, an entire informal social network that permitted him to function. Emigration brought destruction of his network and necessitated reintegration into a new network elsewhere.

The intellectual subtleties of the reconstruction process demanded by emigration are the subject of the next few days of this symposium. Clearly, the social and intellectual histories of the process are intimately related. Reception of the émigré was influenced by the degree to which his discipline was understood, by the state of knowledge and research interests in the institutions or academic departments open to him, and by the style or trends in plastic or performing works that prevailed in an art market at a given time and place.

Yet, even where conditions for the reception of a style or branch of inquiry were favorable, the market conditions were severe for the intellectual and artistic migrant. The same academic overpopulation that existed in Germany was found in most, if not all, countries of the Western world. With sixteen thousand unemployed musicians in Great Britain, Lord Beveridge stated, it was hard to convince authorities to admit refugee musicians and give them work permits. In the United States student enrollments decreased in the 1930s because of the low birthrate caused by World War I, with the result that the number of American college and university instructors who lost their jobs between 1933 and 1936 amounted to the same number of persons then believed to have been dismissed from German universities—two thousand academics (including a few women). In Great Britain, before the Red Brick explosion of higher education, university appointments—except for the very prominent professors—were limited.

The political pressures resulting from these and similar economic stringencies appear to offer sufficient reason for the slowness and inactivity, if not outright and deliberate dilatoriness, of parliamentary bodies and executive branches of government in responding to calls for aid to the intellectual refugee. That in spite of these difficulties a considerable number of intellectual and artistic refugees could be placed was to the credit of a large number of private individuals and agencies in most countries of the Western world.

Agencies were set up in the United States, Great Britain, France, Switzerland, Holland, Belgium, and other countries. One association of refugee intellectuals in Zurich, the Notgemeinschaft Deutscher Wissenschaftler im Ausland, helped in the placement of over two thousand persons. The British Society for the Protection of Science and Learning reported (in 1939) that it had placed 524 persons permanently and 306 persons temporarily in various countries of the world. This figure included not only German and Austrian but also Italian, Spanish, and other victims of totalitarianism. In Britain alone, 492 scholars who had been assisted by the society were in positions in industry, museums, publishing, the colleges, and universities.

In the United States, placement figures are available from such established institutions as the Rockefeller Foundation, the Emergency Committee in Aid of Displaced Foreign Scholars, the Oberlaender Trust, and the American Friends Service Committee. Over

56

and above these major agencies, however, aid to intellectual and professional migrants from Germany or Austria was provided by a vast array of volunteer organizations and ad hoc committees of professors, librarians, psychiatrists, physicians, lawyers, musicians, film people, and many religious and nonsectarian groups. The deep popular outpouring of voluntary aid to the displaced student, intellectual, or artist may be glimpsed in a recent documentation on the archival resources available for the study of this period.[2] This grassroots effort, especially in response to the burning of the synagogues and the attendant pogroms of November 1938, must be seen in the context of the grim facts of the economic market and the government policies related above. The as yet unwritten history of this effort will reveal American humanitarianism at one of its finest hours.

VI The reconstruction of the social networks destroyed by persecution and emigration took, of course, more than one form. The most favorable transfer occurred when an entire institution succeeded in relocating. This was the case with the (small) Warburg Institute, which moved from Hamburg to London, and the Institut für Sozialforschung, which shifted from Frankfurt via Paris and Geneva to Morningside Heights in New York. Socially similar in terms of network support were situations involving the appointment of a group of scholars to an existing university or college. In this country, the best-known (if as yet inadequately described) group appointments took place at the University in Exile at the New School for Social Research, and at the Institute for Advanced Study in Princeton. Similar to such group appointment patterns were those involving universities appointing a larger number of refugee scholars in some schools or departments—for example, in art history, applied mathematics, or social science.

Abroad, the hiring of approximately one hundred refugee professors at the Universities of Ankara and Istanbul, and the founding, by Paul Hindemith and Carl Ebert, of the music conservatory in Istanbul, are the best-known examples of such group appointments. Similarly, neither the growth of the Hebrew University in Jerusalem from a small institution teaching two hundred students in 1933 to a full-fledged university nor the growth and differentiation of its medical departments was unrelated to refugee appointments: by 1939, more than thirty professors from German universities had   57 found a niche in Jerusalem, followed by others and by younger generations of scholars during and after the war.

For the majority of displaced intellectuals, finding a new position in another country offered a unique opportunity to confront their cultural past with the opportunities of their new environment. Many of the prominent among them found positions with the assistance of the large relief agencies. No overall analysis of the intellectual or social place of these immigrants in American life or academic history, or in the intellectual history of other countries, has ever been attempted.

In many fields, our information suggests the younger and less prominent also made contributions, related their own and their parents' cultural impulses to their native training, teaching, or research, and provided a multiplying factor to the process of cultural transfer. Without considering their history, the account of the cultural migration of the Nazi period and its aftermath will remain incomplete.

VII   One final remark: the political periodization of the historic process that here concerns us obscures, to some extent, the larger context in which the migrants of the Hitler period will ultimately have to be placed. Before Hitler's appointment as the German chancellor on January 30, 1933, research had already begun to transcend the boundaries of the political units—the nation-states—that had emerged from the nineteenth century. As research was becoming international, the researcher, too, began to transcend national boundaries: Albert Einstein's personal history demonstrates in an admittedly unusual and idiosyncratic way a broader characteristic of twentieth-century cultural history. Following World War II, professionals and intellectuals, business managers and technical personnel began to follow the earlier example of musicians, painters, the plastic arts fraternity, and the motion picture community and moved across national boundaries. Study abroad, partly furthered by government-established agencies or private institutes of international education, led innumerable students—by no means only from the newly established postcolonial states—to foreign universities. Even before the military-industrial interests sought to attract foreign scientists for national purposes, political upheavals or economic limitations had motivated scientists to seek placement in intellectual or academic environments conducive to productive work. For many fields,

58

this new internationalism of the intellectual signaled the end of provincialism. Could it be that, by a "cunning of history," the massive flight of the intellectual from Nazi Europe will ultimately find its historic place in this as yet inadequately conceptualized and explored new internationalism of the Western world, the Atlantic civilization?

Notes

For a detailed discussion of the "Jewish Emigration from Germany: Nazi Policies and Jewish Responses," see my articles by that name: 1: *Yearbook, Leo Baeck Institute* 25 (1980):313–61; 2: ibid. 26 (1981):323–409.

1. *International Biographical Dictionary of Central-European Émigrés 1933–1945 (Handbuch der deutsch-sprachigen Emigration 1933–1945)*, vol. 1: *Politik, Wirtschaft, Gesellschaft*, ed. Werner Roeder and Herbert A. Strauss (sponsored by the Institut für Zeitgeschichte, Munich, and the Research Foundation for Jewish Immigration, New York, 1980); vol. 2: *The Sciences and the Arts*, ed. Herbert A. Strauss and Werner Roeder (sponsored by Research Foundation for Jewish Immigration, New York, and Institut für Zeitgeschichte, Munich, 1983); vol. 3: Index volume, 1983.

2. Herbert A. Strauss, ed., *Jewish Immigrants of the Nazi Period in the U.S.A.* (sponsored by the Research Foundation for Jewish Immigration, New York), vols. 1–3 (1978–82), vols 4–6 (in preparation).

59

American Refugee Policy in Historical Perspective

ROGER DANIELS

Most of this colloquium, quite properly, is not only a commemoration of the Einstein centennial; it is also an entirely appropriate celebration of the extraordinary infusion of learning and talent that the barbarism of the Old World sent to the New. Yet, as we all know, those who escaped were only a tiny remnant of the whole. The horrible story of how the governments of the English-speaking nations hardened their hearts and all but closed their doors to the victims of what the world would eventually name genocide has been told in frightful detail by historians. A.J. Sherman and Bernard Wasserstein have well covered the British experience; Arthur Morse, David Wyman, Henry L. Feingold, and Saul S. Friedman have chronicled and commented on the American aspect of the tragedy; while Irving Abella and Harold Troper, in a stunning 1979 article in the *Canadian Historical Review*, have shown how strikingly similar Canadian policy was to the American.[1] That the United States, Britain, Canada, and other nations not under the Nazi yoke could have, and should have, done more, is axiomatic. As Vice President Walter Mondale put it recently, the nations of asylum simply "failed the test of civilization."[2]

My purpose today is not merely to rehearse that sorry chronicle of events, which, as David Brody demonstrated seventeen years ago, was not solely the fault of gentiles,[3] but rather to ask two questions about that experience: first, what had American policy toward refugees been; and second, how did it change under the successive impacts of the closing of the frontier, the struggle to fulfill the promise of American life, depression, and war.

Although President Jimmy Carter claimed that the United States was and always has been "a nation of refugees," such a conclusion requires a straining of the evidence.[4] It is true, however, that refugees have been received, and sometimes welcomed, from the earliest years of our existence as a nation. The assumption here is that a refugee was, in the common dictionary definition, "a person who flees from one's home or country to seek refuge elsewhere, as in time of war, or political or religious persecution." Applying this definition to our first century we find royalists and republicans, ousted slaveholders and Bonapartists, all finding asylum here. During the waning days of Federalism, and especially in the administration of John Adams (1797–1801), some concern was expressed over the allegedly subversive activities of certain French and Irish resident aliens, some of whom were or became refugees, but that was a short-lived aberration. Refugees were treated no differently from other immigrants, and, in fact, the term *refugee* does not appear in American immigration law until 1934, so that prior to that date there is no legal distinction whatever between "immigration policy" and "refugee policy."[5] Throughout the first half of the nineteenth century, those who could obtain transportation came here, and no federal statutes existed to curtail or regulate their coming. Despite America's relatively wide-open door, Great Britain rather than the United States became, throughout the century, the mecca for European political refugees. Relatively large numbers of Latin American refugees arrived here, exiles who can be counted in hundreds rather than in dozens. The most significant of these groups were Cubans, centered in Tampa and New York City, who conducted propaganda and even waged war against their colonial overlords until the Spanish were driven out in 1898.

In the meantime, a body of immigration law was developing in the United States, law that would, willy-nilly, shape refugee policy.

That law can best be understood as representing an accretionary body of prohibited and excluded categories. The first of these were created in 1875 when the entry of "women for the purposes of prostitution" and criminals "whose sentence has been remitted on condition of immigration" were barred by statute.[6] Seven years later, the passage of the Chinese Exclusion Act for the first time singled out an ethnic group for exclusion.[7] Two other statutes in the 1880s barred "contract labor," while in 1891 the list of reasons for exclusion was broadened to include

all idiots, insane persons, paupers or persons likely to become a public charge, persons suffering from a loathsome or contagious disease, persons who have been convicted of a felony or other infamous crime or misdemeanor involving moral turpitude, [and] polygamists.[8]

In 1903, in the wake of the murder of President William McKinley by an American-born anarchist with a Polish name, Congress broadened the excluded list to encompass

anarchists, or persons who believe in or advocate the overthrow by force and violence of the Government of the United States. . .or the assassination of public officials.[9]

All of these prohibitions became an ongoing part of American immigration law, and many of them were utilized as devices to bar refugees in the 1930s. Particularly significant were the economic restrictions (the "likely to become a public charge" or "l.p.c." clause probably kept out more otherwise qualified immigrants than did any other), the restrictions about crimes and misdemeanors involving "moral turpitude" (some would-be refugees in the 1930s were denied visas because of their violation of the Nuremburg Laws of the Third Reich), and the political and ideological prohibitions that some U.S. consuls extended to members of socialist as well as communist parties.

As can be inferred from the increasing amount of anti-immigration legislation in the late nineteenth and early twentieth centuries, there was a growing disenchantment with immigration in the United States, particularly among the elite. In 1894, a group of Harvard men organized the Immigration Restriction League, which provided a kind of intellectual leadership for the anti-immigrant movement.[10] One of the factors that fed the growing resentment of immigration was its steadily growing volume. About half of all the people who have ever immigrated to the United States came in the years between 1880 and 1924. When we think of that era of immigration today, Emma Lazarus's now famous poem of 1886, "The New Colossus"—   63

Give me your tired, your poor,
Your huddled masses yearning to breathe free,
....
I lift my lamp beside the golden door.

—comes almost immediately to mind. Yet, as John Higham has
shown, that verse was not at all representative of the contemporary
climate of opinion, and it became popular only in the 1930s.[11] More
representative of the era of immigration restriction was a lesser verse
by the genteel poet Thomas Bailey Aldrich called "The Unguarded
Gates." Published in the *Atlantic Monthly* in 1882 it decried the

... wild motley throng,
....
bringing with them unknown gods and rites
....
In street and alley what strange tongues are these,
Accents of menace to our ear,
Voices that once the Tower of Babel knew.

In addition to sheer numbers, the negative attitude toward immigration was undoubtedly exacerbated by the closing of the frontier
and the psychic strains of increasing industrialization and urbanization. These factors helped produce a kind of American *Kulturkampf* (cultural struggle) between an old-stock, Protestant, rural-
oriented America and an immigrant, non-Protestant, urban-oriented
America. Immigration policy was but one of the battlegrounds of
that struggle, a struggle that was heightened by the strains and stresses
arising out of the nationalism and antiforeign reactions set off by
World War I. It was not merely a coincidence that in February 1917,
just prior to American entry into the war to make the world safe for
democracy, Congress added a literacy test to the immigration statutes. Woodrow Wilson, like William Taft and Grover Cleveland
before him, had vetoed the measure on the ground that literacy was
an indication of opportunity rather than of intelligence, but more
than two-thirds of both houses overrode that argument. Prospective
immigrants to the United States, unlike those to Great Britain, could
choose to be examined in any "language or dialect, including Hebrew
or Yiddish."[12] Although it had been a bone of contention for decades,
the literacy test itself proved to be of little real effect in stemming
the tide of immigration. During fiscal year 1921, for example, more
than 800,000 immigrants were admitted. About 1½ percent of these,
13,799 persons, were denied admission on some grounds, with a

64

mere 1,450 barred because they failed the literacy test. Yet, despite its ineffectiveness, the passage of the literacy test in 1917 was an important symbolic victory for the restrictionist forces and presaged even more important triumphs in the postwar era.

Separate immigration statutes in 1921 and 1924 transformed the immigration policy of the United States from one that admitted immigrants with certain specific exceptions to one that allowed the admission of strictly limited numbers of persons from particular places.[13] As Representative Albert Johnson, a Republican from Washington and chief author of the 1924 legislation, put it:

... the myth of the melting pot has been discredited. ... The United States is our land. ... We intend to maintain it so. The day of unalloyed welcome to all peoples, the days of indiscriminate acceptance of all races, has definitely ended.

While vice president, Calvin Coolidge, who signed the 1924 act into law, had published an article entitled "Whose Country Is This?" in which he made clear not only his adherence to the theory of Nordic supremacy but also his notion that intermarriage between Nordics and other groups produced deteriorated offspring.[14]

The drastic reorientation of American immigration policy, although triggered by wartime nationalism and postwar disillusion, was a logical continuation of trends begun in the late nineteenth century. Since no distinction was made between refugees and other immigrants, the 1924 act was crucial in setting out what became the parameters of refugee policy in the 1930s. The legislative debates that preceded the act show little awareness of potential refugee problems. One leading nativist did envisage a future refugee influx that restrictive legislation might prevent. Madison Grant wrote, in late 1918, that:

When the Bolshevists in Russia are overthrown, which is only a question of time, there will be a great massacre of Jews and I suppose we will get the overflow unless we can stop it.[15]

However, I have seen no evidence to suggest that such anticipations were widespread. Many Americans and most of the Congress did want to cut down on the volume of immigration and also to restrict drastically immigration from southern and eastern Europe. Almost all of those who participated in the great debate over immigration policy in the 1920s assumed that the future would resemble the past, that most of those who would try to come to the United States would be attracted for largely economic reasons.

65

What the new immigration law did was set a limit on the number of immigrants who could enter the United States in any one year and then subdivide that number into quotas for individual countries supposedly based upon the relative number of persons from that country who had been here in 1890, the last census taken before very heavy immigration from eastern and southern Europe had occurred. Immigrants from Canada and Latin America were not subject to quotas, but all previous restrictions did apply. At the time Hitler came to power, the number of immigrants who could enter the United States annually was limited by presidential proclamation to 153,849. Of those spaces, 65,721 were reserved for Great Britain and Northern Ireland, 25,957 for Germany, 17,853 for the Irish Free State, and 7,441 for the nations of Scandinavia. This amounted to more than 75 percent of the quota.[16] In 1920, the last year of relatively unrestricted immigration, these same nations had accounted for only 14 percent of immigration. There was no transferability of quotas from one nation to another, and throughout the 1930s the number of persons admitted was well below quota. Even the German quota, for example, was filled in only one year of the 1930s. For the fiscal years ending June 30, the number of German immigrants was as follows:

1933	—	1,919
1934	—	4,392
1935	—	5,201
1936	—	6,346
1937	—	10,895
1938	—	17,199
1939	—	33,515
1940	—	21,520
Total		100,987

Had all the German quota spaces been filled, the total would have been 211,895.[17]

The accession of Franklin Roosevelt to the presidency inaugurated changes in almost every aspect of American life. There was not, however, even a semblance of a new deal for immigration. From his very first days in office, FDR was made aware of what was happening to Jews in Germany, and, as a humane liberal democrat, he deplored it.[18] As chief executive, however, he did almost nothing and for years took the advice of his conservative State Department. When, for example, Felix Frankfurter and Raymond Moley urged him to send representatives to a 1936 League of Nations conference on Jewish and non-Jewish refugees, and, if possible, to appoint Rabbi Stephen M. Wise to the delegation, Roosevelt instead followed the State Department's recommendation to send only a minor functionary as an observer.[19] In an election year, FDR endorsed Secretary of State Cordell Hull's narrow view of executive power. Hull had written to him:

The agenda of the conference calls for discussion only of matters pertaining to the legal status of German and other refugees. As far as this country is concerned, the status of all aliens is covered by law and there is no latitude left to the Executive to discuss questions concerning the legal status of aliens. It does not appear advisable, therefore, for the Government to place itself in the position of even appearing to have any authority or discretion in connection with the status of other than American citizens.[20]

Similarly, when Herbert Lehman, FDR's successor as governor of New York, wrote him about the difficulty German Jews were having in getting visas from American consulates in Germany, Roosevelt, on two different occasions in 1935 and 1936, sent replies that had been drafted by the State Department. In each instance, the response assured Lehman of FDR's "sympathetic interest," but insisted that

the Department of State and its consular officials abroad are continuing to make every effort to carry out the immigration duties placed upon them in a considerate and humane manner.

Lehman was also assured that a visa would be issued in any instance

when the preponderance of evidence supports a conclusion that the person promising the applicant's support will be likely to take steps to prevent the applicant from becoming a public charge.[21]

Irrefutable evidence exists in a number of places to demonstrate that, despite these assurances at the very highest levels of government, the U.S. Department of State consistently made it difficult for most refugees to enter this country. Let me illustrate what I mean by a brief description of the problems encountered by Hebrew Union College (HUC) in Cincinnati in its Refugee Scholars Project. These incidents, which were all too typical, are taken from an excellent essay on the project by Michael A. Meyer.[22] The project, which was operational between 1935 and 1942, eventually brought eleven refugee scholars to Cincinnati. Most of those came under the provisions

67

of a special section of the 1924 act, which exempted from quota restriction

an immigrant who continuously for at least two years immediately preceding the time of his application for his admission to the United States has been, and who seeks to enter the United States solely for the purpose of, carrying on the vocation of minister of any religious denomination, or professor of a college, academy, seminary or university; and his wife, and his unmarried children under 18 years of age, if accompanying or following to join him.[23]

Such a provision was almost providential for the kinds of scholars HUC wanted to bring out, but the State Department, and especially Avra M. Warren, head of its Visa Division, continually raised—one is tempted to say invented—difficulties. In most instances, the college, sometimes with the help of influential individuals, managed to overcome them. In the cases of Arthur Spanier and Albert Lewkowitz, however, the difficulties proved insurmountable. Spanier, the former Hebraica librarian at the Prussian State Library and later a teacher at the former Hochschule für die Wissenschaft des Judentums in Berlin, had been sent to a concentration camp after *Kristallnacht*. The guaranteed offer of an appointment from HUC was enough to get him released from the concentration camp but not enough to get him a visa from an American consulate. A visit to the State Department by HUC president Julian Morgenstern was necessary before the reasons for refusal could be discovered. According to Warren, Spanier was primarily a librarian. His teaching at the Hochschule was not acceptable to the State Department because in 1934 the Nazis had demoted the Hochschule to the status of a Lehranstalt (institute), and an administrative regulation of the State Department, not found in the law, held that the grant of a nonquota visa to a scholar coming from an institution of lesser status abroad to one of higher status in the United States was not acceptable. Spanier and the other scholar, Albert Lewkowitz, managed to reach the Netherlands. It seemed then that Lewkowitz, at least, was likely to get out since he had been a teacher of Jewish philosophy at the Breslau Jewish Theological Seminary, an institution whose status the State Department did not question. But the German bombing of Rotterdam in May 1940 destroyed the copies of Lewkowitz's records, and the American consular officials there insisted on new documents from Germany. Five years earlier, in peacetime, Roosevelt had assured Lehman that

68

consular officials have been instructed that in cases where it is found that an immigrant visa applicant cannot obtain a supporting document normally required by the Immigration Act of 1924 without the peculiar delay and embarrassment that might attend the request of a political or religious refugee, the requirement of such document may be waived on the basis of its being not "available."[24]

No such waiver was made for Lewkowitz. Neither he nor Spanier obtained visas, and both were sent to Bergen-Belsen sometime after the Nazi occupation of the Netherlands. Lewkowitz was one of the few concentration camp inmates exchanged in 1944, and he was permitted to enter Palestine. Spanier died in Bergen-Belsen.

In early 1938 the White House began a series of executive actions designed to alleviate the refugee crisis. FDR, however, never made a move to disturb the seemingly sacrosanct quota system. As his spokesman, Myron C. Taylor, explained in a radio address on November 25, 1938:

Our plans do not involve the "flooding" of this or any other country with aliens of any race or creed. On the contrary, our entire program is based on the existing immigration laws of all the countries concerned, and I am confident that within that framework our problem can be solved.

Roosevelt's confidence was misplaced. Nothing short of a drastic revision of American immigration regulations could have saved substantial numbers of additional refugees after 1938, and this the administration was not willing to make. The president did take some initiatives leading to an almost meaningless conference at Evian, France, in 1938, and later that year, in the wake of *Kristallnacht*, he directed that political refugees on visitor's visas could have those visas extended every six months. This eased the situation of perhaps fifteen thousand persons who were already in the United States, but it did nothing for those still abroad. After the fall of France, FDR asked his Advisory Committee on Refugees to make lists of eminent refugees and then instructed the State Department to issue temporary visitor's visas to those individuals. The State Department's own reports, which are not always reliable, indicate that it issued 3,268 such visas to

those of superior intellectual attainment, of indomitable spirit, experienced in vigorous support of the principles of liberal government and who are in danger of persecution or death at the hands of autocracy,

but that only about a third of them were used.[25] In addition, there   69 were chimerical proposals to put refugees in Alaska, in various parts of Latin America, and even to establish a refugee nation somewhere in Africa.

With the coming of war, another phobia was used as a rationale to keep the bars up against refugees: the fear that Nazi agents would sneak in among them.[26] Only in 1944, when the incredible dimensions of the Holocaust began, reluctantly, to be realized in the West, did any meaningful action occur. On January 22, 1944, President Roosevelt established the War Refugee Board.[27] Although the board did not bring refugees to the United States, it did, with public and private funds, manage to aid in the rescue of the remnants of European Jewry. In terms of relaxation of the rules, Roosevelt made one more exception. In early June 1944, in a move masked by D-Day, he announced the establishment of a temporary "haven" at Oswego, New York, where 987 "carefully selected" refugees were brought, not for admission, but to be "interned," as if they were prisoners of war or enemy aliens. Had such expedients been adopted earlier, the wartime refugee story might have been substantially different.[28] As it was, the total number of refugees who came to the United States between Hitler's assumption to power and the end of the war in Europe was, almost certainly, well under two hundred thousand, or fewer than seventeen thousand per year.

The United States, therefore, went through all of World War II without developing a real refugee policy, using instead only an immigration policy slightly adapted for special conditions; it would get a refugee policy only in the postwar era and only after almost three years of political struggle. The end of the war found the United States and its allies confronted with the problem of some eight million displaced persons in Europe. Although perhaps seven million of them were eventually repatriated, the remaining million, plus millions of *Volksdeutsche* from former German territories and enclaves and new refugees from eastern European regimes, made for a postwar refugee population that approached ten million persons. Only a minor fraction of these were Jewish survivors of the Holocaust.

When Harry S. Truman became president, his initial response was similar to that of his predecessor—verbal sympathy, but little action outside of the quota system. In late 1945 and early 1946, he proposed reserving half of the existing European quotas for displaced persons and expressed the hope that this would bring some forty thousand refugees here annually. However, only about five thousand displaced persons entered the country in the first nine months of 1946, so, just before the fall elections, Truman began to talk about bringing in displaced persons outside of the quota system. In his January 1947 State of the Union message, the president urged Congress to "find ways whereby we can fulfill our responsibilities to these homeless and suffering refugees of all faiths." Shortly thereafter, Representative William Stratton, an Illinois Republican, introduced a bipartisan measure calling for one hundred thousand displaced persons to be admitted over and above the quotas for each of four successive years. This proposal set off a long and bitter debate that resulted in the passage of the Displaced Persons Act of 1948, the first piece of legislation in our history that can be described as setting refugee policy instead of immigration policy. The act accepted the definition of "displaced persons" that had been adopted by the International Refugee Organization (IRO), which the United States had joined in 1947.[29] "Displaced persons" were those who were

victims . . . of the nazi or fascist . . . or . . . quisling regimes . . . [or] Spanish Republicans and other victims of the Falangist regime in Spain . . . [or] persons who were considered refugees before the outbreak of the second world war, for reasons of race, religion, nationality, or political opinion . . . who [have] been deported from, or obliged to leave [their] country of nationality or of former habitual residence.[30]

To this basic IRO definition were added, in the 1948 act and by various amendments up to 1951, *Volksdeutsche*, Polish veterans in exile, Greek displaced persons, European refugees from China, Italian refugees from the Venezia-Giulia, and post-1948 refugees from Czechoslovakia.[31]

Rather than the 400,000 envisaged by the Stratton bill, the 1948 law authorized the admission of almost 250,000 displaced persons over the next two fiscal years.[32] All of the restrictions of the 1924 law in regard to health, ideology, and financial condition still applied. In an essentially face-saving measure, the law "maintained" the quota system by charging most displaced person entries to some existing quota, but allowing quota mortgaging. Within four years, to cite one extreme but not isolated case, the Latvian quota of 286 per annum had been mortgaged up to the year 2274.[33] Predictably, having gotten only roughly half of what they wanted, those who wished to liberalize refugee admissions continued their fight. In June

1950, the 1948 act was amended to run for two more years, and the authorized total was raised to just over 415,000.[34] As it turned out, the total number of persons of all kinds admitted as refugees from the end of the war until the expiration of the Displaced Persons Act in June 1952 has been calculated at 378,623. Diehard restrictionists, like Senator Pat McCarran (D.-Nev.) continued to complain that the "floodgates of the nation were being pried open for the entrance of millions," but the legislative history of the two acts shows a new, if limited, sense of responsibility for refugees on the part of the American government.[35]

As the provisions of the Displaced Persons Act were running out, Congress passed the first general immigration act in twenty-eight years. This 1952 act, to the disappointment of most who had been fighting for a liberalized immigration policy, maintained the old quota system with few modifications, although it is important to note that the total exclusion of most Asians was ended as were racial bars to naturalization. Although the word *refugee* does not appear in the act, one provision was to be of great importance for future refugee policy. The attorney general was given explicit power "to parole into the United States . . . for emergency reasons or for reasons deemed strictly in the public interest" any alien. What this came to mean in practice was that the executive branch could act—for Hungarians, Cubans, for Tibetans, for Vietnamese—and that Congress could later pass legislation regularizing their entry. No longer could a Cordell Hull counsel a president that "no latitude" was left for executive action.[36]

The following year a new refugee program was enacted. The Refugee Relief Act of 1953 authorized the admission of 205,000 non-quota persons between mid-1953 and the end of 1956. The cold war origins of the act may be seen in its definitions of the kinds of persons to whom it would apply: "refugees," "escapees," and "German expellees." A refugee was defined as

any person in a country or area which is either Communist or Communist-dominated, who because of persecution, fear of persecution, natural calamity or military operation is out of his usual place of abode and unable to return thereto, who has not been firmly resettled, and who is in urgent need of assistance for the essentials of life or for transportation.

Similarly, an "escapee" was one who had "fled from the [USSR] or other Communist, Communist-dominated or Communist-occupied area of Europe including those parts of Germany occupied by the" USSR, and a "German expellee" was any refugee of German ethnic origin . . . who was born in and was forcibly removed from or forced to flee from Albania, Bulgaria, Czechoslovakia, Estonia, Hungary, Latvia, Lithuania, Poland, Rumania, Union of Soviet Socialist Republics, Yugoslavia, or areas provisionally under the administration or control or domination of any such countries.

In addition, for the first time, Asians were officially denominated admissible refugees; two thousand visas were authorized for "refugees of Chinese ethnic origin," as long as they were vouched for by the Nationalist Chinese government, and three thousand visas were authorized for other refugees indigenous to the Far East.[37] In 1956, the definition of "refugee-escapee" was broadened to include persons "from any country within the general area of the Middle East"—defined as stretching from Libya to Pakistan, from Turkey to Ethiopia and Saudi Arabia—"who cannot return . . . on account of race, religion or political opinion."[38]

In 1962, with the passage of the Migration and Refugee Assistance Act, Congress recognized that refugee problems were going to be continuous and, for the first time, created legislation that did not have a self-contained deadline. In line with traditional Democratic faith in presidential power, it delegated broad executive powers, not to the attorney general, but to the president and, reflecting recent events in Cuba, extended the whole concept of refugees for the first time to those who had "fled from an area of the Western Hemisphere." Congress also authorized the expenditure of up to $10 million annually for the emergency use of refugees.[39]

In 1965 Congress totally revamped the 1952 Immigration Act by abolishing the national origin quotas as of June 30, 1968, and, while keeping most of the economic and ideological prohibitions of the old statutes, it set up a complex system of preferences. The new law reserved 120,000 spaces annually for natives of the Western Hemisphere, with no limitation on the number from any one country; 170,000 spaces were reserved for natives of the Eastern Hemisphere, with an annual limit of 20,000 from any one country. Preferences within and over and above that system are complex, and there are numerous and complicated exceptions that have made the practice of immigration law a growth industry. Regular immigration has brought around 400,000 persons annually into the United States since 1968. Many of those who enter under regular immigration law are refugees, but no one knows how many. But in addition to these numbers are persons admitted under various refugee programs.[40]

73

As one final example, I will mention the act of November 2, 1966, which regularized the status of Cuban refugees who had been admitted to the United States under the special parole authority of the attorney general. The new law authorized the attorney general to issue these Cubans documents, backdated to their time of entry on parole, making them resident aliens eligible, among other things, for naturalization.[41] Similar statutes have been enacted for Hungarians and other groups, and, barring the passage of a comprehensive refugee statute, more will probably be enacted in the future.

Thus, by the middle of the 1960s, the United States had evolved a fairly comprehensive and flexible refugee policy under which somewhere between a million and a half and two million refugees have been admitted since 1948. Obviously, had there been any kind of reasonable and humane refugee policy in the 1930s and early 1940s, there would be even greater refugee accomplishments to celebrate here. During that period, the United States was no longer, in the words of George Washington, "open to receive . . . the oppressed and persecuted of all nations and religions." While our new refugee policies tend to have finite limits for specific groups, those policies have been made flexible and reasonably responsive. There are still problems over definition—are, for example, persons fleeing abominable economic conditions in Haiti to be considered refugees?—over scope, and over intent.[42] In the final analysis, refugee and immigration policy is likely to be a reflection of foreign policy, as the recent disgraceful hysteria about the visas of Iranian students so clearly demonstrated. It is, I suppose, rather unreasonable to expect that it be otherwise.

Notes

1. A.J. Sherman, *Island Refuge: Britain and Refugees from the Third Reich, 1933–1939* (Berkeley and Los Angeles, 1973); Bernard Wasserstein, *Britain and the Jews of Europe, 1939–1945* (Oxford, 1979); Arthur D. Morse, *While Six Million Died* (New York, 1967); David S. Wyman, *Paper Walls: America and the Refugee Crisis, 1938–1941* (Amherst, Mass., 1968); Henry L. Feingold, *The Politics of Rescue: The Roosevelt Administration and the Holocaust, 1938–1945* (New Brunswick, N.J., 1970); Saul S.

Friedman, *No Haven for the Oppressed: United States Policy toward Jewish Refugees, 1938–1945* (Detroit, 1973); Irving Abella and Harold Troper, "'The Line Must be Drawn Somewhere': Canada and Jewish Refugees, 1933–9," *Canadian Historical Review* 60 (1979): 178–209.

2. Mondale speech text, Office of the Vice President's Press Secretary, July 1979, for release Saturday, July 21, 5:00 P.M.

3. David Brody, "American Jewry, the Refugees and Immigration Restriction (1932–1942)," *Proceedings of the American Jewish Historical Society* 45 (1955/56): 219–47.

4. Carter speech as reported in the *New York Times*, July 29, 1979.

5. 48 *Stat.* 477. In the era of the American Civil War, there was a special use of the term *refugee*, as in the Bureau of Freedmen, Refugees and Abandoned Lands, which is ignored here.

6. 18 *Stat.* 477.

7. 22 *Stat.* 58.

8. 23 *Stat.* 332, 24 *Stat.* 414, and 26 *Stat.* 1084.

9. 32 *Stat.* 1213.

10. Barbara Miller Solomon, *Ancestors and Immigrants* (Cambridge, Mass., 1956), provides an excellent analysis of the league.

11. John Higham, "Emma Lazarus. . .," in Daniel Boorstin, ed., *An American Primer* (Chicago, 1966), pp. 458–463.

12. 39 *Stat.* 874.

13. 42 *Stat.* 5, and 43 *Stat.* 153.

14. As cited in Roger Daniels, *Racism and Immigration Restriction* (St. Charles, Mo., 1974), p. 10.

15. Letter to Prescott F. Hall, Oct. 21, 1918, cited in John Higham, *Strangers in the Land* (New Brunswick, N.J., 1955), p. 306. Higham's work remains the premier study of the flowering of American nativism.

16. *President's Proclamation No. 1953*, June 19, 1931.

17. For 1938–40, because of the *Anschluss*, the Austrian quota of 1,413 annually is added.

18. See, for example, William Phillips to Louis M. Howe, Mar. 31, 1933, and Franklin Roosevelt to I.C. Blackwood, Apr. 12, 1933, printed in Edgar B. Nixon, ed., *Franklin D. Roosevelt and Foreign Affairs* (Cambridge, Mass., 1969), 1:31, 51.

19. Raymond Moley to Marguerite LeHand, Apr. 4, 1936, printed in Nixon, *Roosevelt and Foreign Affairs*, 3:278–80.

75

20. Cordell Hull to Roosevelt, Apr. 21, 1936, printed in Nixon, *Roosevelt and Foreign Affairs*, 3:282–83.

21. Herbert Lehman to Roosevelt, Nov. 1, 1935, and June 15, 1936; and Roosevelt to Lehman, Nov. 13, 1935, and July 2, 1936; printed in Nixon, *Roosevelt and Foreign Affairs*, 3:50–52, 64–66, 123–24, 341–43.

22. Michael A. Meyer, "The Refugee Scholars Project of the Hebrew Union College," in Bertram Wallace Korn, ed., *A Bicentennial Festschrift for Jacob Rader Marcus* (New York, 1976), pp. 359–75.

23. 43 *Stat.* 153, Sec. 4 (d).

24. Roosevelt to Lehman, Nov. 12, 1935, printed in Nixon, *Roosevelt and Foreign Affairs*, 3:65.

25. Robert A. Divine, *American Immigration Policy, 1924–1952* (New Haven, 1957), pp. 98, 102–3.

26. See, for example, a State Department–inspired article by Samuel Lubell, "War by Refugee," *Saturday Evening Post*, Mar. 29, 1941.

27. *Executive Order 9417*, Jan. 22, 1944.

28. Feingold, *Politics of Rescue*, pp. 248–94, contains a good account of the WRB.

29. 61 *Stat.* 241.

30. Constitution of the International Refugee Organization, annex I, secs. A and B.

31. These categories are taken from both the 1948 and 1950 acts, cited below in nn. 32 and 34.

32. 62 *Stat.* 1009.

33. Frank Auerbach, "Who Are Our New Immigrants," *Department of State Bulletin* 26, no. 678 (June 23, 1952).

34. 64 *Stat.* 219.

35. Divine, *American Immigration Policy*, pp. 110–34, is the best complete account of the displaced persons acts, but recent work by two scholars is beginning to give us a fuller picture. See Leonard Dinnerstein, "Anti-Semitism in the Eightieth Congress: The Displaced Persons Act of 1948," *Capitol Studies* 6 (Fall 1978):11–26; and Amy Zahl Gottlieb, "Refugee Immigration: The Truman Directive," *Prologue* 13 (Spring 1981):5–17. Dinnerstein's book, *America and the Survivors of the Holocaust* (New York, 1982), was published as this went to press. The following table, from Divine, p. 141, shows the numbers authorized for admission under the 1948 and 1950 acts.

76

Category	1948 Act	1950 Act
IRO displaced persons	200,000	301,500
Volksdeutsche	27,377	54,744
Polish veterans in exile	—	18,000
Greek displaced persons	—	10,000
European refugees from China	—	4,000
Venezia-Giulia (Italians)	—	2,000
Displaced orphans	3,000	5,000
Other European orphans	—	5,000
Recent refugees	2,000	500
Adjustment of status (persons in U.S. on temporary visas, etc.)	15,000	15,000
Total	247,377	415,744

36. 65 *Stat.* 163, sec. 212, para. 31 (d) (5).

37. 67 *Stat.* 401.

38. 71 *Stat.* 639.

39. 76 *Stat.* 121.

40. 79 *Stat.* 911.

41. 80 *Stat.* 1161.

42. For an up-to-date survey of contemporary refugee problems, see the Spring 1981 issue, vol. 15, no. 1, of *International Migration Review,* entitled "Refugees Today" and edited by B.N. Stein and S.M. Tomasi.

"Wanted by the Gestapo: Saved by America"— Varian Fry and the Emergency Rescue Committee

CYNTHIA JAFFEE McCABE

France's capitulation to Hitler in June 1940 trapped more than four million refugees in its "unoccupied" southern provinces—refugees whom the French government might have been required to "surrender on demand" under the ominous Article 19 of the Franco-German Armistice. Among them were some of the outstanding figures of modern art: Jean Arp, André Breton, Marc Chagall, Marcel Duchamp, Max Ernst, Wifredo Lam, Jacques Lipchitz, André Masson, and Henri Matisse. Nonetheless, the March 1942 exhibition of fourteen "artists-in-exile" at the Pierre Matisse Gallery in New York included Lipchitz, Breton, Masson, Ernst, and Chagall, all of whom had reached safety in the United States. Lam, by this time, was in his native Cuba, and Duchamp would arrive in New York within three months. Each of these artists owed his freedom, if not his life, to the Emergency Rescue Committee and its remarkable emissary in France, Varian Fry.

From August 1940, when he arrived in Marseilles, until his expulsion thirteen months later, Fry, a thirty-two-year-old Harvard-trained classicist on leave from an editorship at the Foreign Policy Association, together with a small, devoted staff, helped more than one thousand carefully screened artists, musicians, writers, scholars, politicians, labor leaders, and their families to leave France either legally or illegally. *Wanted by the Gestapo: Saved by America* headlined a 1940 Emergency Rescue Committee fund-raising pamphlet that asked for contributions of $350—the price of the life of one escapee.

The Emergency Rescue Committee (ERC) sprang into existence three days after France fell. At a New York dinner organized by the American Friends of German Freedom to honor newscaster Raymond Gram Swing, a prestigious national committee headed by Dr. Frank Kingdon, president of the University of Newark, was assembled. Five other college presidents—Robert Hutchins of the University of Chicago, Alvin Johnson of the New School for Social Research, William A. Neilson of Smith College, George Schuster of Hunter College, and Charles Seymour of Yale University—were also actively involved. Dorothy Thompson, Elmer Rice, and Swing were strong voices from the media.

On June 27, Fry and Karl Frank ("Paul Hagen"), research director of the American Friends of German Freedom, were sent by the ERC to meet with Eleanor Roosevelt in Washington. They had two goals: to seek Mrs. Roosevelt's recommendations for an ERC envoy to Vichy France and to enter into discussions with the White House about the visa situation in the United States and abroad. On July 7, Fry received a brief letter from Mrs. Roosevelt indicating that the president "will try to get the cooperation of the South American countries in giving asylum to the political refugees."

This was the opening round in the committee's unending battles on behalf of its "clients" to obtain overseas visas, the most critical of the many necessary documents of survival. The fall of France had coincided with the transfer of the immigration service from the Department of Labor to the Department of State, where Assistant Secretary Breckinridge Long was a virulent foe of foreigners. As a result, rules for the issuance of visitor's visas to persons who could return to their homelands as well as transit visas to those en route to third countries were severely tightened. Moreover, although an Emergency Visitor's Visa Program was instituted, its criteria, as stated in a Department of State press release, were stringent:

In exceptional circumstances, Visitor's Visas may be useful in saving persons of exceptional merit, those of superior intellectual attainment, of indomitable spirit, experienced in vigorous support of Liberal government and who [are] in danger of persecution or death at the hands of autocracy.

Applications had to be approved by the President's Advisory Committee on Political Refugees, or a related agency, cleared by the Justice and State departments, then passed on to the American consuls overseas, who had ultimate responsibility for granting or denying the visas. Although onerous, this emergency policy was especially important to the ERC in the early months of its rescue mission since, for almost all of the people it aimed to help, the 1940 immigration quotas had already been filled.

By mid-July the ERC had set up headquarters at 122 East Forty-second Street, New York. Since no experienced underground worker had been located and every day lost was crucial, Fry, who spoke French and German and who could obtain credentials as a social worker from the International YMCA, was appointed its European director.

His objectives were outlined in a letter of instruction from Mildred Adams, the committee's secretary:

Your task for us in Europe is exploratory on the one hand and specific on the other. You are: A) to find out and report to us the conditions under which refugee and rescue work must be carried on in the territories you cover, with particular attention to transportation, money transmittal, personal surveillance, attitude of American and foreign officials, etc. B) to attempt to locate, and to aid with counsel and money as directed, certain individuals whom this committee will specify, so that they may reach Lisbon or Casablanca and thereby be in a better position to be transported to this continent. C) to investigate and recommend individuals in such centers as Lisbon, Toulouse, Marseilles, etc. whom we may in the future designate as agents to act for us in those centers.

Fry was expected to fly by Pan American Clipper from New York to Lisbon on August 5 and to return by the same route on August 29. In addition to the dress shirts purchased at Brooks Brothers during his last hours in New York, Fry carried with him a master list of individuals in the gravest jeopardy, a list culled from the many supplied by a group of influential advisors. There was the Museum of Modern Art's list, compiled by director Alfred H. Barr, Jr., and his wife, Margaret Scolari Barr, who became a key ERC worker on the artists' behalf. Thomas Mann's extensive roster included Nobel laureate novelist Josef Wittlin; publishers Kurt and Helen Wolff, Jacques Schiffrin, and Franz Pfemfert; film critic Siegfried Kracauer; playwright Walter Hasenclever; writers Lion Feuchtwanger, Hans Sahl, Walter Mehring, Anna Seghers, Alfred Döblin, Alfred Polgar, and Alfred Neumann from Germany, Hertha Pauli and Ernst Weiss from

81

Austria, Valerie Marcu from Rumania, Hans Habe from Hungary, and Hans Natonek from Czechoslovakia; as well as Mann's elder brother Heinrich, son Golo, and brother-in-law Peter Pringsheim. Max Ascoli and Pertinax added Italian and French authors, respectively, while Karl Frank noted his own comrades in the German Social Democratic Party, in addition to the leaders of other Russian, Polish, Austrian, Italian, and Spanish political groups. The American Federation of Labor's operative in Marseilles, Frank Bohn, had yet another list, which Fry took over when Bohn was forced home— Konrad Heiden, Hitler's biographer; political scientist Hannah Arendt; German Finance Minister Rudolph Hilferding; Italian Socialist Party leader Giuseppe Modigliani; Austrian Secretary of State and poet Guido Zernatto; Largo Caballero, exiled prime minister of the Spanish Republic. The Nazis, too, had a list—Joseph Goebbels's death list—and the overlap was not coincidental: Hilferding and Caballero died at their hands; Hasenclever committed suicide after being captured and interned, Weiss when the Germans entered Paris.

Upon debarking in Lisbon, Fry traveled by train with two Rockefeller Foundation doctors whose company he credited with the fact that he was not searched at the Franco-Spanish border. Thus, his lists and instructions, together with three thousand dollars in cash, arrived safely in Marseilles. The city that confronted Fry, a rather naive and shy American, in August 1940 was not what he expected. There were no hungry children in the streets yet and no flagrant lawlessness. This blockaded port, however, seethed with people in flight. As ex-Bolshevik Victor Serge wrote in *Memoirs of a Revolutionary,* they were

a crowd of refugees of first-rate brains from all those classes which have ceased to exist through the mere fact of daring to say no, most of them rather quietly, to totalitarian oppression. In our ranks are enough doctors, psychologists, engineers, educators, poets, painters, writers, musicians, economists and public men to vitalize a whole great country. Our wretchedness contains as much talent and expertise as Paris could summon in the days of her prime, and none of it is visible, only hunted, terribly tired men at the limit of their nervous resources.
Here is a beggar's alley gathering the remnants of revolution, democracy and crushed intellect. We sometimes tell ourselves it would be tremendous if only five in a hundred of these forsaken men could manage to come across the Atlantic and thereby rekindle the flame of battle. If it had not been for Varian Fry's American [sic] Rescue Committee, a goodly number of refugees would have had no reasonable course open to them, but to jump into the sea from the height of a transport bridge, a certain enough method.

CYNTHIA JAFFEE McCABE

After abandoning his initial idea of bicycling around Unoccupied France seeking out the individuals on his list, Fry set up temporary offices in the Hotel Splendide. Word of his arrival spread instantly around the city. Writer Sahl heard from poet Mehring "that there was an American here to rescue us"; "you're mad," was Sahl's reply. In his memoirs, *In Search of Myself*, Natonek described the situation:

We had no exit visas and even had we had them there were no ships.

Like the first bird note of a gloomy morning a rumor ran through the cafes of the *vieux port* and Cannibière. It was said that an American had arrived with the funds and the will to help. . . .

I tramped the thirty blocks between my apartment and Mr. Fry's address without being aware of the time or my exertions. . . . Few of us, actually, had hopes of living. We struggled but it was a reflex action. Mr. Fry greeted me when I entered the room.

"Hello," he said.

He was casual, but he locked the door carefully behind us. Then he approached his desk.

"I've been looking for you," he said. . . .

He handed me a list, *the* list. There was a name inscribed on it with a cross and a question mark. The shape of the name was the shape of my own. . . .

"Leave Marseilles at once," Fry advised. . . . "You must chance the crossing into Spain."

The confusion that characterized the early months of Marshal Philippe Pétain's government worked to Fry's advantage. "One always tends to overestimate the tentacles of a totalitarian regime," notes Professor Albert O. Hirschman of the Institute for Advanced Study. A twenty-six-year-old German political refugee who had fought with the Spanish Republicans and in the French army, Hirschman, known as "Beamish" to readers of Fry's brief volume, *Surrender on Demand,* was his chief assistant for illegal operations. Hirschman traded currency on the Marseilles black market, obtained forged documents for ERC "clients," and devised methods of transmitting messages to New York on strips of paper inserted into toothpaste tubes or shoe polish cans carried by departing refugees. He also explored escape trails over the mountains, one of which he himself used in December 1940 en route to the University of California at Berkeley, which had offered him a Rockefeller Foundation fellowship in economics.

As a cover for these illegal activities, Fry established a genuine relief organization, the Centre Américain de Secours (CAS), at 16 rue Grignan. Here a staff headed by Daniel Bénédite, a young Frenchman who had dealt with many refugees at the Paris Prefecture of

83

Police, together with his English-born wife Theodora and others could screen potential "visa cases," while social workers unaware of any covert operations helped other refugees by dispensing free meal tickets or, whenever possible, the small sums of money that forestalled incarceration in an internment camp.

Miriam Davenport, who had studied art history at Smith College and was fluent in French and German, soon joined them. Arriving initially with a message from Mehring, whom she had met during the exodus from Paris, Davenport was responsible for interviewing refugee artists. When an unknown artist, portfolio in hand, came to the CAS office, she frequently sent the individual to the Vieux Port to sketch. The drawings thus produced were a determining factor in her decision about the artist's credibility. Davenport introduced Fry to Mary Jayne Gold, another young American, whose autobiography *Crossroads Marseilles 1940* colorfully depicts the situation from a singular perspective. Gold contributed much-needed funds to the ERC operation and, in turn, brought with her a teenaged refugee from Danzig, Justus Rosenberg. "Gussie," who now heads the Languages and Literature Division at Bard College, Annandale-on-Hudson, New York, became the center's office boy.

Mehring, arrested at the border as a petty thief in the fall, returned to Marseilles, where a refugee doctor testified that he was bedridden and could not be moved. During the following year, as a committee member, he sometimes acted despotically, according to photographer Hans Namuth, a grateful ERC visa recipient, who passed through Marseilles after being demobilized from the French Foreign Legion. Sahl, whose knowledge of the German literary scene was a great asset to Fry's team, has in an unpublished essay described the intense pressures exerted in the course of "A Day at the Rue Grignan." Sixty to eighty cases would often be handled during office hours. Then, when the doors were finally closed, the inner circle of "conspirators" would meet with Fry to determine which artists, writers, and others might qualify as ERC "clients," and their names would then be cabled to New York for initiation of the laborious process of gathering affidavits, funds, sponsors, and visas.

The Emergency Rescue Committee broke into public attention in the United States in October 1940, when, within a period of ten days, first Lion Feuchtwanger, then Heinrich Mann, his wife Nelly, and nephew Golo (Thomas's son), as well as Franz and Alma Mahler Werfel arrived in New York. In a daring rescue, U.S. Vice Consul Miles Standish had abducted Feuchtwanger from the internment camp at Les Milles and brought him to Vice Consul Hiram Bingham's villa, where he stayed in hiding until Fry sent him to Lisbon in the company of a Unitarian minister.

Upon arriving in the United States, Feuchtwanger was all too eager to detail his escape. Such outspokenness, his rescuers feared, could jeopardize their entire operation. And, in fact, it did result in the tightening of border regulations.

The previous week, Fry had personally supervised the escape of the Manns and Werfels over the Pyrenees. The plan was for the entire group to take the train from Cebère to Port Bou. Before then, some refugees who lacked exit visas had been allowed through, but now at the Franco-Spanish checkpoint the French were no longer so lenient. So the party, including Heinrich Mann, nearly seventy, and Werfel, who had a bad heart, decided to attempt the mountain climb. An experienced ERC guide, Leon Ball, accompanied them to the border. Each climber carried only a rucksack, Alma Mahler Werfel's containing Franz Werfel's draft of *The Song of Bernadette* and the score of Anton Bruckner's Third Symphony.

Fry, meanwhile, as the possessor of the only valid exit visa in the group, took all the luggage through on a train. Upon crossing into Spanish territory, the refugees presented themselves, as was mandatory, to the authorities. Then, as Alma Mahler Werfel wrote in *And the Bridge Is Love,*

like poor sinners, we sat in a row on a narrow bench, while our papers were checked against a card index. Heinrich Mann, greatly endangered because of his leftist tendencies, was travelling with false papers under the name of Heinrich Ludwig. Werfel, travelling under his own name, had heard in Marseilles that Hitler himself had put a price on his head. Golo Mann was in danger because he was his father's son. Yet Golo sat quite calmly, reading a book, as if the whole business did not concern him. . . .

Nelly Mann had half-carried her aged husband over this thistly mountainside, and her stockings hung in shreds from bleeding calves. After an agonizing wait, we all got our papers back, properly stamped, and were free to continue through Spain. When I think how many killed themselves up there on the hill, or landed in Spanish jails, I see how lucky we were to have our American scraps of paper, honored by the officials at Port Bou.

On October 13, exactly a month after they left Marseilles, the Manns and Werfels, together with ten other committee protégés, disembarked from the Greek liner, *Neo Hellas*, in Hoboken, New Jersey, where Thomas Mann, Frank Kingdon, and the members of the press awaited them.

"Wanted by the Gestapo: Saved by America"

Unlike Feuchtwanger, "all members of the group questioned yesterday refused to give details of their escape, saying there were others who hoped to follow them," a *New York Herald Tribune* reporter noted.

When Mr. Werfel, a short plump man with shell-rimmed glasses and curly black hair, was asked to describe his escape, he remained silent for a long period. He then shrugged his shoulders. "I can't speak," he said. "Most of us are still in France. My friends are all in concentration camps."

While escorting the Manns and Werfels, Fry used the opportunity to check out conditions in Barcelona, Madrid, and Lisbon and to interview escaping clients about their experiences. He also met with the British ambassador to Spain, who offered him ten thousand dollars in exchange for his assistance in getting stranded members of the British Expeditionary Forces out of France. The money was to be paid to the ERC's account in New York for later conversion to black-market francs.

Heinrich Mann, Werfel, and Konrad Heiden, author of a devastating biography, *Der Fuehrer*, who arrived in New York shortly afterwards, were the guests of honor at an ERC dinner at the Hotel Commodore on October 31, Thomas Mann, W. Somerset Maugham, and Dorothy Thompson were the principal speakers. This and similar dinners were apparently among the committee's most successful fund-raising activities. By early 1941, an ERC booklet could announce "602 Lives Saved."

While Fry's band of celebrities was being feted in New York, European borders were tightening further. As a consequence of Heinrich Himmler's visit to Madrid, all applications for Spanish transit visas had to be submitted to the capital, obviously so that the Gestapo could review them. The Portuguese imposed similar regulations, with the effect that only people who already had visas on their passports were being processed. A pattern became familiar to the committee during its two-year history: day by day the rules changed, and day by day innumerable regulations were drastically altered. The staff at the Centre Américain de Secours had to stay aware of each shift of governmental policy and had to calm its hysterical clients as each new rumor swept through Marseilles.

By mid-autumn 1940, Fry was finding the work load and pressures in Marseilles totally exhausting, and his staff began to look for a suburban retreat. The Bénédites, according to Daniel's unpublished autobiography, "Entre Parenthèses," found a large, unoccupied house,

Varian Fry, seated right, with four Emergency Rescue Committee clients—(from left) Max Ernst, Jacqueline Breton, André Masson, and André Breton—at the Villa Air Bel outside Marseilles. (Photo by Ylla. Courtesy of Annette M. Fry.)

the Villa Air Bel, a half-hour's tram ride outside the city; Mary Jayne Gold, too, was involved in this discovery.

Fry rented the villa, renamed by Victor Serge "Château Espèr-Visa." Its initial residents included Serge and his family, the Bénédites with son Pierre, Jean Gemahling from the ERC staff, and André Breton, demobilized as a physician from the French Army, with his wife Jacqueline and daughter Aube. For Fry, it served as a telephone-less weekend retreat.

With their leader, Breton, in residence, "the entire Deux Magots crowd, mad as ever," as Fry characterized them, assembled around Air Bel. André Masson and his family found shelter there, as did Max Ernst, when he was finally released from the internment camp at Les Milles. Together with Wifredo Lam, Victor Brauner, Jacques Herold, Oscar Dominguez, Benjamin Peret, and Remedios Varo, all of whom were living nearby, they revived the Surrealists' collaborative activities such as the creation of Exquisite Corpses; in these drawings and collages, one artist would work on the top portion, which was then folded down, and the others would contribute successively, without knowledge of the previously rendered components. Led by Jacqueline Lamba Breton, they also produced a set of tarot cards, known as the "jeux de Marseilles." On Sundays, the Surrealists mounted exhibitions and held auctions that attracted such visitors as Kay Boyle, Consuelo de Saint-Exupéry, and Peggy Guggenheim.

Guggenheim, who was reintroduced to Ernst at the villa, played a pivotal role in supporting the committee. She not only covered Ernst's Clipper flight to America but also paid the transatlantic passage of the Bretons and Massons. In addition, she helped Marc Chagall exchange his currency from francs into dollars in a U.S. bank.

The activities at Air Bel, however, also drew the attention of the Sûreté Nationale. Thus, less than a month after settling into the villa, Fry, Gold, Serge, and most of its other residents were arrested by the Sûreté. Before being searched, Fry managed to destroy most of his financial records and lists of clients as well as a Surrealist manuscript entrusted to him by Breton. For three days during the visit of Marshal Pétain to Marseilles, they were held incommunicado aboard the S.S. *Sinia* docked in the harbor. Some twenty thousand people were caught in police "râfles" that first week in December 1940, but Air Bel, site of a bombing eight years earlier, was especially suspect.

Even as Sûreté and Gestapo raids increased and the population of concentration camps swelled, some of Fry's potential clients refused assistance. Believing that their stature would assure protection from arrest, André Gide and Henri Matisse declined aid; however, both declared their sympathies by joining the ERC's Comité de Patronage. The aged Aristide Maillol, too ill to contemplate leaving his home in Banyuls, proposed that his model Dina Vierny, now a Paris art dealer, serve as an ERC border guide and personally showed her the best route over the mountains.

Although Gide, Matisse, and Maillol, as non-Jewish Frenchmen, were not harmed by the Nazis, several of Fry's political clients, thinking themselves too prominent to be extradited, lingered too long or too openly in Marseilles. Giuseppe Modigliani, painter Amedeo Modigliani's brother and a noted Italian labor leader, refused for months to abandon his eye-catching fur coat, a gift of the American Federation of Labor, or to change his appearance and shave off his beard; he and his family eventually reached safety in Switzerland, but Rudolf Breitscheid and Rudolf Hilferding, two of Germany's most important Social Democrats, were seized on the eve of their departure. Alfred Apfel, a Berlin attorney who had defended George Grosz, died from a heart attack in the office of the Centre Américain de Secours upon hearing about the extradition of Breitscheid and Hilferding.

Equally reluctant to leave but also in peril were Marc Chagall and Jacques Lipchitz—both Jewish, Russian-born, naturalized French citizens. Fry spent a weekend with Chagall in Gordes, trying to convince him that there were cows and pastures in America. When the painter was caught in a police roundup, Fry obtained his release by threatening to telephone the story to the Vichy correspondent for the *New York Times*.

To obtain Chagall's visa, Fry went to Vice Consul Bingham in January 1941 with only an affidavit of his own that Chagall was of moral character and would not be an encumbrance on the United States, and within a short time the artist had a regular visitor's visa. A concurrent application with all the proper documents for Chagall's emergency visitor's visa took six weeks to be processed in Washington.

Lipchitz, initially concerned solely for the safety of his art, had left Paris only when friends, the Pierre Chareaus, refused to go without him. In hiding in Toulouse, he continued to draw but made only one surviving sculpture, *Flight*. Lipchitz landed in New York aboard   89 the S.S. *Nyassa* on June 13, 1941; by day's end, according to art historian Meyer Shapiro, he and the sculptor had met. *Arrival*, the companion bronze to *Flight*, was created shortly thereafter. Through the remainder of his life, Lipchitz referred to Fry as "un héros légendaire."

The situation on April 19, 1941, with respect to many of his artist clients is summarized in Fry's cable of that date to MODERNART NEW-YORK:

YOUR LETTER MARCH TWENTYFOURTH BRETONS MASSONS ENROUTE MARTINIQUE CHAGALLS LEAVING INCESSANTLY [IMMEDIATELY?] ARPS SOON AS GET EXITVISAS KANDINSKYS NOTTILL AUGUST stop ELEANOR [ROOSEVELT] RIGHT ABOUT LOU ERNST UNABLE POSE AS STILL MAXS WIFE stop ACCORDING BRETON ELUARDS BEING KEPT ARREABY HAVE NO WISH LEAVE BUT ILL WRITE MAKE SURE stop WILL TRY HELP LEONOR FINI

By September 1941 France considered Fry's presence in Marseilles intolerable, and the U.S. government, for the sake of diplomatic relations, would not come to his aid. In fact, a letter from Eleanor Roosevelt stated explicitly that there was nothing further to be done. When Fry asked the French at the time of his expulsion why he was being persistently hunted, the reason given was that he had aided the Jews and anti-Nazis.

When he was forcibly escorted across the French border by the Sûreté in September 1941, Marcel Duchamp's name was still on Fry's rescue list. The ERC office was able to effect the escape of Duchamp, harpsichordist Wanda Landowska, curator Charles Sterling, art critic Paul Westheim, novelist Jean Malaquais, sculptor Bernard Reder, and some three hundred others before it was raided and closed by the police the following June.

With Duchamp's arrival the ranks of the School of Paris in New York were virtually complete. By war's end their presence had permanently transformed that once-provincial city into the art capital of the world. Similarly, if less fundamentally, the German-speaking intellectuals who established a bastion in southern California influenced American literature and film. Almost forgotten is the fact that Fry's former clients dominated both groups.

In retrospect, we can see that during a period of less than two years, the small team led by Varian Fry, supported by a devoted and knowledgeable group of Americans operating in New York and Washington, achieved a notable victory against the Nazis and Vichy France. Five months after his arrival in Marseilles, Fry had prepared

90

a detailed report of the situation there that was smuggled to the Emergency Rescue Committee's New York office. He wrote at that time,

this job is like death—irreversible. We have started something here we can't stop. We have allowed hundreds of people to become dependent on us. We can't say we are bored and are going home!

Many of Europe's finest creative spirits lived to attest to his tenacity.

THE MUSES IN AMERICA

Adaptation and Influence

German Émigrés in Southern California

JARRELL C. JACKMAN

In January 1980 I spent an evening with the émigré Marta Feucht-wanger at her home in Pacific Palisades. We stood on the terrace looking out at the ocean under a starry sky—a scene most serene and beautiful. Other guests were present that evening, all of us captivated by the setting, all of us aware that this once had been a center of exile activity: the home where the novelist Lion Feucht-wanger entertained émigrés during the 1940s. Still clear-minded at ninety-one, full of life and memories, Mrs. Feuchtwanger is living history; she enjoys showing her deceased husband's extensive collection of books, each one of them with a story behind it, many of them rare first editions and inscribed copies by fellow émigrés such as Thomas Mann.[1]

In this castle-by-the-sea one cannot help but ask the question: is this what exile was like in southern California? If so, can this even be called "exile," and how typical was it of the émigré experience? After spending an afternoon at Feuchtwanger's, the émigré author Herman Kesten left amazed by what he had seen: a twenty-room Spanish-style home with a view of the mountains and ocean; all kinds of fruit trees; a garden filled with flowers; a park with benches and breakfast tables. As Kesten said, "What a life!"[2] It undoubtedly had its comforts, and there must have been occasions when Feucht-

Émigré Lion Feuchtwanger and his wife Marta at their home in Pacific Palisades, California. (Courtesy of Marta Feuchtwanger.)

wanger thought to himself that all the troubles he had had to endure in escaping the Nazis were worthwhile—if this was the end result.

But, of course, the end result was not the same for all the émigrés. While Feuchtwanger lived in luxury, writers such as Heinrich Mann, Alfred Döblin, and Bertolt Brecht struggled to eke out an existence in their small bungalows and apartments. Employed by the film studios as scriptwriters, they had to bear the full brunt of adapting to a new life in a strange and frightening world. In some cases they were too old to learn English and too set in their ways to interact with the new environment. They had not been interested in America, nor had they had an audience for their works here, before emigrating—in contrast to Feuchtwanger.

So they arrived in southern California, unprepared for what they encountered. That the region is located at one of the westernmost points of the New World is important because, as individuals steeped in their Old World culture, they traveled almost the length of Western civilization, across the Atlantic Ocean, then clear across the continental United States, with each mile separating them further from the Old World and its cultural traditions. They had to adapt to a warm environment after the cold and bracing climate of Germany.[3] They glimpsed a new cultural landscape filled with bungalows spread across the vast Los Angeles basin, and connected by highways swarming with automobiles. On the streets they saw Californians dressed casually, wearing short-sleeved shirts and knickers.[4] In the studios they witnessed a hyperactive, frantic business world. Everywhere they looked they saw evidence that this was the New World, and they experienced a real sense of being cut off from their past.

How well the émigrés adapted to this new environment depended in part on their attitudes toward southern California. If an émigré viewed himself as the standard bearer of "high culture" and southern California as "lowbrow," then there were bound to be some problems.

Such was the case with the émigré composer Arnold Schoenberg, who was often appalled by what he saw in southern California. He wrote, at one point, to Oskar Kokoschka in New York:

You complain of lack of culture in this amusement-arcade world [of America]. I wonder what you'd say to the world in which I nearly die of disgust. I don't only mean the "movies." Here is an advertisement by way of example: There's a picture of a man who has run over a child, which is lying dead in front of his car. He clutches his head in despair, but not to say anything like: "My God, what have I done?" For there is a caption saying: "Sorry, now it is too late to worry— take out your policy at the XX Insurance Company in time." And these are the people I'm supposed to teach composition to![5]

The local hedonistic mass society so offended his German sensibilities that Schoenberg could not help believing that "everything was all wrong" in Los Angeles, and while the local residents could be very "kind and helpful," he found them "mostly inferior."[6] He did not want to be influenced by this world and rejected the notion that the physical environment had affected him: "If immigration has changed me," he wrote, "I am unaware of it. Maybe I would have written more when remaining in Europe, but I think: nothing comes out what was not in [sic]. And two times two equals four in every climate."[7]

Schoenberg received his inspiration from the German classical music tradition in which he fervently believed. That was the main reason for his feeling so strongly about his work as well as for his reacting so bitterly to the world of southern California. But, of course, Schoenberg was always the temperamental genius and had previously bemoaned the lack of recognition he had received in Europe. His music, too controversial for many conductors and composers and too dissonant for the conventional tastes of listeners, was never performed enough to satisfy him. In Los Angeles the same proved true: Schoenberg complained that, "Mr. Wallenstein [conductor of the Los Angeles Philharmonic] is here six years. . .and has not yet played one piece of mine."[8]

This hurt not only his artistic pride, but his pocketbook. After retiring from teaching composition at the University of California at Los Angeles, Schoenberg was financially insecure. Still, he could not bring himself to write music for Hollywood films. This would have been selling out and beneath him. And who is to say he was wrong in making the choice he did? The fact was, he became bitter about his situation and wrote:

there will certainly be in perhaps twenty years a chapter in the musical history of Los Angeles: "What Schoenberg has achieved in Los Angeles"; and perhaps there will be another chapter, asking: "What have the people and the society of Los Angeles taken of the advantage offered by Schoenberg?"[9]

In answer to his question, it can now be said great advantage has been taken of his presence—but unfortunately Schoenberg, who suffered from a heart condition during his exile years, did not live to experience it. More than two decades after his death, a Schoenberg Institute on the campus of the University of Southern California (USC) was erected. A splendid edifice, it houses many of his manuscripts, recordings, paintings, and other materials; there is also a concert hall where Schoenberg's music is frequently performed and symposia are held. The institute, moreover, publishes a journal on

The Arnold Schoenberg Institute on the campus of the University of Southern California, named after the émigré composer who during his years in Los Angeles felt isolated and neglected. (Photo by Christine Del Villar. Courtesy of the Arnold Schoenberg Institute.)

his life and work and has received financial support from Germany as well as from a consortium of local universities.[10] The irony of all this is obvious: a composer who often felt isolated and neglected in Los Angeles is now receiving more attention than he might ever have hoped for. And why has this happened? One reason is the influx of émigré composers and musicians who have had a major impact on the local music community. These émigrés have been responsible for raising the level of music in the region, a direct result of which has been an appreciation of Schoenberg and his achievements. Another reason is that his genius inspired his students, one of whom, Leonard Stein, is the director of the institute. So this monument on the campus of USC stands in honor of Schoenberg, who in 1951 died in Los Angeles in relative poverty with few people attending his funeral.[11]

Not all the composers, however, suffered as much as Schoenberg, in part because they had a different attitude toward their exile situation. Quite a few of them accepted the challenge of trying to work in Hollywood and, while not as brilliant as Schoenberg, they were talented men, trained in the serious music tradition. Among the most successful were Erich Korngold, Franz Waxman, Ernst Toch, Friedrich Hollander, and Ernest Gold, all of whom received nominations for or won Academy Awards. Perhaps the most satisfied with his Hollywood career was Korngold, the onetime Viennese *Wunderkind*, who won two Academy Awards and lived in a spacious home in Toluca Lake. His wife wrote:

He experienced the satisfaction of receiving unusual recognition for his musical creations in America. Thousands of letters arrived from all over the United States, later even from Europe and South America. . . . Korngold fan clubs were founded; Erich received gifts from all parts of the United States at Christmas and on his birthday.[12]

Like Korngold, other émigrés earned huge salaries at the studios, but unlike him, they were more alienated from the work and more unhappy with the way they were treated. The grandson of Ernst Toch recorded that the composer's "early enthusiasm for the artistic cross-fertilization possible in film gradually soured into bitter disillusionment. . ., and he came to despise the necessary prostitution of his talents."[13]

Those émigrés who worked in the studios were, for the most part, well-educated, serious musicians representing high culture, while the people they worked for were usually men of little education who produced films for popular consumption. As members of the German cultural elite, the émigrés were accustomed to being treated with a certain amount of respect, but found themselves frequently insulted by their Hollywood bosses.

Friedrich Hollander described in his autobiography some of the problems with which he had to contend.[14] Initially he was hired by Twentieth-Century-Fox, where he was given his own office with a piano; he was then approached by a producer who asked him to score a film, which he did, and which became a successful movie. Hollander's mistake, though, was not asking his department head for permission to do the score. Even though the music and the movie were well received, Hollander was fired for not having gone through proper channels.

Later, however, he was hired by Paramount, and again given an assignment. His film score was played through for several executives, the composer waiting anxiously in the wings for their reaction. After a long silence at the end of the movie, one of the executives stood up and said: "Piss in ice water."[15] Aghast, Hollander stood there dazed, certain his Hollywood career was over. Then someone else added that it was not really so bad, and the group decided to use the score without any changes. The upshot of this incident was that the very man who had reacted so crudely to his first work did more than anyone else to promote Hollander's Hollywood career. Hollander and most of the émigré composers learned to expect the unexpected, and with a healthy check coming in every week, they swallowed their pride and did the work assigned. The émigrés ended up making a major contribution to the scoring of films (in some cases, their music being the only redeeming quality of the movies they worked on).

The great advantage the émigré composers and musicians had over writers and actors was not being bound to language for economic survival. Except for Schoenberg, the émigré composers were also more positive in their attitudes toward southern California than were most of the writers, who did a great deal of moaning and groaning about Hollywood and cultureless Californians, even though many of them had been given one-year contracts as scriptwriters. This grousing is understandable considering some of their situations as exiles. What should be kept in mind is that there has been a long line of American and European writers who have come away from Hollywood disgusted by the experience. The letters and diaries of Bertolt Brecht, Leonhard Frank, and a number of other émigrés are replete with snide and angry comments about Hollywood and southern California.[16] These men, like Schoenberg, considered themselves artists and representatives of "German culture," and they resented being told what to create.

They resented, too, being cut down to size by Americans they felt were their intellectual inferiors. That happened to the émigré Frederick Kohner the first time he met Harry Cohn, president of Columbia Studios.[17] Kohner wanted to thank Cohn for hiring him, and when shown into the president's office, he expressed his gratitude. Cohn growled back that if Kohner did not produce he would be "kicked in the pants" out the door.[18] Kohner, having earned a Ph.D. in Europe, felt affronted; as he got up to leave, Cohn told the "Herr Doktor" that he had better get used to the way people talked in Hollywood. He did eventually and decided that the money made this life bearable, an attitude also shared by a number of émigré

101

writers, some of whom made lasting contributions to the Hollywood film industry. Among the most famous was Billy Wilder, who began as a scriptwriter and later directed *Sunset Boulevard* and *Lost Weekend*, two of the finest movies to come out of Hollywood in the 1940s and 1950s.

Frederick Kohner also made his mark in Hollywood, as a scriptwriter and later as a novelist. One of the more interesting facts of the German immigration to southern California is that the émigré Kohner wrote in English the novel *Gidget* (1957), which in addition to selling millions of copies in America and abroad was made into a successful movie and television series.[19] The novel portrays the southern California surfer world, in which what mattered most was one's suntan. The favorite pastimes of Gidget's friends were "shooting the breeze," "making out," "tooling down the main drag," "getting annihilated on beer," or "fractured on wine," to quote some of the phrases used in the novel. These were the activities of young teenagers totally oblivious to anything except their hedonistic lifestyle. Having raised a daughter in this environment, Kohner cashed in on being able to capture the experience in his novel, and he lives today a rather affluent life in his Brentwood home.

Several other émigré writers also achieved a similar level of affluence. In the 1940s, Bruno Frank, Franz Werfel, Thomas Mann and Lion Feuchtwanger bought homes in Beverly Hills or Pacific Palisades. Frank, Werfel, and Feuchtwanger wrote for or sold stories to Hollywood, but Mann depended on the royalties from his works in translation and the salary he received as a consultant to the Library of Congress on German literature.

There was considerable contact between these men, who also hobnobbed with some of the important names in Hollywood.[20] The interaction between the Germans and the Americans remained generally informal, and the intellectual impact they had on one another was minimal. The Germans depended on one another for intellectual stimulation because of common interests in politics and cultural matters. In a few cases, living in southern California did influence their writings. Feuchtwanger, for example, wrote a short story on Venice, California, a beach community south of Pacific Palisades, and Werfel's last novel, *Star of the Unborn*, has some descriptions of life in Beverly Hills.[21] Yet, for the most part, the émigrés continued to write their fictional works on subjects relating to Germany or Europe, while limiting their reactions to southern California to letters and diaries. The most extreme example of this was Thomas

102

Mann, who lived more than ten years in southern California and wrote nothing about America in his fiction. The only American influence he could attribute to his novel *Joseph the Provider* (1943) was that it had been written under "the Egyptian-like sky of California."[22]

An individual as steeped in the German language and German history as Mann was could not be expected to abandon them in exile. He explained in a lecture at the Library of Congress in 1942:

A work must have long roots in my life, secret connections must lead from it to earliest childhood dreams if I am to consider myself entitled to it, if I am to believe in the legitimacy of what I am doing. The arbitrary reaching for a subject to which one does not have traditional claims of sympathy and knowledge, seems senseless and amateurish to me.[23]

So Mann never attempted to synthesize his California and German experiences and went on after *Joseph the Provider* to write *Doktor Faustus* (1947), probably the most German novel ever written. But, of course, this work was not created in an intellectual vacuum: a German exile community, estimated by one émigré to number ten thousand,[24] surrounded Mann in southern California, allowing him to consult with individuals such as the émigré sociologist and musicologist Theodor Adorno. Mann and Adorno discussed among other subjects the musical twelve-tone system that Mann went on to write about in *Doktor Faustus*. Mann also read passages from his novel to friends and colleagues at his own home, at Lion Feuchtwanger's, and at other émigré gatherings. On these evenings, German culture was being kept alive some six thousand miles from its place of origin.

Mann himself was keeping it alive as much as any single individual. He remained German to the core, as did others, including his elderly brother Heinrich and the émigré novelist Alfred Döblin. What distinguished Thomas Mann from some of the other émigrés was that his preoccupation with his own cultural heritage did not lead him to criticisms of America or Americans. In fact, he had a basic respect for things American and a real fondness for southern California. Granted, he did not have to face working inside the studios every day or walk the streets of Hollywood, which might have tried his patience, as it did that of Carl Zuckmayer, the émigré poet and dramatist.

Among the émigrés it would be difficult to find anyone more bitter than Zuckmayer. From the day he arrived in southern California, he felt alienated from his surroundings, especially in Hollywood   103 where he lived and worked. He became so unnerved by the frantic pace inside the studios that he insisted on staying home to do his scriptwriting.[25] But he could not escape the world outside the studios, which also struck him as chaotic. The women in stores and restaurants seemed plastic and made up like dolls; they chewed gum incessantly while awaiting the big moment of discovery by some movie mogul. After only a few months in Hollywood, Zuckmayer decided he had better return to New York before he went mad. Of his last day in southern California, he wrote:

I saw Hollywood one last time in all its horror. Artificial Christmas trees with electric candles in all imaginable colors, chiefly pink, orange, and silvery blue, stood in front of the houses. I had been invited to a party given in the Beverly Hills Hotel. A slide had been covered with artificial snow and men in bathing trunks, women in silk jersey, skied down it directly into the cocktail tent. Huge crimson poinsettias bloomed in all the gardens. The sight of all this nauseated me.[26]

Zuckmayer had not been very successful as a screenwriter, but it would leave a false impression to conclude that those who succeeded in Hollywood did not complain, while those who failed did complain. There were several well-paid émigré scriptwriters including Curt Goetz, as well as other writers not dependent on Hollywood, who found southern California a mind-boggling experience. Erich Maria Remarque, for example, recorded how the people on a southern California beach affected him:

Unemployed extras were strutting about, hoping to be discovered by a talent scout. The waitresses in the restaurants and snack bars were all waiting for the great moment, meanwhile consuming lavish quantities of make-up, tight-fitting pants and short skirts. The whole place was one giant lottery: Who would pick the winning number? Who would be discovered for the movies?[27]

There have been so many lines like this written about Hollywood and southern California that it would have been surprising had the émigrés not chimed in with their criticisms. While the émigrés themselves can be criticized for their ingratitude to Hollywood, which, after all, had literally saved some of their lives by providing them with jobs in the studios, their anger is understandable in light of the traumas most of them had gone through as exiles. Their egos had been substantially deflated in southern California, where the local denizens had very little interest in German culture. In fact, Germany was the enemy that America, after 1941, was intent on destroying, and it would have seemed a contradiction in terms—at least to the popular mind—to be interested in preserving German culture in America.

Yet this did not stop certain émigrés from trying to transplant their culture to the New World environment of southern California. Perhaps the most enthusiastic in attempting this was the brilliant émigré theater director Max Reinhardt. He told Klaus and Erika Mann:

You simply must stay here [in southern California]. It's going to be a new center of culture. America is going to take over the cultural heritage of Europe, and there is no more hospitable landscape, none lies under happier stars, than the Californian. Here is a youthful country. European and American scientists and artists will meet to prepare a home for our old culture and for the new one that is coming into being here.[28]

In the early 1930s Reinhardt had been invited to southern California to stage *A Midsummer Night's Dream* at the Hollywood Bowl. A major success, the play was later made into a movie starring Mickey Rooney as Puck. One would have thought that Reinhardt's return in the 1940s would have been equally promising. He certainly was not lacking in enthusiasm for southern California. Unfortunately, when he set up an actor's school in the 1940s, the response to his efforts was only lukewarm, and the plays he directed were not particularly successful. By 1945 Reinhardt had become totally disillusioned and returned to New York, where he died shortly thereafter.

There were also efforts by other Germans to transplant a theater tradition to southern California, all of which met with little response, except for one case: Die Freie Bühne (The Free Stage), organized and operated by the émigré actor Walter Wicclair. Wicclair had a great desire to keep alive German theater in exile, and his efforts turned out not to be in vain. He began staging plays in German, employing émigré actors, and later he also did plays in English.[29] His company survived into the 1950s, and, up until a few years ago, Wicclair was still participating in local theater, especially in his favorite work, August Strindberg's *Dance of Death*.

And what happened to the many other émigré actors who ended up in Hollywood? To their good fortune, after 1941, Hollywood began producing a series of anti-Nazi films and employed the German actors, whose accents were perfect for the parts. Another irony of the German emigration was the casting of these émigré actors as

105

Nazis, their archenemies.

Occasionally, a German actor distinguished himself in a Hollywood role, as did Albert Bassermann. Frederick Kohner remembered a scene shot at Warner Brothers for the movie *Dr. Ehrlich's Magic Bullet*, in which Bassermann played a German scientist. Bassermann had learned the part with a German translation accompanying it, so that he knew what he was saying. When it came time for him to deliver his lines, he did so flawlessly. Kohner described the scene as follows:

When Bassermann had finished his rather lengthy speech, something quite extraordinary happened. Hands started to clap in approval. The applause was coming from the toughest audience imaginable: from the grips on the rafters—the most cynical, hard-boiled workmen among the ranks of studio employees. They certainly had never heard of Albert Bassermann before, but instinctively they knew that they had witnessed a master's performance. They recognized an actor's ability to be more human than humanity. . . . The applause was picked up by everyone on the set—the camera crew, the make-up people, the assistants, the script girls. And finally, the director, producer, agent and even Jack Warner joined in.[30]

The great acting ability of Bassermann had overcome the language barrier, but the German actors could not hope to lose their accents, which meant they would only be able to play in movies with German or foreign parts. As a result, most of the émigré actors left after the war in the hope they would be able to resume their careers in Europe.

The German exile experience in southern California ran the gamut between sheer agony and pleasant living. The Germans were fortunate in having so many of their fellow countrymen around them, so that if they could not adapt to certain conditions in exile, they at least had someone with whom to commiserate. But in the world of southern California, they had to learn to accept what they encountered or suffer the economic consequences. Sometimes they did a little too much "nose-thumbing" and could be ridiculously arrogant in their attitude toward America. It helped if the émigré had a positive feeling for his home in exile, but this did not guarantee ultimate success.

The ability of the émigrés to assimilate into the cultural life of southern California was determined by a set of factors: age, facility in English, profession, temperament, and attitude toward his home in exile. On the whole, it can be said that most were able to assimilate—as teachers in local universities, as musicians and composers, as novelists, as movie actors, directors, and screenwriters. At the same time, southern California allowed the Germans to intermingle freely and in the process guaranteed that a certain amount of their culture would be preserved. Today there are archives containing émigré manuscripts and other material at the Universities of California at Santa Barbara and Los Angeles and at the University of Southern California. Through these archives a part of German culture survives in the region, as does an academic interest in the émigrés' years in Los Angeles. A permanent exile research center at USC is being planned, for example, around the book and manuscript collection of Lion Feuchtwanger, and on the USC campus the Schoenberg Institute is preserving and perpetuating German serious music in southern California. As stated in the pamphlet issued by the institute:

The inexhaustible legacy of Arnold Schoenberg will benefit scholars
and artists who wish to gain an insight into the main cultural flow
of our age. Here at the Institute for the world to study and enjoy, and
from which to gain inspiration, is perhaps the richest endowment
any musician has ever left to posterity.[31]

Even with all of these activities, there are still large unexplored areas in the history of the exiles in southern California. To date most of the interest in the émigrés has been among German scholars working in this country who, understandably, tend to approach the subject of émigrés from the perspective of their own intellectual interests in German culture. However, there also exists a need to examine the exile experience in the context of California and American history; so far the émigrés have received little attention in local histories, and only recently has a historian offered a course at UCLA on the émigrés in southern California.

I have suggested how some of the better-known Germans adapted to the region, yet there are thousands of lesser-known émigrés including women and children whose lives were permanently altered by exile, and whose story has only been partially told. This part of the history should also be recorded, but before it can be done, a comprehensive list still has to be compiled of the German émigrés who ended up in southern California. This perhaps could be one of the first projects undertaken by the future exile research center at USC.

107

While there is still much research to be undertaken, from our present historical vantage point we can begin to understand the significance of the German immigration to southern California in the 1930s and 1940s. On one level, it provided a boost to the cultural life of the region, illustrating once again the ability of America to absorb other cultures and to benefit from them. On another level, the German migration bridged two cultures separated by thousands of miles. What resulted was an interaction between the émigrés, who represented an Old World culture dating back centuries, and southern California, a New World future-oriented region. It appeared on the surface that these two forces were irreconcilable—the Germans bound to the past, the southern Californians forward-looking. But in actuality the threads connecting them became strong, and an actual cultural synthesis took place when the émigrés composed for Hollywood, when Frederick Kohner wrote his novels, and when Walter Wicclair staged his plays. But still something was lost—a number of careers were ruined and full advantage was not taken of the émigrés by the region. Such was the price to be paid for Hitler's expulsion of the German cultural elite.

A return to Marta Feuchtwanger's terrace in Pacific Palisades is a fitting place and way to conclude this essay. Outside on that terrace once stood Thomas Mann, Bertolt Brecht, and numerous other important German intellectual figures of the twentieth century, and from that terrace they could look out over the Pacific Ocean with the blue sky above. Externally, all appeared calm and serene, but internally the émigrés were caldrons of emotions. Their hearts were laden with past painful experiences; they could not forget the turn of events that had uprooted and transplanted them to America. Yet, for all their personal problems and the difficulties they faced in working for Hollywood, one is left with the impression that the émigrés had been rather fortunate in being exiled in the Lotus Land of southern California.

Notes

1. Marta Feuchtwanger, interview at her home, Pacific Palisades, California, Jan. 4, 1980.

2. Herman Kesten quoted in Lothar Kahn, *Insight and Action: The Life and Work of Lion Feuchtwanger* (Cranbury, N.J., 1975), p. 300.

3. Quite a few Germans complained that the southern California climate sapped their creative energy. I talk about that in my article, "Exiles in Paradise: German

Émigrés in Southern California," *Southern California Quarterly* 61 (Summer 1979): 189–90.

4. The casual dress of southern Californians contrasted sharply with the formal attire worn by Germans such as Thomas Mann and Arnold Schoenberg. In almost every photograph taken of these two men in southern California, they are wearing coat and tie.

5. Arnold Schoenberg, *Letters* (New York, 1965), p. 242.

6. Quoted in Hans Heinz Stuckenschmidt, *Schoenberg: His Life, World and Work* (London, 1977), p. 475.

7. Quoted in Walter H. Rubsamen, "Schoenberg in America," *The Musical Quarterly* 37 (Oct. 1951):485–86.

8. Schoenberg, *Letters*, p. 265.

9. Quoted in Martin Bernheimer, "Tardy Tribute to Genius of Schoenberg," *Los Angeles Times*, Jan. 20, 1974, Calendar sec., p. 44.

10. On Jan. 3, 1980, I was given a tour of the institute by Clara Steuermann and also interviewed Leonard Stein, its director.

11. Stuckenschmidt, *Schoenberg*, p. 523.

12. Luizi Korngold, *Erich Korngold: ein Lebensbild* (Vienna, 1967), p. 80.

13. Lawrence Wechsler, Introduction to Ernst Toch, *The Shaping Force in Music* (New York, 1977), p. x.

14. Frederick Hollander, *Von Kopf bis Fuss, Mein Leben mit Text und Musik* (Munich, 1965).

15. Ibid., p. 337.

16. The émigré reaction to Hollywood and southern California is discussed in detail in my Ph.D. dissertation, "Exiles in Paradise: A Cultural History of German Émigrés in Southern California, 1933–50" (University of California, Santa Barbara, July 1977).

17. Frederick Kohner, interview, Brentwood, California, Jan. 3, 1980.

18. A similar incident with Harry Cohn was related to me by another émigré, Paul Elbogen, who remembered being called into the president's office and told by Cohn, who was brandishing a two-foot shoe horn, that he (Elbogen) had better produce or expect to get fired. Paul Elbogen, interview, San Francisco, Dec. 18, 1973.

19. Frederick Kohner, *Gidget* (New York, 1957).

20. There were some trying experiences for the more formal Germans who attended Hollywood parties. The émigré author Joseph Wechsberg was horrified by an incident involving a Hollywood producer who walked up to Thomas Mann at a party, slapped him on the back, and addressed him as "Tommy." Joseph Wechsberg, *The First Time Around: Some Irreverent Recollections* (Boston, 1970), p. 212.

109

21. The Feuchtwanger short story was published in Lion Feuchtwanger, *Stories from Near and Far* (New York, 1945). Werfel's *Star of the Unborn* was published in New York in 1946.

22. Thomas Mann, "Joseph and his Brethren," p. 10 (Manuscript of lecture delivered at the Library of Congress, Nov. 17, 1942), Manuscript Collection, Library of Congress, Washington, D.C.

23. Ibid.

24. A more precise number of émigrés who ended up in southern California has yet to be determined. The ten thousand figure is the number estimated by the émigré actor Walter Wicclair in his book *Von Kreuzberg bis Hollywood* (Berlin, 1975), p. 163.

25. Carl Zuckmayer, *A Part of Myself*, trans. Richard and Clara Winston (New York, 1970), p. 345.

26. Ibid., p. 352.

27. Erich Maria Remarque, *Shadows in Paradise* (New York, 1972), p. 205.

28. Quoted in Erika and Klaus Mann, *Escape to Life* (Boston, 1939), p. 265.

29. Marta Mierendorff, *Fifty Years in the Theater: A Publication Celebrating Walter Wicclair's 70th Birthday* (Los Angeles, 1971).

30. Frederick Kohner, *The Magician of Sunset Boulevard: The Improbable Life of Paul Kohner, Hollywood Agent* (Palos Verdes, Calif., 1977), p. 118.

31. "Arnold Schoenberg Institute at the University of Southern California" (Pamphlet issued on the occasion of the opening of the institute, Los Angeles, Feb. 20, 1977).

Social Theory in a New Context

H. STUART HUGHES

Sometime in the year 1941 a distinguished American sociologist wrote, in behalf of an Austrian-born colleague who was himself to become equally distinguished:

In spite of the fact that he has lived in this country for seven years or more, he has a distinctly foreign appearance and speaks with a strong accent. This prejudices some people against him, and I think some are further prejudiced because they feel that there is occasional arrogance in his manner. Actually, P. is one of the most modest of men, but he does have a rather heavy Germanic way of presenting a topic which tends to make some people feel that there is not as much in the topic as the difficulty in following him would suggest. I think such critics would be occasionally right, but I can testify from experience that there is plenty of pure gold in them thar hills.

The letter is a delightful period piece. It suggests how exotic the émigré scholars still seemed nearly a decade after Hitler's advent and how cautiously those among the native-born who respected them felt they had to proceed in championing the newcomers—even to the point of closing with a stale old-West turn of phrase. It may serve to introduce the central problem in the confluence of American and German social theory: What made it possible for two such contrasting traditions to reach mutual understanding? What circum-

111

stances led to an interpenetration of assumptions and methods that at certain points amounted almost to symbiosis?

For the more active and imaginative of the émigrés, the difficulty of working with Americans could be summed up in the word *positivism*. Our countrymen struck them as naive fellows, pedestrian, commonsensical, down-to-earth, and hypnotized by "facts." While such a string of adjectives frequently had about it an air of caricature, it was unquestionable that most American social theorists subscribed to the central positivist tenets: they took for granted that the data they were seeking were "out there" and ready for immediate interpretation; it seldom occurred to them that their own mental activities figured in the proceedings. And this philosophical laziness they dignified with the eminently respectable term *empiricism*. Now the German- and Austrian-born were by no means uniformly antiempiricist. Some of them—particularly those who had studied in Vienna—had come under the influence of a scrupulous form of neopositivism in logic and epistemology. But one and all they insisted that a mere grubbing for facts would not do: they believed it incumbent on them to adopt a professorial tone toward their hosts—to teach the basics of Kant and Hegel, Marx and Weber, to reluctant listeners, to insist on a rigorous *Fragestellung*, or posing of the question, before the empirical work could begin. Hence the "arrogance" and "heavy Germanic way of presenting a topic" on which the writer of the letter felt obliged to comment. Hence also the annoyance— for the most part unexpressed—of Americans relegated to the rank of schoolboys.

Yet when the Second World War ended, four years after the writing of the letter in question, the émigrés not only had learned to speak our language (with a "strong accent" no longer cause for suspicion or reproach); they also had found common ground on which they and their hosts could approach the study of society. How had this intellectual miracle come about?

First for the preconditions. If we ask what were the circumstances that facilitated the exchange of ideas between émigrés and Americans, we can find at least five special conditions, heterogeneous to be sure, but in most cases mutually reinforcing.

Initially it was necessary for the newly arrived themselves to make an effort. They got nowhere if they simply squatted close to some campus in the expectation that their international renown would automatically procure for them a university chair. A few eminent examples of this sort—fortunately of men with private means—were enough to deter the rest. If one wanted to insert oneself into American intellectual life, one was obliged to make a minimum of concessions—at the very least to simplify one's idiom and to become informed about what (however little) had been accomplished on this side of the Atlantic. One could not go on forever standing (or sitting) as a symbol of the superiority of Old World culture. In short, one needed to open one's mind.

If a certain adaptability was a prerequisite for finding an American audience, so too was a suitable locale. Geography exerted a crucial effect on the distribution and reception of talent. The older intellectual centers did not necessarily prove the most favorable; the Boston-Cambridge area is a case in point. Newer, warmer milieus seemed better able to provide pleasant and easy access between émigrés and native-born. The vast southern California beachhead on which the Germans and Austrians encamped is too well known to require elaboration here. Perhaps less familiar is the role played by the nation's capital. As, after Pearl Harbor, the war agencies sprouted, Washington became the place where those whom the universities had rebuffed could find a job: economic necessity and zeal for the struggle against fascism went hand in hand. And an expert knowledge of central Europe had overnight become a precious commodity. In the informal, frequently chaotic, and benignly tolerant atmosphere of the war agencies, the émigrés encountered native-born Americans who had themselves traveled and studied in their lands of origin. These latter were usually younger than the émigrés—and correspondingly willing to learn. They too had been uprooted—if less drastically—from their familiar environments. It was only natural, then, that open, spontaneous exchanges between these two varieties of scholar should have resulted.

All of which suggests a third precondition. If intellectual exchange went on more freely in a locale unfamiliar to both partners in the conversation, it similarly prospered where the institutional setting was new. The great northeastern universities found room for only a select few among the refugee scholars from central Europe. Still more significantly, the émigrés made only a small dent in such universities' academic procedures. The same was true in Washington. The personnel of the regular government departments changed surprisingly little during the war years: at State, the dominance of

113

Foreign Service types remained unchallenged; in the Pentagon, one could visit office after office without hearing a "strong accent." In these familiar bastions of government—as, more covertly, in the Ivy League institutions—doubts about the suitability (or possibly loyalty?) of the émigrés lingered longer than in the newer agencies. It was in the interstices of what had not yet come to be called the American "establishment" that the refugees from Germany and Austria found their niche; where bureaucracies or academic departments stood entrenched, they experienced a cool reception.

So much for geography and institutions. What of the "welcoming committee"? Just as the émigrés did best where institutional restraint was light, so the native-born who became their unenrolled "students" were seeking, not always fully consciously, to break the bonds of their previous training. To fields of study where young Americans were in a state of dissatisfaction or revolt, the scholars from central Europe came as heaven-sent messengers of a deeper wisdom. I can testify from personal experience to the staleness and flatness of graduate work in history in the late 1930s. I suspect that dozens of my contemporaries felt the same way about American sociology and political science. A fourth clue to the success of the émigrés may be discerned in the fact that they arrived just at the right time—just at the moment when a new generation of scholars was thirsting for what they had to offer. To us, their native-born juniors, the teaching they imparted was a heady brew, as learned as it was bold, that ranged freely over the whole field of social investigation. It mattered little whether the newcomers were professionally labeled sociologists, historians, or political scientists; the tradition they brought with them scorned such petty-minded demarcations.

A final precondition concerns the critical mass of the émigrés themselves. In order to bring their collective influence to bear, they needed to be concentrated in sufficient numbers. By the same token, there needed to be enough of them in each place or institution to provide mutual support, whether intellectual or emotional. But the optimum situation occurred when their mass was not overwhelming. In a setting where central Europeans outnumbered the native-born, life became deceptively easy for them: in enclaves of this sort, they might go for weeks without a serious conversation in English, visiting cosily back and forth much as they had done before their emigration. The balance between enough and too many was always delicate. It is a crucial consideration to keep in mind when we begin to assess the achievements and failings of the more prominent locales in which the émigrés congregated.

Two institutions in particular may strike us as having been over-saturated with central Europeans—the New School for Social Research and the Institut für Sozialforschung. About the New School, it is difficult to generalize. Its midtown location in New York City admirably equipped it to attract a highly motivated part-time student body of adults. Its faculty, although constantly shifting and uneven in quality, included at one time or another a large number of the leading scholars in the emigration. But its influence remained diffuse: with its curriculum a miscellany of courses and its students for the most part only fleetingly in contact with their teachers, it was in no position to elaborate a common intellectual program. In this case, then, the preponderance of émigrés was of little significance; the achievements of the New School were those of individual scholars, working as well as they could on low pay and in makeshift facilities.

Quite different was the Institut für Sozialforschung, which resembled the New School only in that it had the words *social research* in its title and was located, temporarily at least, in New York. One prime distinction between the two was that while the New School was always threatening to go broke, the Institut usually had plenty of money. Originally based in Frankfurt—hence the name "Frankfurt School" that became associated with its labors—it had fled Germany early enough to save its endowment. And the money traveled with it again when it moved a second time—perhaps predictably—from the cold winds of Morningside Heights to the more inviting landscape of southern California.

Whether in New York or on the Pacific Coast, the Institut was defiantly and uncompromisingly Teutonic. Its prime movers, Max Horkheimer and Theodor W. Adorno, defined their task in characteristically complex fashion as one of mounting an avant-garde assault on mass culture while preserving what was best in the tradition from which they had sprung. In neither role were they particularly concerned about their public. Indeed, their audience existed chiefly in their imaginations and did not materialize until the 1950s. Horkheimer and Adorno composed their most important works in German; their masterpiece, *Dialectic of Enlightenment*, although substantially completed in 1944, did not see the light until three years later and languished untranslated for a quarter century thereafter. During the Institut's New York phase, Herbert Marcuse had been associated with it, collaborating with Adorno and Horkheimer in developing its basic concepts. One reason why Marcuse's ideas burst with such explosive force on American readers in the 1960s was that these readers knew nothing that had come before; they never suspected that much of what struck them as totally novel in Marcuse's writings had been common intellectual property within the Institut a generation earlier. For—again unlike the New School—the Institut had a coherent program, which its individual members elaborated as personal whim might prompt.

The central feature of this program was an effort to accommodate the teachings of Sigmund Freud to those of Karl Marx. Such an aim, as Adorno and Horkheimer saw it, debarred them from theoretical exchanges with Americans; ever alert to the danger of shocking their hosts, the leading figures of the Institut went to absurd lengths to conceal their Marxist sympathies. A similar caution did not apply in the case of Freud. And it was in the realm of psychology alone that the Frankfurt School proved willing and able to reach out to American co-workers. The one significant Institut project that involved native-born collaborators was the investigation of "fascist potential" eventually published in 1950 under the title *The Authoritarian Personality*. The book turned out once again to be a curious period piece—or, rather, hybrid. The American and the German contributions never fused; they remained quaintly juxtaposed. On the quantitative, interview-based findings of the experimental psychologists he had recruited, Adorno superimposed an elaborate philosophical gloss that he could just as well have written without them.

In the field of psychology, the émigrés never outnumbered the native born. Here they acted as a leaven rather than an invading force. The subdiscipline of psychoanalysis is perhaps the "human" science most often cited as invigorated and raised to new heights by the arrival of the central Europeans; it also offered the classic example of young Americans eagerly awaiting the message from overseas. In the psychoanalytic institutes of our major cities, the émigrés quickly attained positions of commanding influence. It is astounding to learn of the apparent effortlessness with which a figure such as Heinz Hartmann, newly arrived from Europe in 1941, began to write lucid English and to overawe his colleagues by the power

Herbert Marcuse in Switzerland on his eightieth birthday, July 17, 1978. He first met H. Stuart Hughes at the Office of Strategic Services in Washington, D.C., during World War II, and they remained friends until Marcuse's death in 1979. (Photo by Isolde Ohlbaum.)

of intellect alone. The explanation, of course, is that the native-born were deferential to a fault: uncertain of the rigor of their own training, they were only too happy to let the Viennese and the Berliners tell them what to do. Thus, the institutional setting that may seem at first glance to have provided the most favorable mix of a majority of Americans stimulated but not overpowered by the émigrés proves on closer inspection to have been somewhat less idyllic. The difficulty here was that the newcomers did most of the talking.

Was true reciprocity ever possible? A fourth and last setting—necessarily less well known than those discussed up to now—suggests that intellectual exchange might proceed best when it came as a by-product rather than the ostensible purpose of an exercise. When Adorno and Horkheimer moved their Institut to California, their colleague Marcuse, following his friend the political scientist Franz Neumann, decided to go to Washington instead. Here Marcuse and Neumann eventually found their way into the Research and Analysis Branch of the newly founded Office of Strategic Services (OSS). The parting from their former associates crucially changed

117

their lives. No longer were they to live in an enclave of central European society, speculating in Olympian fashion on the origins and future of mass culture: they had now become civil servants, yoked to the task of winning the war. In the OSS they encountered a host of fellow émigrés, amply sufficient to form a "critical mass." But far more significantly, they learned to work closely and harmoniously with native-born scholars on projects whose urgency left little room for theoretical hair-splitting.

There was time, however, for conversation—fleeting, fragmentary, inserted once again in the interstices of the job. The subculture of the OSS's Research and Analysis Branch took the form of an ongoing if ever-interrupted seminar. The Americans might listen more than they spoke, but they were seldom deferential. They even gently teased the émigrés about central European mannerisms and complained about the opacity of Teutonic prose—something that I find difficult to imagine happening in a psychoanalytic institute. Thus on the one hand, the Research and Analysis Branch provided free of charge a second graduate education to young political scientists, historians, or sociologists who were to go on to become professors at major universities. On the other hand, the émigrés who worked with them enjoyed a rare opportunity to familiarize themselves with American manners and values under conditions that minimized occasions for wounded sensibilities or hurt pride. The interchange succeeded for the very reason that it was unintended: neither side needed to be self-conscious about a process that occurred so naturally that only long after the fact did its importance become manifest.

We might conclude that the history of émigré influence in social theory is impossible to write, since what was most rewarding in it was so informal that it went largely unchronicled. It may be worthwhile, however, to draw up a rough balance sheet. Initially, we should distinguish between the intellectual stratosphere and the more mundane plane of practice in the individual disciplines. On the level of grand theory, the philosophically inclined among the newcomers never got very far. The vast majority of their hosts remained unconvinced of the virtue of majestic thought-structures. Hegel tarried in the backwaters; the truly professional study of Marx began only in the late 1960s, and at the hands of young scholars almost totally free from émigré influence. In the pantheon of German social spec-

118

ulation, Max Weber alone became a naturalized American. And this happy result was in part due to Weber's work having had a firm foundation in empirical research. Moreover, it had never claimed to be an all-encompassing system; it could be—and was—appropriated piecemeal. What the native-born found in Weber was above all a new mental set: they learned to question what they meant by a "fact" and to subject to rigorous scrutiny the implicit value assumptions lurking behind an ostensibly factual inquiry. The Americans who had been persuaded to study Weber could never again be quite as simple-mindedly positivist as they had been before. That was the fundamental lesson of émigré social theory that took root in our country's scholarship.

On the level of individual labors in the several disciplines, we could always reel off a catalog of names. Such listings already exist in the standard works on the subject. In the present context, however, it is more helpful to mention a handful of figures whose influence lingered on long after the emigration experience in the narrower sense was over. In the field of history, Hajo Holborn and Felix Gilbert—both of whom had worked in Washington—continued to act as kind and discreet mentors to the native-born friends they had met in government service. Their characteristically European conviction that the writing of history was above all a process of thought—of imaginative reconstruction—little by little became second nature to those whom they counseled. In the field of sociology, Paul F. Lazarsfeld enjoyed a comparable position as someone whose advice was constantly sought and usually acted upon. Among émigré sociologists, Lazarsfeld was distinguished by his forthright empiricism; this gave him from the start a kind of acceptability with the native-born that eluded his more dogmatic colleagues. But Lazarsfeld wore his empiricism with a difference: he insisted that one should not proceed with an investigation until its methodological assumptions had been clearly staked out. The contemporary, sophisticated study of voting behavior sprang largely from his precept and example.

When one turns to the great success story of émigré influence—the theory and practice of psychoanalysis—the name of Heinz Hartmann once again inevitably comes to mind. And with it comes the realization that all is not well in psychoanalysis today. Its current difficulties are by no means entirely of its own making: a number can be ascribed either to financial stringency or to a disquieting current of anti-intellectualism in the psychiatric profession. But some part directly derives from the triumph of the central Europeans.   119

Scrupulously loyal to Freud's legacy, Hartmann and his co-workers refused to discard any of the intellectual baggage they had taken with them across the Atlantic. Still more, they lovingly elaborated what they already had. The result was an ever wider gap between the complexities of theory and the simpler, more verifiable insights of clinical practice. Their work also debarred American psycho-analysis from fully absorbing a body of work that might have helped to close that gap—the work of the British school of W. Ronald D. Fairbairn and D.W. Winnicott, whose allegiance to the basic Freudian discoveries was tempered by the hard-won knowledge they had wrung out of their own professional experience.

Must the verdict, then, be ambivalent? Must we substitute for the word *miracle* some cautious or guarded term to describe what émigré influence accomplished? I hesitate to go that far. As a living example of intellectual enrichment through the emigration, I have a vested interest in holding onto what I learned three decades ago. I suggest, rather, that this experience—like all good things—finally reached its end and that the termination occurred in the 1970s. As the émigrés died off or retired, and as other scholars who had sat at their feet became the older generation of scholars, the link that had held the German and American traditions together began to wear thin. Even at its best it had never been as strong as it appeared; only in the sort of privileged instances to which I have alluded had assumptions and methods been truly shared. Thus, as a younger generation of Americans who had no direct knowledge of the emigration came of age, its lessons began to be forgotten. Witness the current recrudescence of positivism in social science. Witness the renewed tendency to slice up the study of society into clearly demarcated disciplines and subdisciplines.

But one achievement no amount of intellectual erosion can destroy: from the emigration experience American social theory emerged deprovincialized. And that it has remained.

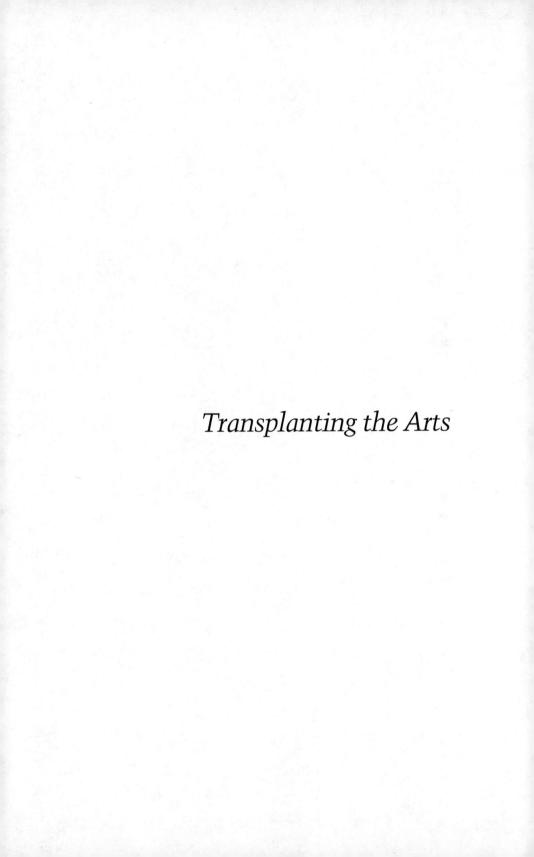

Transplanting the Arts

The European Writers in Exile

ALFRED KAZIN

Sigmund Freud. Thomas Mann. James Joyce. Samuel Beckett. Bertolt Brecht. Vladimir Nabokov. Erich Auerbach. Ernst Cassirer. Claude Lévi-Strauss. Maurice Maeterlinck. Jules Romains. Georges Bernanos. Jacques Maritain. Erwin Panofsky. Karl Wolfskehl. Elsie Lasker-Schuler. Paul Tillich. Américo Castro. Hermann Broch. André Breton. Erik Erikson. Franz Werfel. Elias Canetti. Sigrid Undset. Robert Musil. Oskar Maria Graf. André Maurois. St. John Perse. Arthur Koestler. Renato Poggioli. Erich Maria Remarque. Wilhelm Reich. Hannah Arendt. Erich Heller. Herbert Marcuse. Nelly Sachs. Michael Polanyi.

These at least made their way to safety. But others didn't: Ernst Toller, dead by his own hand in New York; Kurt Tucholsky in Sweden; Stefan Zweig in Brazil; Walter Benjamin after being turned back on the French-Spanish frontier; Egon Friedell in Vienna; Paul Celan in Paris . . . Theodore Lessing, murdered in Prague as he sat at his desk; Erich Mühsam, tortured to death in Oranienburg; Anne Frank, fifteen years old when she died in Belsen; Simon Dubnow, author of the greatest history in Russian of the Jews, eighty-four when he was shot to death in the Riga ghetto. Max Jacob died in Drancy; Simone Weil in London of malnutrition induced by her solidarity with the occupied French. We do not know just how many writers in Yiddish, Hebrew, Russian, Lithuanian, Latvian, and Polish died in the gas chambers. We do not know the fate of those gifted young children who were smuggled out of the Vilna ghetto so that they at least could continue the story of their people.

We will never know the full score of the Hitler horror. What began in 1933 did not end in 1945. To discuss the particular talents that made it to America, to our and the world's good fortune—Mann, Brecht, Nabokov, Arendt, Auerbach, Maritain—is to recall not only the many who did not but the unequal contest between the individual talent and murderous totalitarianism. To have been of age during the Hitler period is to be stamped forever with the image of an unlimited destructiveness that now seems no less grotesque for being so suicidal.

In what many consider the greatest German poem of the Holocaust, "Todesfuge," Paul Celan wrote of the death inflicted on so many helpless people.

wir trinken und trinken
Black milk of dawn we drink it at dusk
  we drink it at noon and at daybreak we drink it at night
  we drink and we drink
  we are digging a grave in the air there's room for us all.

Johann Wolfgang von Goethe said that the "shudder of awe" was man's highest tribute to the power of the universe. That shudder we still feel at the proscription, exile, hardships, and death of so many gifted people.

Yet just now I prefer to think of a German philosopher someone told me of. He guarded his family in an Amsterdam attic near where the Otto Frank family was betrayed. With a rifle on his knees day after day he wrote a philosophical treatise—and lived to publish it. I think of Thomas Mann, in Princeton and in Pacific Palisades, completing the great Joseph tetralogy and going on to write *Dr. Faustus;* of Erich Auerbach, for me the greatest of modern literary scholars, writing his magisterial study of representation, *Mimesis.* Auerbach was grateful that the Turkish libraries were so poor; he was not distracted by secondary literature. Simone Weil, first on Riverside Drive in New York, then in London, was working out that extraordinary personal theology, *L'Attente de Dieu, La Connaissance Surnaturelle,* that was to have such a marked effect on T.S. Eliot and so many English, French, and American intellectuals. Sigmund Freud was in London, stoically enduring the pain of cancer

ALFRED KAZIN

in his jaw, for which he would not take even aspirin lest it diminish the lucidity with which, at eighty-three, he was still seeing patients and rewriting *Moses and Monotheism*. Describing himself as "an island of pain in a sea of indifference," he was to die just as Hitler unleashed his war.

The most gifted of Russian writers in exile, Vladimir Nabokov, while still in Paris, had begun to write his first novel in English, *The Real Life of Sebastian Knight*. He wrote it in the bathroom of a tiny flat so as not to disturb his infant son Dmitri. When the Nazis overran France in 1940, Nabokov had to save his Jewish wife; he was able to get on one of the last ships to America thanks to a Jewish rescue service that gratefully remembered the support given to persecuted Jews under tsarism by Nabokov's father, an aristocratic liberal whose real legacy to his son was the Russian democratic tradition. Nabokov in America was bitterly to complain to his good friend and sponsor Edmund Wilson that American intellectuals seemed to know nothing of this tradition, thoughtlessly disseminating the Leninist lie that Russian exiles were all "white guards." No other writer in exile was to make such brilliant use of the English language and the American scene.

After passing through Denmark and the Soviet Union, Bertolt Brecht was in Hollywood. He was to pass through America, too. In a litany addressed to those who come after us, *An Die Nachgeborenen*, Brecht cried: "Truly, I live in dark times—*Wirklich, ich lebe in finsteren Zeiten* . . . Whoever laughs/ Has simply not yet received/ The dreadful news . . . Accidentally I have been spared./ The roads led into the swamps in my time/ Language betrayed me to the butcher. . ./ We passed—changing countries more often than shoes/ . . . Yet we know well enough/ Hatred of baseness, too,/ Distorts one's features."

Hannah Arendt, who had taken her doctorate at Heidelberg under Karl Jaspers with a famous thesis on St. Augustine's concept of love, was on West Ninety-fifth Street in New York, struggling with her adopted English to write *The Origins of Totalitarianism*. She was an editor at Schocken Books, where her passion for Kafka, for her the greatest modern writer in German, had much to do with his influence on American writers. As soon as the war ended, she devoted herself to Jewish Cultural Reconstruction, striving to locate, and to find safe homes for, the libraries and religious articles stolen en masse by the Nazis. With her philosopher husband Heinrich Blücher, a German Protestant, she was now devoting herself to political phi-

The European Writers in Exile

losophy. Totalitarianism was the central fact of the era that she was determined to trace to its roots in the alienation of modern society and thought from tradition. For her, this went deeper than the Marxist description of the worker's estrangement from his daily task.

Herbert Marcuse of the Frankfurt Institut für Sozialforschung, headed by Max Horkheimer and T.W. Adorno, was soon to mix Freud and Marx into a cumbersome potion that would be swallowed easily, especially in California, by young American Ishmaels looking for a Captain Ahab to direct their life voyage. Wilhelm Reich, a left-winger amid conservative Freudians, a determined radical visionary who extended Freud's dictum of sexual repression from a bourgeois nineteenth-century problem into the twentieth-century malady that explained the proliferation of all disease, even fascism, was to find a small fanatical audience here for his apocalyptic vision. The orgone energy at large in the universe was not being sufficiently absorbed by traumatized slaves of a sexual inhibition programmed by capitalism's work ethic.

Claude Lévi-Strauss was at the New School for Social Research, sometimes moonlighting as a French cultural attaché, spending his limited funds on the vast literature of Indian ethnology. Erwin Panofsky at the Institute for Advanced Study was helping to make art history a significant American enterprise. The French poet and diplomat St. John Perse (Alexis Léger) was in Washington writing *Exil, Vents, Amers;* Franz Werfel was in California, publishing *The Forty Days of Musa Dagh* and writing *The Song of Bernadette.* Nelly Sachs was in Stockholm, recovering from the shock of her transplantation and the revelations of Treblinka and Auschwitz to write with a piercing new simplicity based on the Psalms and mystical imagery of Hasidic origin. The Holocaust almost literally drove her out of her mind, but she recovered by writing the poems *In den Wohnungen des Todes* (In the Apartments of Death), of which she said, "If I could not have written, I could not have survived .... Death was my teacher ... my metaphors are my sounds."

Freud said that intelligence is weak but persistent. These writers were weak and vulnerable, struggling with new countries, new customs, often enough a difficult new language to write in, but they were persistent. A common theme in the face of Nazi destructiveness was history as the human memory, our common past, the human labyrinth. Think of Freud's insistence that our past is always within us, of Thomas Mann's concern in the Joseph novels with what he called the deep well of the past, of the Greek polis as the background

126

of Hannah Arendt's political philosophy, of the way in which tradition haunted Nabokov and Lévi-Strauss no less than the Germans.

Continuity means not just the past but the past behind the past we think we know. The real drama of European exiled writers in America—I limit myself to Mann and Arendt—is the contrast between their instinctive European sense of history and the optimistic American belief (should I call it the old American optimism?) that the future is as real as the present. Only a great European poet, Rainer Maria Rilke, could have defined poetry as "the past that breaks out in our hearts." Huck Finn, on learning that the Bible story he was forced to learn dealt with characters dead a powerful long time ago, said that he took no stock in dead people. Americans, especially of recent immigrant vintage, thought of the past as a mistake. The America that began to rearm in 1940, miraculously recovered from the Depression, had a bounce, a new faith in progress as its destiny, that contrasted with the exhaustion and fearfulness of many exiles.

In any event, severe German intellectuals like Thomas Mann and Hannah Arendt had to acquire a taste for America. Mann, somehow protected from many disorderly things in the New World by his outward propriety, gave the impression in Princeton and Pacific Palisades between 1938 and 1953 of being as rigid as Gustav von Aschenbach on his arrival in Venice. This may just have been his favorite disguise; Mann liked to think of himself as antibourgeois, a literary subversive, a mischievous satirist who just happened to look like a German field marshal with a taste for reading. He certainly made the best possible use of his contradictions. A novelist where there had been so few German novelists before him, a natural conservative who had astonishingly begun his career, at twenty-five, with *Buddenbrooks* (whose theme is the decline and fall of his tradition), Mann knew how to make exemplary fiction by playing on a reality that, as German philosophy and poetry have demonstrated, may not be taken literally, that literally may not even exist.

The great work of Mann's life, *Joseph and His Brothers*, was appropriately begun in the year Hitler came to power, 1933, and was completed in 1942. The novel owes more than we will ever know to an exile like the biblical Joseph's—and to the wayward, mischievous family loyalty that Joseph chose over religious loyalty to the monotheism that his father Jacob represents as the last of the patriarchs and the wrestler with God to whom God gave the name Israel. At the end of *Joseph the Provider*, when after more than a

127

Thomas Mann in his library at his home in Pacific Palisades, 1946.
His "outward propriety," according to Alfred Kazin, protected Mann
from many of the disorderly experiences of exile. (Thomas Mann Archiv.)

thousand pages Joseph is united with the father who never ceased to mourn his favorite son, "the son of the promise," Jacob nevertheless reminds Joseph that the latter's success has been worldly; it is not a part of the spiritual epic begun by Abraham.

So one can say of Mann's achievement, incomparable in its modern rendering of the biblical story, that it triumphs as a story because it is detached. Although there is something symbolic in Mann's spending so many of the Hitler years writing his book, Mann did not consciously write it as an act of participation and sympathy. He stands outside the Bible's claim to revelation and the religious destiny of mankind; he is preoccupied, literally and almost dreamingly, with the biblical world as a storybook, a mythical coat of many colors. Did all that actually exist? If any of it did, how can we reach it? History may be the greatest fiction, and thus an invitation to write fiction that weaves speculation, legend, and the prototypes within our own minds.

What his God was to Jacob—the mysterious, unspeaking but audible force of destiny, the mystery of mysteries because He is One yet his works are forever contradictory—the most ancient world is to Mann the storyteller, who works here as a sorter-out of myths, creating his story by examining and reviewing one myth after another. There is a pattern here, but what is it? The "ironic German," as the critic Erich Heller has called Mann, is not likely to believe that his characters are as God-appointed as they say they are. Jacob, Esau, Laban, Leah, Rachel, Joseph, Benjamin, Reuben become more real to us than ourselves, as is required in a great novel. But to wonder what they are, with all their exaltations, jealousies, sufferings, and wanderings up and down that hot desert—this is to make us wanderers ourselves. Early in the first volume, *Tales of Jacob*, Mann likens himself to Jacob the wanderer, who preferred to dwell in tents. "As for me," he writes at the close of his wonderful opening meditation on the pastness of the past,

I will not conceal my native and comprehensive understanding of the old man's restless unease and dislike of any fixed habitation. For do I not know the feeling? To me too has not unrest been ordained, have not I too been endowed with a heart which knoweth not repose. . .? For the storyteller makes many a station, . . . pauses only tent-wise, awaiting further directions, and soon feels heart beating high, . . . a sign that he must take the road, toward fresh adventures which are to be painstakingly lived through, down to their remotest details, according to the restless spirit's will.

The European Writers in Exile

Mann surely owed this to his inner homelessness in America. Nabokov came here in 1940 prepared to write in English, to teach in America, to learn all he could from America; he certainly got the native scene down cold in *Lolita, Pnin, Pale Fire*. But of course Nabokov was unknown and had to make his way; Mann, sixty-three when he arrived, was not without a German sense of his own importance. His publisher, Alfred Knopf, may have called him "Tommy," but I am sure no one else would have thought of it. Mann was an American citizen when he returned to Switzerland in 1953 by way of East Germany; he disappointed many of his admirers by responding pessimistically to American disorder during the McCarthy madness instead of absorbing older traditions of liberty that he never really understood.

Yet *Joseph and His Brothers*, and of course *Doctor Faustus*, came out of Mann's intellectual alienation from America as well as his unrealizable hopes for Germany. It is not necessary for a great artist to be at home in exile, perhaps just the contrary. Adroit and even devilish in his quick use of parody of the American scene, Nabokov already had been twice exiled—from Russia and Germany—before he came here from France. Nabokov's fiction, especially in English, is relativistic, duplicitous in technique, devoted to protagonists driven by *idées fixes*. It was easier for Nabokov than for Mann to get absorbed in America; his sense of the comic and the perverse, plus his need to show off all he learned from a language and culture not his own, fed on America. And he too ended up in Switzerland!

Mann's unweaving the Bible into a modern novel somehow depended on his ability to live in Princeton and Hollywood without quite taking in the sounds around him. Henry Kissinger's brother, asked why he spoke without an accent, is reported to have said, "I played with the boys on the block." This may not be the way to ultimate success.

In *Joseph and His Brothers*, it is not only Joseph who is in exile but also, by extension, his lonely God-intoxicated father. The Hebrew God Himself, we learn in two extraordinary passages, is notoriously jealous because He is alone, having promised Himself to this one family. Only Mann, with his knowing humor at the expense of self-importance, has developed—perhaps from some old Jewish legend—a long-buried fact in the story of Potiphar's wife, who is mad for Joseph: Potiphar is a court eunuch. When Mann's Joseph learns this, he reflects that Potiphar must be lonely, as lonely as God:

130

Yes, God too, the Lord, was lonely in His greatness; and Joseph's blood and his memory spoke in the realization that the isolation of a wifeless and childless God had much to do with the jealousy of the bond He had made with man.

Later Joseph astonishingly says to Potiphar:

Our God has dedicated Himself to us, and is our blood-bridegroom in all jealousy, for He is solitary and on fire for our loyalty. And we for our part are the bride of His loyalty, consecrate and set apart.

No Jewish writer coming out of the terrible years, whether as victim or survivor, could have described the Hebrew God with such mischief. The destruction, to use a term more fitting than the outworn and unprovoking term Holocaust, sent many baptized Jews, like Arnold Schoenberg, back to their Old Testament God. In the immense loneliness of Jewish history, there has often been no one else to turn to.

Like most modern Jewish thinkers, but more especially German Jewish thinkers, Hannah Arendt was more influenced by Christianity than by Jewish tradition. Her first work had been on St. Augustine; she and Hans Jonas, who was to become the great authority on the Gnostics, were the only Jews in Rudolf Bultmann's famous New Testament seminar at Marburg. Arendt was also profoundly indebted to the classical tradition. Her first book in English, *The Origins of Totalitarianism* (1951), was based on unfashionable perspectives. In the face of all the usual left- and ex-left-wing illusions about communism, she believed that totalitarianism was the same everywhere if it meant absolute one-party rule; this suggestion was still too shocking for students of Nazism in the early 1950s. In Franco's Spain some power centers that were not entirely creatures of the state, remained, so there was not the total kind of domination that in the last and best chapters of *The Origins of Totalitarianism* she ascribed to the Nazi and Leninist policy systems. She convincingly demonstrated their fatal resemblance.

The Origins of Totalitarianism began with the so-called Jewish problem and its relation to the German catastrophe. Unlike so many other exiled writers, Arendt faced this issue directly. She had never been a radical even during the Weimar period and was not under the illusion, familiar in Marxist literature from Marx to Isaac Deutscher, that the "problem" was merely a reflection of social and economic tensions. On the other hand, Arendt did not comprehend from within the Jewish tradition the extent to which the Jewish masses of eastern Europe, faithful to their religion, had no problem; just enemies.   131

Kafka, a writer whose superiority to Thomas Mann was with Arendt an article of faith, was willing to suffer his Jewishness but not to accept it. Arendt was religious in a very private sense. Her emerging political philosophy, drawn from a host of classical authorities, Montesquieu, Alexis de Tocqueville, John Adams, and other conservatives, came down to a vision of the Greek polis as the great political condition and to the rootlessness of the individual, the incessant struggle of politics, as symbols of some underlying modern disorder.

She was indeed very theoretical. Even her acquired taste for republican liberty rather than social meliorism reflected her basic conditioning in the profound sense of the self at the heart of German Protestantism and German philosophy. Her constant maxim was "we must think what we are doing." Ralph Waldo Emerson (who, as his admirer Nietzsche said, had only one fault: he had been too much influenced by German philosophy) characteristically said that to think is to be free. That was Arendt's profession of faith, her life, her example to many American writers who learned from her that there was indeed another Germany.

Hannah Arendt became a remarkably vivid figure at Berkeley, Chicago, and Columbia; as the first woman professor at Princeton; and at the New School for Social Research. She seemed to be not another scholar-in-exile but rather a personality as only America could make from a European inheritance and so gifted and fearless a mind. What America did for her was to give her still another intellectual loyalty and an audience that was even more literary than it was scholarly. Writers responded to her, and she to writers, in a way that professional scholars never could. She would not have been altogether pleased to register the fact that she was actually more of a writer than a philosopher and historian. She set great store by her philosophical training, her long relationship with Karl Jaspers, her ambitious treatises such as *The Human Condition* (1958), and her last unfinished three-volume work, *The Life of the Mind* (1978). But only a writer would have been sent by the *New Yorker* to cover the Adolf Eichmann trial, and only a writer would have tossed off the fatal phrase "the banality of evil."

Hannah Arendt was a great moralist. She held very firm views on what the condemned Jews should have done in the face of the Hitler terror. One reason *Eichmann in Jerusalem* (1963) disturbed many people was its unrecognized German *Egoismus*, from the sidelines of philosophy, at the expense of people who were not in a condition to "think" freely. Although she disparaged the historic tendency of

Hannah Arendt and her husband philosopher Heinrich Blücher in Paris in the late 1930s. Émigré Arendt "became a remarkably vivid figure at Berkeley, Chicago, and Columbia; as the first woman professor at Princeton; and at the New School for Social Research." (Courtesy of Literary Trust of Hannah Arendt Blücher.)

German intellectuals to live above the battle and professed admiration for the opposite trait in American intellectual life, in the end she could not avoid the noble German trap: to think is to think yourself free. To think and to think well was not the prerogative of the Nazi murderers any more than it was of their victims. The theoretical nature of her approach to the destruction of European Jewry was in contrast to the passion with which she described the terrible events themselves.

When I first read *Eichmann in Jerusalem,* I was overwhelmed by the power with which Arendt reported the court testimony and the mountain of records that the Nazis themselves left of their crimes. I remember in particular her account of one Private Schmidt, who alone on the eastern front seems to have asserted his conscience as a Christian and refused to kill; he was beheaded. I did not understand the "banality of evil" thesis and, in view of the facts, wondered whether she altogether understood what such a phrase implied. Her gift as a writer was indeed superior to her philosophizing about what Churchill called the worst episode in human history. Her lifelong refrain, we must think what we are doing, when applied to Eichmann and his murder squads, simply meant: they were too ignorant, coarse, bureaucratic—in a word, unthinking. Therefore, the extermination of even a million children could seem "banal," like a computer error.

So we are led back to that fatal discrepancy between German intellectuals and political beastliness. I do not know how much her gratitude for America included the recognition that her admired John Adams was in politics all his life or that the noble Thomas Jefferson, our Goethe, was not ashamed to play the political game. His only regret, shared by us today, was that inferior men played it more successfully.

Can we always think what we are doing? No. But can we do what we have been thinking? William James said we should. So did Ralph Waldo Emerson, Henry David Thoreau, John Quincy Adams, and Abraham Lincoln before him. Now, however, pragmatism has an ugly sound, and in the hands of many Americans totally absorbed by the commercial culture, it should. It may be that modern-day Americans are too far removed from the Enlightenment even to vote for the Bill of Rights. The idea of a republic, of republican liberty, thrilled Hannah Arendt and made her passionate about her citizenship. She quoted the great German historian of antiquity, Theodore Mommsen—"My great dream was to live in a free German republic; lacking that, I wrote the history of Rome." Perhaps in the end, she was too impatient with her old German political frustration, but too devoted to German intellectual *virtu*, to accept the mediocrity that so many of us do accept in the face of a commercial rapacity that invades every aspect of American life.

Arendt did not accept mediocrity; she did not really understand it. When the great Jewish scholar Gershom Scholem, an old friend, reproached her for not sufficiently loving the Jewish people, she tartly responded that the expression was nonsense—one could love God, not a people. The austerity of this is breathless. It is positively unthinkable among American intellectuals just now. Even to recall a perception like this is to remember how different the European writers-in-exile could be. How much we owe them.

The Music World in Migration

BORIS SCHWARZ

I am speaking to you from personal experience. My own musical career was halted when Hitler came to power in 1933, and three years later I had no choice but to emigrate. Fortunately for me, my paternal friend, Professor Albert Einstein—with whom I had played chamber music since I was a teenager—came to my rescue and enabled me to join him in the United States.

In 1933, I was a young violinist in Berlin, playing concert engagements in Europe, performing regularly on German radio, and teaching a group of students. At the same time, I was a matriculated student at the University of Berlin, working toward my Ph.D. in musicology. In less than a year, all my professional work had stopped: My German engagements were cancelled; the radio no longer invited me nor any other Jewish artists to perform; my German students were forced to switch to other teachers; my Jewish students dispersed. My foreign concert tours became increasingly difficult, since I was deprived of my German passport by the simple process of "denaturalization"—I had been a resident of Berlin since 1912 but was a Russian by birth. My only reason for wanting to remain in Berlin was my desire to complete my Ph.D.; this, too, became impossible when, my dissertation already accepted, I was refused admission to the oral examination. This happened in March of 1936; in July of that year, I landed in New York, ready to begin a new life. Little did I think at the time that it would lead to a first violin chair in Arturo Toscanini's NBC Orchestra, a Ph.D. at Columbia University, and a professorship at Queens College.

What kept me and other Jewish musicians afloat in Germany in the years after 1933 was a kind of Jewish self-help: the German-Jewish communities organized the Jewish Cultural Association (Kulturbund), which enabled Jewish artists to perform for an exclusively Jewish public in community centers, in synagogues, and sometimes in private homes. But the Jewish population of Germany was quickly decimated through emigration and deportation, and after 1938 the cultural activities came to a halt. The director of the Kulturbund, Dr. Kurt Singer, perished in 1944 in the concentration camp of Theresienstadt.

The Nazi purge of Germany's musical life was executed swiftly and ruthlessly, legally or violently. Demonstrations by brownshirts were staged against "undesirable" conductors, operas, and stage performances. Existing professional organizations (e.g., the Deutsche Konzertgeberbund) were dissolved and replaced by new organizations to which only "pure" Germans were admitted (e.g., the Reichsmusikkammer). Great artists, rooted in German tradition, were dismissed overnight, mostly on racial grounds—one Jewish grandparent could contaminate the "Aryanism" of the accused. Having been affiliated with a leftist political party or associated with Jewish or radical artists was also sufficient cause for discharge. Tenure rights were abrogated, and appeals were ignored, although everything went through pseudolegal "channels." The Nazis coined the term *Kulturbolschewismus* (cultural bolshevism) to denote a type of unacceptable modernism or leftist tendency. Whether performers or composers, critics or authors, publishers or impresarios, teachers or scholars, everybody was subjected to questionnaires, investigations, and denunciations. *Musik im Dritten Reich,* a book of documents assembled by Joseph Wulf and published in West Germany in 1963, reveals a cesspool of intrigues, baseness, and barbarism.[1]

Of course, there were some Germans who tried to take a stand. The conductor Wilhelm Furtwängler, for example, addressed an open letter to Reichsminister Joseph Goebbels (dated April 11, 1933) appealing for the right of great artists such as Bruno Walter, Otto Klemperer, and Max Reinhardt to be heard in Germany. Goebbels's answer was smooth and misleading. In the meantime, other artists, including Fritz Kreisler, Bronislaw Hubermann, and Artur Schnabel, cancelled their appearances with the Berlin Philharmonic Orchestra. Furtwängler protected several leading players of the Philharmonic and held onto his trusted secretary, Berta Geissmar, as long as their safety was not endangered, but eventually he had to yield. Other German artists, such as Fritz Busch, simply packed and left Germany. But there were also many ugly cases of opportunism—e.g., violinist Gustav Havemann and composer Paul Graener, who turned against former colleagues and bullied their way to the top. As Goethe once said, "There is nothing more dangerous than ignorance in action."

And so an important segment of Germany's music world began to migrate. On the surface, the fate of a musician forced to emigrate seems less onerous than that of an actor, writer, or scientist. Music is an international language; a musician—with his instrument in hand—can play and be understood in Paris, New York, or Rio, without the need to communicate through spoken words. Singers tend to be multilingual. Composers are more difficult to transplant: there are subtle national differences in musical tastes and customs; besides, creative musicians are apt to "dry up" when they are removed from their native land. Sergei Prokofiev, for one, admitted to this "drying up" when he decided to return to Russia after a fifteen-year absence; other émigré composers suffered without admitting it. Only a few exceptional composers—Igor Stravinsky, Béla Bartók, Arnold Schoenberg, Paul Hindemith—carried their roots with them wherever they went.

Even more difficult was the situation for musicologists, music critics, teachers, and academicians, for their effectiveness depended on verbal communication—and a very subtle kind of communication at that. But the question of emigration was one of physical survival; the problem was where to turn in order to escape. No European country was willing to accept very many refugees, regardless of their musical talent. If they had valid passports, they might be admitted to visit, but not to work. Palestine (then a British mandate) and the United States were the two favorite destinations. American immigration policy was based on a quota system. I was lucky, having been born in Russia, for the comparatively small Russian quota was not fully utilized. A nonquota immigration visa could be obtained if evidence of an appointment by an academic institution of higher learning could be provided; this approach proved useful for quite a few scholars and composers. My own visa was arranged on the basis of a personal affidavit of Professor Einstein. I still remember the scrutiny of the American consular official in Berlin: "How well do you know the professor?" Fortunately I had photographs to prove our long-standing association, which continued, I'm happy to say, in Princeton until the professor's death.

Let me divide the musicians into three large categories—performers, composers, and musicologists, with teaching done in all three specialities. The virtuoso performers were natural travelers, and America had always offered the most lucrative concert tours. In the past, the successful virtuosos took their hard-earned dollars and returned immediately to Europe, not without blasting concert conditions in America as a kind of "penitentiary." This was the case, in the nineteenth century, with Anton Rubinstein, Hans von Bülow, and Henri Vieuxtemps. In the twentieth century, an increasing number of artists including Mischa Elman, Fritz Kreisler, Efrem Zimbalist, Josef Hofmann, and Eugène Ysaye found this "penitentiary" more attractive, and they settled here. During the 1920s, the Russian Revolution caused a great migration of musicians to America, led by the veteran violinist-teacher Leopold Auer (who brought the prodigy Jascha Heifetz). The Russian émigrés were quickly absorbed by the American scene, especially during a decade of prosperity. When the German wave of musicians arrived in the 1930s, conditions had changed, for the United States had just experienced a serious depression, and jobs were scarce.

Besides, the migration of the 1930s was different; these central European musicians came with musical tastes that were more sophisticated and more purist than the customary level of American concert life. There was a higher percentage of academically trained musicians. Many had left tenured positions of high prestige and found themselves teaching beginners at some settlement school. Orchestral jobs were controlled by local musicians' unions, and the more desirable positions were protected by waiting lists—up to a year in the highly competitive field of film music in Hollywood.

But it was soon recognized that the newly arrived European musicians had something important to contribute to American musical life. Their performances stressed musical values rather than brilliant virtuosity, and their programs leaned toward chamber music (in which they received great support from Mrs. Elizabeth Sprague Coolidge). This shift in emphasis brought about a sociological change in the concert-going public, particularly in New York City. The German émigrés, musically cultured and selective, began to dominate the concert halls where good music rather than virtuoso display was offered. The newly founded chamber music society, New Friends of Music, was called facetiously the "old friends of Schnabel." Indeed, the pianist Artur Schnabel became the symbol of the high-principled artist. Equally serious was the art of Rudolf Serkin. The violinists Adolf Busch and Joseph Szigeti and the cellists Gregor Piatigorsky and Emanuel Feuermann settled in America, as did the Budapest Quartet, the Roth Quartet, the Kolisch Quartet, the Albeneri Trio. The arrival of the violin pedagogue Ivan Galamian created a new school of American violin playing.

The newly arrived conductors contributed their share to shaping the musical taste of American audiences. Foremost was Bruno Walter, formerly of Berlin and Leipzig, who led in paving the way for a full appreciation of Gustav Mahler's music; his Mozart interpretations, too, were exemplary. Otto Klemperer exerted his influence on the musical life of Los Angeles. George Szell became associated with the Metropolitan Opera and later built the Cleveland Orchestra to its present excellence. William Steinberg accomplished the same for the Pittsburgh Symphony. Pierre Monteux shaped music in San Francisco. Fritz Stiedry built a fine chamber orchestra for the New Friends of Music and later joined the Metropolitan Opera. Erich Leinsdorf and Julius Rudel came to the United States at comparatively young ages and fused their Viennese heritage with American ingeniousness; they contributed significantly to opera and concert life. Joseph Rosenstock conducted for many years at the Metropolitan Opera, as did Maurice Abravanel. Efrem Kurtz was active in Houston and Kansas City, Antal Dorati in Minneapolis and Washington, Paul Paray in Detroit, Max Rudolf in Cincinnati, and Dimitri Mitropoulos in New York. And finally let us not forget the greatest of the great—Arturo Toscanini, who challenged both Mussolini and Hitler with his anti-Fascist stance.

It is true that the orchestral scene in America was traditionally dominated by foreign-born conductors—Leopold Stokowski, Willem Mengelberg, Eugene Ormandy, Serge Koussewitzky and before them Karl Muck, Gustav Mahler, Anton Seidl, and Artur Bodanzky. But the migration of the 1930s and 1940s brought new ideas and an unusual, very "middle European" type of program building. However, the recently arrived conductors showed comparatively little interest in furthering the cause of modern American music, to the distress of indigenous composers. Only Koussewitzky was consistent in encouraging younger American composers, not only in Boston but also in Tanglewood, and he set an example for others, especially Mitropoulos.

139

How did the European composers fare in this era? In Berlin around 1932, the highest posts were occupied by Franz Schreker, director of the Hochschule für Musik; Arnold Schoenberg, professor at the Academy of Arts; and Paul Hindemith, teacher at the Hochschule. Among the notable freelancers were Kurt Weill, Ernst Toch, Karol Rathaus, Stefan Wolpe, and Ernst Krenek. Except for Schreker, who died a broken man in 1934, all the above-named came to the United States and became established as composers and teachers. They were joined from other parts of Europe by Igor Stravinsky, Darius Milhaud, Béla Bartók, Bohuslav Martinů, Jaromir Weinberger, Erich Wolfgang Korngold, Karl Weigl, Miklos Rozsa, Alexander Tansman, and Benjamin Britten. Some returned to Europe after the war, but not without contributing to the American scene and being enriched in turn by the American experience. Only one departed in bitterness, the remarkable composer Hanns Eisler. Active in New York and Hollywood from 1935 to 1948, he had to leave the United States under the terms of "voluntary deportation" because of his alleged communist sympathies. His humiliating experience before the House Committee on Un-American Activities in September 1947 made him into a *cause célèbre*.[2] Eisler died, highly honored, in 1962 in East Berlin.

Most characteristic was the fate of Arnold Schoenberg, who was blacklisted by the Nazis for being a "cultural bolshevik" as well as a Jew. (Incidentally, Schoenberg was converted early in life but resumed his Jewish faith in 1933.) Dismissed from his professorship in 1933, Schoenberg's departure from Berlin resembled a flight. Stranded penniless in Paris, he received an unexpected offer to teach at a small private conservatory in Boston, founded and directed by the cellist Joseph Malkin. He accepted and arrived in New York on October 31, 1933. The first winter was not easy: Schoenberg battled with the harsh climate, the English language, the insufficiency of students, and the indifference of conductors. But he also found adherents, supporters, and friends, and he was met with an open-mindedness that was sadly lacking in Berlin as well as in Vienna. And he admitted that he enjoyed the actual teaching. He acquired a new American publisher, G. Schirmer, Inc., whose president, the distinguished scholar Carl Engel, became his staunch supporter and friend. Because Schoenberg's fragile health could not withstand the cold climate of the East Coast, he moved with his family to Los Angeles, where he lived from 1934 until his death in 1951. In 1935, he was appointed professor of music at the University of Southern Califor-

Arnold Schoenberg with his weekly private composition class at his home in Brentwood, California, late 1940s. After a short stay in Boston, the famous twelve-tone composer moved to Los Angeles where he spent the last seventeen years of his life. (© 1953, renewed 1981, Richard Fish. Reprinted with permission.)

nia; in 1936 he accepted a similar post at the University of California at Los Angeles. An attempt by Metro-Goldwyn-Mayer to draw Schoenberg into writing for films failed because the composer set an exorbitant price (fifty thousand dollars) in the hope that it would not be accepted.

Although Schoenberg is known to have been rather uncompromising in his musical views, he did make some concessions so that his writing would be more accessible to the American public, particularly to young American musicians. Thus, in 1934 he wrote a piece for student orchestras, the Suite for String Orchestra, describing it as "tonal." There is also the Theme and Variations for band, op.43A (1943), which served a "pedagogical task" but which he wrote "with great pleasure." But on the whole he remained true to himself: he produced some of his most important works during the California years (opp.36–50), mastered both written and spoken English, and was an active participant in the American musical scene. As the   141 originator and master of the dodecaphonic system (Composition with 12 Tones), he exerted a strong influence on a generation of American composers. Schoenberg became an American citizen in 1941, and in 1949 he made peace with his native city of Vienna by accepting honorary citizenship there. His collection of essays, *Style and Idea*, which was published in New York in 1950,[3] did not appear in Germany until 1976. Many of his manuscripts are in a special collection at the Library of Congress; others are preserved in the Arnold Schoenberg Institute on the campus of the University of Southern California (completed 1976 and directed by his former student and associate Leonard Stein).

Born in 1895, and some twenty years younger than Schoenberg, Paul Hindemith was of pure German ethnic background, but his was a case of guilt by association: he performed with Jewish artists (the string trio of Goldberg-Hindemith-Feuermann was famous in its day), and he stubbornly refused to sever these (and other) relationships. A teacher at the Berlin Hochschule from 1927 to 1934, he was mainly known as the leader among young German modern composers. Voices in the Nazi-controlled press argued that Germany could ill afford to lose him, and Furtwängler went to battle for him, but Goebbels decided otherwise. Hindemith's position became untenable—he was branded as one of those "cultural bolsheviks"—and he came to America in 1937. His American debut took place at the Library of Congress on April 10, 1937, when he played his own unaccompanied Viola Sonata. Yale University was his center of activity in the United States; he was professor of music there from 1940 to 1953 and built a department that reflected his ideas on the craft of musical composition. Hindemith was a beneficial influence on a generation of young American composers: he extolled solid craftsmanship and debunked the ivory-tower approach to composition. His books on harmony and musicianship, published in English in the 1940s, are still widely used.[4] Beyond his compositions and his teaching, he conducted the Yale Collegium musicum and played a vital part in the revival of Renaissance and baroque music. While in America (he became a citizen in 1946), Hindemith wrote some of his most spontaneous and effective music; his somewhat crabby modernistic style became more pliable and ingratiating, and he rediscovered tonality. As was the case with Schoenberg, the contact with American students—receptive but less sophisticated—contributed to this development. For a time, Hindemith was one of the most widely performed composers in this country. Invited to return to Germany after the war ended, he went merely for a concert tour. Although he accepted a professorship at Zurich in 1953, he continued to visit America for concerts as guest conductor. He died in Frankfurt in 1963.

Among the most eminent non-German composers who settled in the United States in the 1930s were Béla Bartók, Darius Milhaud, and Igor Stravinsky, each of whom had his personal reasons for leaving Europe. Bartók was a confirmed anti-Fascist and felt oppressed by the rise of fascism in his native Hungary. Leaving just ahead of the Nazi invasion, he arrived in New York in 1940. His American debut as a pianist-composer took place on April 13, 1940, at the Coolidge Festival at the Library of Congress; his partner was a fellow Hungarian, the great violinist Joseph Szigeti, and the program consisted of music by Beethoven, Debussy, and Bartók. (This historic concert, thanks to the initiative of Harold Spivacke, is preserved on a recording.) Unfortunately, Bartók's remaining years (he died of leukemia in 1945) were none too happy. He refused an offer to teach composition at the Curtis Institute—he believed that composition could not be taught—and preferred to accept a modest research grant at Columbia University in the field of folk music. He had hoped for concert engagements and commissions but was largely disappointed. Bartók suffered from "overwhelming homesickness," as his wife Ditta described it. Living in the big city of New York was strange, almost abhorrent to him. Despite his unhappiness and failing health, Bartók created some of his most inspired works while in America—the Concerto for Orchestra, commissioned by Serge Koussewitzky for the Boston Symphony (1943); the Sonata for Solo Violin, commissioned by Yehudi Menuhin (1944); the Piano Concerto no. 3, premiered posthumously in 1946. The world is richer for the sublime works created by Bartók during his last years while his strength was ebbing.

Fate was more generous with Stravinsky. Having left his native Russia in 1912, at the age of thirty, he was a citizen of the world. Until the late 1930s, he spent most of his time in Paris, except for the World War I years, when he was in Switzerland. He first visited America in 1925, when he played his own Piano Concerto in Boston under Koussewitzky, and he continued to fulfill American commissions, as well as making a concert tour in 1937–38. While he was in the United States during the academic year 1939–40 to give the Charles Eliot Norton Lectures[5] at Harvard University, Stravinsky decided to remain because of the outbreak of World War II, settling in California and becoming an American citizen in December 1945. In a burst of newfound patriotism, Stravinsky harmonized and orchestrated the *Star-Spangled Banner*, but his version was so outlandish that the traditional edition was hurriedly substituted at the second performance (1944). Stravinsky's other "Americana" were more successful—e.g., his amusing *Circus* Polka, "composed for a young elephant," commissioned by Ringling Brothers Circus (1942), and the *Ebony* Concerto for clarinet and swing band, premiered by Woody Herman at Carnegie Hall (1946).

Stravinsky's years in California are richly documented in the six volumes of dialogues and reminiscences that he wrote in collaboration with his young American associate, Robert Craft. (We need not enter into the current dispute as to how authentic the utterances of Stravinsky are; they were published, after all, during Stravinsky's lifetime, and he could have discontinued publication after the first volume if he felt misquoted.) It was in America in the 1950s that he underwent his astounding stylistic change to twelve-tone serialism. (While living in Los Angeles, Schoenberg and Stravinsky avoided personal contacts though they had known each other in Europe.) Although Stravinsky never taught, he was taken as a model by many American composers of all ages: his ability to grow, to develop, to change, and to experiment delighted his admirers and followers. In 1962, Stravinsky accepted an invitation to visit Moscow after a fifty-year absence, and the eighty-year-old maestro conducted some of his own works, putting an end to years of vituperations exchanged between himself and the Soviet musical world.[6]

Darius Milhaud, the distinguished French composer, belonged to an old Jewish family from Provence. He arrived with his wife and son in New York on June 15, 1940, virtually on the last boat from Lisbon. On the dock to greet him were old friends and fellow émigrés, the composer Kurt Weill and his wife Lotte Lenya. Neither North nor South America was unfamiliar to Milhaud; he was in Brazil during World War I and had visited New York in the 1920s. He became particularly fascinated with American jazz—the "pure" variety as played in those days in New Orleans and Harlem—and used some of the jazz idiom in his music of the 1920s (e.g., *La Création du Monde*, a ballet, 1923). While in the United States, he also appeared as conductor, lecturer, and interpreter of his own music: he visited Philadelphia, New York, Boston; he was at Harvard, Princeton, and Vassar. In 1940, Milhaud's destination was Mills College in California, which had offered him a teaching post just before he

144

left Europe. He was quite happy in the intimate setting of a small liberal arts institution (a college for women, by the way), and he remained there until 1947. More easygoing than, say, Schoenberg, Milhaud did not mind teaching amateurs as long as they were serious about their work. In fact, he spoke with admiration about the American system that permitted nonprofessionals to study music as a cultural endeavor. How much Milhaud enjoyed his students at Mills is evident in this affectionate quote from his autobiography, *Notes without Music:*

American women students are usually extremely gifted, but I can never get over the surprise of seeing with what ease . . . they carry out their assignments. . . . They are self-confident and free from complexes and inhibitions. Composition [is] something to be done . . . with ease and gusto . . . Each year my students take part in two public concerts.[7]

Milhaud composed music with prodigious facility and could write a piece on command within hours—not always inspired but technically masterful. His first American opus was a string quartet (his Tenth) for Mrs. Coolidge's birthday; it was played at the annual birthday concert she offered at the Library of Congress on October 30, 1940. Milhaud's compositions were performed frequently (two of his symphonies were commissioned by the orchestras of Chicago and Boston), the Columbia Broadcasting Orchestra invited him repeatedly to conduct his music, and the League of Composers in New York arranged special programs of his works. He, in turn, reciprocated with a full heart: he wrote music especially scored for American school bands and orchestras (*Suite Française, Kentuckiana*), songs and choral music for colleges, and such oddities as a Concerto for Marimba for the St. Louis Orchestra. The Mills College student song, *Pledge to Mills,* is his composition (1946). For Temple Emanuel in San Francisco, he wrote a Sabbath Morning Service. He also wrote one film score, *Bel-Ami,* for Hollywood. After the Milhauds returned to Paris in 1947, he made arrangements to come back regularly to the United States and also taught at the newly established arts center in Aspen, Colorado.

Three other composers, former students of Franz Schreker, settled in the United States: Stefan Wolpe, Ernst Krenek, and Karol Rathaus. The Berlin-born Wolpe (1902–72) came to America via Palestine in 1938. His compositions are highly valued by connoisseurs of modern music. He made his impact primarily as a teacher of composition and held appointments at the Philadelphia Academy of Music, at Black Mountain College in North Carolina, and at Long Island University. Among his students are some of America's important composers: Ezra Laderman, Ralph Shapey, David Tudor, and Morton Feldman.

The Viennese Ernst Krenek (b. 1900) achieved sensational success in Europe with the jazz opera *Jonny spielt auf* (1927) but then turned to a more complicated style of composing. He came to the United States in 1937, taught for a time at Vassar College, headed the music department at Hamline College in Minnesota (1942–47), and then moved to California. He presently divides his time between Europe and America, composing, writing on musical subjects, conducting his own music. In 1979, the Santa Barbara campus of the University of California organized the most comprehensive survey of Krenek's creative work as a celebration of his eightieth birthday, with the indefatigable composer as a participant and listener.

The Polish-born Karol Rathaus (1895–1954) had a significant career as a versatile composer during the 1920s in Berlin, with performances of his works conducted at the Staatsoper and the Philharmonic concerts by Erich Kleiber and Wilhelm Furtwängler. He was also a pioneer in composing for films when the "talkies" were introduced; his score for *Brothers Karamazov* was considered a classic. He left Berlin in 1932, went to Paris, then to London. After a brief stay in Hollywood, he joined the faculty of Queens College of the City University of New York, where he taught from 1940 until his premature death. Here he introduced an integrated composition curriculum and built the college's music department into one of the strongest on the East Coast. In 1952, Rathaus was commissioned by the Metropolitan Opera to produce a new version of *Boris Godunov*, which was given there successfully for several years. As a composer, Rathaus reacted strongly and positively to the American landscape and the English language: his Overture *Salisbury Cove* and his settings of English and American poems for solo voice and for chorus are idomatic and ingratiating. His Fourth String Quartet received the publication prize of the Society for the Publication of American Music.

While Rathaus—though considered a specialist in film music—could not acclimatize himself to the working methods of Hollywood, other European émigré composers made spectacular careers in the film industry. Among them were Erich Korngold (1897–1957), Franz Waxman (1906–67), and Miklos Rozsa (b. 1907). All three continued

Composer Erich Korngold with Bette Davis on the set of *Deception* at Warner Brothers Studios, 1946. Korngold and other émigrés forged successful careers writing Hollywood film scores. (Courtesy of the Korngold family.)

to write music other than for films; in fact, Jascha Heifetz premiered works for violin by these composers with considerable success (the Korngold Concerto in 1947, the Rozsa Concerto in 1956, and Wax-man's *Carmen* Fantasy in 1947).

The most phenomenal case history of a successful Americaniza-tion is that of the composer Kurt Weill (1900–50). At this moment (1980), the revival of his music is the rage of New York: *Mahagonny* is at the Metropolitan Opera, *Silver Lake* at the New York City Opera, and *The Threepenny Opera* is never off the stage for any length of time. After having created a considerable stir with his early operas for the German theater (partly in collaboration with Bertolt Brecht), including *Die Dreigroschenoper* in 1928, Weill and Lotte Lenya came to New York in 1935 by way of Paris and London. His assimilation was facilitated by his having been influenced by Amer-ican folk and jazz idioms while still in Europe. To quote Nicholas Slonimsky, "Quickly absorbing the modes and fashions of American popular music, he succeeded, with amazing fidelity, in creating American-flavored musical plays."[8] In collaboration with American authors, Weill created *Street Scene* (with Elmer Rice, 1947), *Knick-* 147 *erbocker Holiday* and *Lost in the Stars* (with Maxwell Anderson, 1938 and 1949 respectively), *One Touch of Venus* (with S.J. Perelman and Ogden Nash, 1943), *Lady in the Dark* (with Moss Hart and Ira Gershwin, 1941). He also wrote an American folk opera, *Down in the Valley* (1948), based on Kentucky mountain songs. Weill set a new standard of quality for theater music and influenced such American composers as Leonard Bernstein and Marc Blitzstein in their quest for an American lyric style.

While all of the aforementioned composers arrived here as grown men, Lukas Foss, born in Berlin in 1922, was only fifteen when he enrolled at the Curtis Institute in Philadelphia. His career as a pianist, conductor, and composer has led him via California to Boston and New York, where he is now music director of the Brooklyn Philharmonia. His compositional style has evolved from early Americanism in *The Prairie* (a cantata after Carl Sandburg, 1944) to neoclassicism, to "controlled improvisation," and lately to the most advanced devices of compositional techniques. He is a strong influence in the field of modern music, combining European and American traits.

The influence of European émigré composers was great, but even greater was the impact made on the American scene by the arrival of European musical scholars. Before 1930, the branch of humanistic knowledge called *musicology* hardly existed in America. The first American musicologist, Otto Kinkeldey (1878–1966), received his bachelor's and master's degrees in the United States, then went to Berlin in 1909 to obtain a Ph.D. in musicology since no such degree was available in the United States. Even with a Ph.D., Kinkeldey's career was limited to being a music librarian at the New York Public Library and at Cornell University; there was no chair for a professor of musicology. In 1934, the American Musicological Society was founded by nine scholars, including Harold Spivacke, for many years chief of the music division at the Library of Congress; Kinkeldey was its first president. None of the founders was a recent immigrant, though Paul Henry Lang, who was a Cornell graduate with a fresh Ph.D. in musicology (1934), was partly European-trained. Then came the stream of arrivals of European musical scholars. Those born before 1900 brought established European reputations, among them Curt Sachs, Alfred Einstein, Karl Geiringer, Hugo Leichtentritt, Oswald Jonas, Paul Nettl, Willi Apel, and Emanuel Winternitz. The younger among them quickly adapted themselves: Otto Gombosi, Leo Schrade, Felix Salzer, Erich Hertzmann, Manfred Bukofzer, Ed-

148

ward Lowinsky, Hans Tischler, Hans Theodore David, Eric Werner, Hans Moldenhauer, Siegmund Levarie, Hans Nathan, Frederick Dorian, and others. Overcoming linguistic difficulties, most of these scholars obtained positions at American colleges and unversities, usually teaching one or two courses in musicology and some related subjects.

The phenomenal growth of musicological studies in the United States, reflected in the parallel growth of the American Musicological Society (over three thousand members at present), can be traced to the influence of immigrant scholars, mostly of German background. They served as mentors to a young generation of Americans and contributed a new depth to the curricula. But these same scholars profited by the fresh outlook and unprejudiced approach of their American students and younger colleagues. Often, the learned musicologists were assigned to teach lowbrow music appreciation courses to a cross-section of students, with tragicomic results. I remember how Professor Curt Sachs was ready to fail half of his class at Queens College because he did not realize how few of the students could read music. Such experiences certainly sobered the European scholar. On the other hand, the American students were impressed by the exactitude of European musical scholarship.

I can testify to this mutual process of enlightenment since I studied musicology on both sides of the Atlantic. There was monastic seriousness at the Berlin seminar of Arnold Schering, where we students practically stood at attention. German musicology was once described as *Worte ohne Lieder* (Words without Songs), a humorous reversal of Mendelssohn's *Songs without Words*. When I entered Professor Paul Henry Lang's seminar at Columbia, I was amazed by the open-mindedness, the easygoing discussions between teacher and student, the contact with the live world of music, so that musicology did not exist in a vacuum. The informality between teachers and students at American universities was a source of wonderment to many European professors. When I asked my distinguished colleague Rathaus how he felt about his music appreciation class, he looked at me with a wry smile and said, "You know, the other day before class, a student came up to me, slapped me playfully on the back, and asked cheerfully, 'Hi, Doc, what's up today?'" Someone defined the difference between European and American universities in the following way: in Europe, a scholar is surrounded by a group of students; in America, a student is surrounded by a group of scholars. Yes, we are student-centered in America. The term *elective* does

149

not exist in the Soviet curriculum; nor is there much choice in the curricula of central Europe. Excessive authoritarianism is one of the few failings that some European scholars have exhibited. Nevertheless, the influence of European scholarship in music has been enormous, not only through teaching but also in the field of book publications and editing.

All in all, American musical life experienced a period of maturation through its encounter with European musicians. The influence was, in fact, mutual, and both sides emerged immeasurably enriched.

Notes

1. Joseph Wulf, *Musik im dritten Reich* (Gütersloh, West Germany, 1963).

2. See transcript in Nicholas Slonimsky, *Music since 1900* (New York, 1971), pp. 1,394–404.

3. Arnold Schoenberg, *Style and Idea*, ed. and trans. Dika Newlin; 2d. enlarged edition, ed. Leonard Stein (New York, 1975).

4. Paul Hindemith, *Course in Traditional Harmony* (New York, 1943), and *Elementary Training for Musicians* (New York, 1946).

5. Published as Igor Stravinsky, *Poetics of Music* (Cambridge, Mass., 1942 [French] and 1947 [English]).

6. See Boris Schwarz, "Stravinsky in Soviet Russian Criticism," *The Musical Quarterly* 48 (July 1962):340–61.

7. Darius Milhaud, *Notes without Music*, trans. Donald Evans (New York, 1953), p. 284.

8. Nicholas Slonimsky, *Baker's Biographical Dictionary of Musicians* (New York, 1978), p. 1,865.

American Skyscrapers and Weimar Modern: Transactions between Fact and Idea

CHRISTIAN F. OTTO

A handful of Weimar architects arrived in the United States during the late 1930s. Highly experienced as designers, builders, educators, and publicists, they immediately set to work in the New World. Walter Gropius transformed the curriculum in design at Harvard, Ludwig Mies van der Rohe initiated an influential course of instruction at the Illinois Institute of Technology (IIT), and both built extensively. In Chicago, László Moholy-Nagy founded a school that promoted educational ideals derived from the Bauhaus. Marcel Breuer launched a prolific architectural career, and Ludwig Hilberseimer was heard from as a city planner.

The design directions initiated by these individuals were explored by several generations of architects in America. Among many others, Philip Johnson and the huge firm of Skidmore, Owings and Merrill made Mies's steel and glass architecture an American phenomenon. Eero Saarinen, Paul Rudolf, and Roche and Dinkeloo translated aspects of the Weimar inheritance into their own architectural vocabularies, dependent yet distinctive. Some, such as Adolfo Venturi, actively campaigned against aspects of the Weimar program and in so doing confirmed its hegemony. These represent only a few pages in a thick catalog of influences.

The impact of the handful of immigrants on architecture, architectural education, design concepts, and city planning strategies in

151

the United States raises questions that are as compelling as they are difficult to answer. Why was America the architectural mecca for this high-powered Weimar diaspora? What explains the ease with which they were accepted, and their far-reaching influence? How did an architecture embedded in the social and cultural values of the Weimar Republic flourish so voraciously under entirely different conditions?

It would require an extended study to do justice to the complexity of the Weimar legacy in American architecture. One detachable segment of this story, however, will be examined here, namely the impact of Weimar architectural ideas on the American skyscraper.

Although it has become a worldwide phenomenon, the skyscraper is commonly touted as American in origin and evolution. From the 1870s on, American designers had committed themselves in droves to the skyscraper. Their achievements in technical sophistication, plan layout, and formal interpretation were unequaled in the world. Europeans venerated the American skyscraper, which they could experience in cities all over the United States—New York, Chicago, Detroit, San Francisco, Houston, Boston.

Evolving in Europe in the meantime, in the 1920s, was the notion of the tall building as a tower sheathed in a skin of glass sheets and thin metal frames. A reticulated pattern, as flat as graph paper and often sparsely elegant, was stretched over the building from bottom to top, point supports were revealed below, and the whole conveyed the impression of being produced by a highly technological society. These ideas were specifically pursued by Weimar architects, and, within Weimar, most virorously by Ludwig Mies van der Rohe.

Partly persuaded to leave Germany by the circumstances of Nazism and partly cajoled by some American aficionados to come to this country, Mies arrived in Chicago with avant-garde theories about tall buildings; none of his projects had ever been built. He was well enough known in professional circles but was hardly a star like Frank Lloyd Wright. Nevertheless, the Miesian version of the skyscraper, decisively different from its American counterpart, was enthusiastically received in the United States, and for three decades after World War II, during a period of unparalleled building activity, Americans stocked their cities with variations of the Miesian high-rise. The strong, multifarious, indigenous tradition seems to have collapsed

152

Ludwig Mies van der Rohe. Émigrés Mies and Walter Gropius became dominant forces in transmitting the International Style in architecture to the United States. (Courtesy of Hedrich Blessing.)

in less than a decade, and architectural ideas articulated in Weimar became hallmarks of American building from the late 1940s on. In fact, they were declared thoroughly American. How can this extraordinary cultural transference be explained? Did Mies, who began his American career in 1938 as part of the diaspora shaken loose by the political destruction of the Weimar Republic, singlehandedly usurp an entire American tradition? If so, this is a mind-boggling event, the architectural equivalent of something like the Russian Revolution, a phenomenon of apocalyptic proportions for the present and history of the built environment. The annals of twentieth-century architectural history maintain such an interpretation of the transformation of American architectural sensibilities.[1] But since the accepted understanding of the situation, upon reflection, seems to border on the fantastic, I test in this essay the matrix that connects Weimar, Mies, the skyscraper, and America to see whether or not this hypothesis can be confirmed.

American Skyscrapers and Weimar Modern

The skyscraper story consists of a complex set of intercontinental architectural transactions, and the motivations that inform it are many, rich, and intriguing. The salient points concern, first, Mies's research on the tall building during the 1920s in Weimar, and second, American efforts in the 1920s and 1930s to create modern skyscrapers. Proposals to disperse or decongest cities, and an increasing involvement in science and technology also bear on the subject. The conclusion that will be drawn from this review is that the confluence of these concerns produced what is currently referred to as the "Miesian" skyscraper, more so than did Mies himself.

Mies was born in Aachen, Germany, in 1886, and moved in 1905 to Berlin, where he studied architecture with Bruno Paul and Peter Behrens.[2] From 1919 until his departure for America in 1937, he maintained a private architectural practice in Berlin. His fundamental architectural breakthroughs, the bases for work he pursued until his death in 1969, began late in 1920 in response to a competition for a skyscraper.[3] A high-rise building was to be located on a triangular plot on the Friedrichstrasse in Berlin. At this moment in Berlin, notions about tall buildings were generating considerable interest. Architects and critics such as Martin Mächler, Bruno Möhring, and Paul Wittig were lecturing and publishing papers on the advantages and problems of the tall building, as well as considering the impact they might have on the city.[4] That year legislation combining Berlin and the smaller towns around it into the single administrative area of greater metropolitan Berlin had gone into effect, in turn prompting challenges to the zoning ordinances that restricted building height.

Mies's Friedrichstrasse proposal, which filled the triangular site with three faceted triangular units joined to a central core of vertical circulation, was the most radical entry in the competition. He made the walls entirely out of sheets of glass, run without interruption from the bottom to the top of the building. The glass walls dramatized the prismatic shape of the plan, and the razor-sharp vertical edges created a startling contrast to the surrounding buildings. Higher than any other structure around, Mies's skyscraper was a vivid new creation, devoid of all reference to the past. It was so new, in fact, that we cannot even successfully find sources for this design; we have no record that Mies had ever done anything like it before. Just before the outbreak of World War I, some German architects had begun to discuss the possibilities of an architecture of glass, and after the war the architect Bruno Taut published some of his sketches

In Europe Mies's designs for tall buildings such as the Friedrich-strasse Office Building (1919) remained paper projects; in America, after his migration here, Miesian high-rises were erected in New York, Los Angeles, Chicago, and other urban areas. (Ludwig Mies van der Rohe, *Friedrichstrasse Office Building.* Berlin. Project. 1919. Perspective. Charcoal and pencil on brown paper mounted to board, 68¼ x 48". Collection, Mies van der Rohe Archive, The Museum of Modern Art, New York. Gift of Ludwig Mies van der Rohe.)

American Skyscrapers and Weimar Modern

for tall, glass buildings in prismatic shapes. Mies may have been familiar with these drawings—they may even have been a catalyst to his thinking—but this possible connection explains little of Mies's design. Taut's sketches are schematic and small, graphic abbreviations for ideas about a social utopia. Mies, on the other hand, was designing in scale for a specific urban site, using specific materials and structure.[5]

After the competition, which Mies did not win and which in any event never resulted in a building, Mies began constructing models of tall buildings sheathed with glass. He wanted to explore, as he put it, the implications of "over-large glass surfaces." Research revealed new design principles to him. He claimed that glass exposed "the bold structural pattern" of the skyscraper, the structural system, which he maintained was "the basis of all artistic design." Further, as he wrote, he "discovered by working with actual glass models that the important thing is the play of the reflections and not the effect of light and shadow as in ordinary buildings."[6] Often monochromatic, with all ornament expunged from the design, the structures seemed to express the image of a machine, as if they had been extruded from a colossal piece of manufacturing equipment.[7]

Mies did not continue to investigate the design of the tall building after 1922. But later in the 1920s he undertook a series of projects in which he specified the glass cladding of buildings. These were steel and vitreous realizations of what he referred to as "skin and bone construction." Walls consisted of glass panels held in place by a metal frame, clipped to a steel structural cage, which Mies put on display at ground level. With these moves, the elements of the Miesian skyscraper were established: a glass skin patterned by a reticulated cage of narrow steel strips attached to a structural system revealed at ground level by a regular series of slender point supports that seem effortlessly to prop up the light, glass-enclosed volumes above.[8]

In the United States, as head of his own firm and director of architecture at IIT, Mies was given the opportunity to build what in Germany had remained paper projects. He started with one-, two-, and three-story buildings for IIT, and, beginning in the late 1940s, expanded to high-rise structures. Mies's reputation flourished; Park Avenue in New York City became glazed by "Miesian" high-rises (including Mies's Seagram Building), and in urban areas from the District of Columbia to Los Angeles, from Miami to Minneapolis, new skyscraper construction shimmered with glass and steel.

156

American design of the 1920s and 1930s provided the architectural context for the post–World War II situation. During the 1920s, two modes of skyscraper design dominated American work. One was dubbed Vertical Style by critics soon after it appeared; the other we know as Art Deco. A project by a European promoted the one; the other was derived in part from European sources. Yet both were based on American traditions and remained distinctively American.

Eliel Saarinen, Finnish architect and father of the better-known Eero Saarinen, also fathered the Vertical Style.[9] Eliel won second place in the 1922 competition sponsored by the *Chicago Tribune* for its new offices. The unusual features of his project were its stepped massing, emphatic vertical piers, and minimal use of ornament. Louis Sullivan, America's great designer of skyscrapers during the 1880s and 1890s, approved of the project:

Qualifying as it does in every technical regard. . .it goes freely in advance, and with the steel frame as a thesis, displays a high science of design such as the world up to this day had neither known or surmised.[10]

Saarinen, in fact, had profited from Sullivan's handling of the pier and spandrel, which the American architect employed in order to imbue his skyscrapers with a soaring verticality. Many architects in turn were attracted to Saarinen's project, establishing the Vertical Style as a common and popular skyscraper mode in the United States. The results can be seen, for example, in a group of New York City buildings: John Mead Howell's Panhellenic Hotel, begun in 1927; Raymond Hood's Daily News Building, begun in 1929; and Rockefeller Center, begun in 1930 and designed by a consortium of architects. Additional examples can be found in other large American cities, and this design strategy was being pursued as late as the mid-1950s.

Art Deco was an approach to pattern distilled from many sources—in this country, from Frank Lloyd Wright's architectural decoration, and abroad, from the art of the Viennese secession, German expressionism, and French *l'art décoratif*.[11] American designers involved with Art Deco ideas influenced the skyscraper in three ways. First, ornament was considered original, not derived from nor dependent on styles or forms from the past. As such, it was promoted as something contemporary, of and about the modern world, right and proper for dynamic new buildings. Second, it was applied to the bottom and top of buildings, creating interactions on the one hand at the microscale of the street, on the other at the macroscale of the long

American Skyscrapers and Weimar Modern

distance urban view. In the Chrysler Building by William Van Alen, both these innovations can be seen. That part of the dramatic decoration of the building employs automobile wheels, fenders, and gigantic radiator caps as leitmotivs leads to the third point: Art Deco was a response to a machine aesthetic, to the increasing social importance of technology. The shaft of the building reflects this technological frame of mind in its unadorned, utilitarian wall and window architecture, a matter-of-fact cladding of the structural skeleton that we may categorize as "modern of the middle." Chrysler's ornamental forms were derived from new, noncorrosive alloys used on the exterior, and from the processes of working these substances. With enthusiastic conviction, architects attempted to integrate modern ornament with their modern, technological structures. In 1932, the architect Claude Bragdon offered a spirited summary of the contemporary frame of mind. He pointed out that architects were abandoning historical forms in favor of others more rational, more economical, and more expressive of the spirit of a mechanical age. They discovered these same qualities in the skyscraper, "a symbol of the American spirit in its more obvious aspect—that ruthless, tireless, assured *energism*, delightedly proclaiming, 'What a great boy am I!'"[12]

The Vertical Style and Art Deco were accompanied by a cogent and continuous presentation in America of the architecture of the European Modern Movement, buildings conceived as the inevitable products of an industrialized era.[13] The stucco walls were thin, light, flat, unornamented planes; windows were ribbons of glass; roofs were flat; plans were open and without boxed-in spaces; materials were manufactured and displayed no hint of craftwork; and buildings were positioned above the earth on slender, widely spaced supports. According to the assertions of its makers, this new architecture was a direct reflection of its age, a statement and sign of a technological society, its character, and its way of life.

The campaign to educate the public about the virtues of the new architecture began with the opening of the Museum of Modern Art's 1932 exhibition, "Modern Architecture," which was accompanied by Henry-Russell Hitchcock's and Philip Johnson's book, *The International Style: Architecture since 1922*. In both, the tenets of the Modern Movement were vividly expressed in visual and verbal terms. Other Museum of Modern Art exhibits included one in 1941 on the Tennessee Valley Authority ("A new architecture, bold as the engineering from which it springs, is rising in the valley. Look at it,

158

and be proud that you are an American."), another the following year on "What Is Modern Architecture?" and two years later, "Built in USA 1932–1944."[14]

Even before these exhibits, however, publications praising modern architecture from Europe by authors whose works are still influential began to proliferate on the American market. A list of highlights would include:

Henry-Russell Hitchcock, *Modern Architecture: Romanticism and Reintegration*, New York, 1929.
Nikolaus Pevsner, *Pioneers of the Modern Movement from William Morris to Walter Gropius*, London, 1936.
Walter Curt Behrendt, *Modern Building*, New York, 1937.
J.M. Richards, *An Introduction to Modern Architecture*, London, 1940.
Siegfried Giedion, *Space Time and Architecture*, New York, 1941.

In addition to publications and exhibitions, a handful of European modern architects had immigrated to the United States and were putting up contemporary buildings on the West Coast (Richard Neutra's and Rudolph Schindler's houses for the Lovells are still considered major twentieth-century monuments), while on the East Coast a first generation of native American designers began to show the effects of the Europeans' influence.[15] Most of their efforts, found all over the United States, did not involve designing tall buildings. Many projects, such as those by Edward Durell Stone, were for houses; some, such as the Starrett-Lehigh Building by the Cory brothers, New York City, or Wallace Harrison's WFY broadcasting studios in Schenectady, were commercial structures. But there were American practitioners who did attempt to combine modernism and the tall building. Raymond Hood designed the McGraw-Hill Building in 1929, stacking the stories horizontally, stretching thin strips of wall and window around each level, and avoiding ornamental elaboration.[16] That same year, George Howe and William Lescaze undertook the planning of the Philadelphia Saving Fund Society Building (PSFS) in Philadelphia.[17] Lescaze had been trained in Zurich by the early modernist, Karl Moser, but had already arrived in America during 1920. The American-schooled Howe had been converted to modernism during the 1920s, both in his practice and in his espousal in print of a parallel set of architectural principles. PSFS reveals the commitment of its designers to the Modern Movement. It consists of a raised slab that clearly expresses its skeletal structure, employs ribbon windows, puts the mechanical floor on display, and revels in   159 smooth, hard, machined surfaces. In addition, it has been entirely air-conditioned from the beginning, an unusually advanced technological provision.

In discussing Vertical Style, Art Deco, and the presentation of the European Modern Movement, we have pursued a course close to architecture. However, some larger, more general themes are important for an understanding of the American skyscraper. One of these concerns new attitudes toward the city; the other relates to increased industrial and technological involvement in society.

During the 1920s, and continuing into the post–World War II period, attitudes toward the city were stained by increasing negativism generated by overcrowding, expanding slums, vicious traffic congestion, growing air and noise pollution, and high rates of disease and crime. The dispersed city or the decongested city were offered as solutions to these problems.

Many strategies were proposed for achieving the dispersed city;[18] significant plans included Henry Wright's and Clarence Stein's garden cities (e.g., Radburn, New Jersey, begun in 1928), and those of the United States Resettlement Administration (e.g., Greenbelt, Maryland, begun in 1935). Frank Lloyd Wright's Broadacre City, first proposed in 1932, was an effort to disperse all of America consistently over the countryside. And the important voice of critic Lewis Mumford maintained, "Decentralization is a first step towards building up a sound, life-centered civilization."

More dramatic visually were proposals for the decongested city.[19] Taking their clue from Le Corbusier's vision of a City for Three Million—towering cruciform skyscrapers located in a park setting but including superhighways, railroads, and an airport—various American designers generated stunning images of cities composed of supertall buildings and multilevel, at times elevated, highways to permit concentration without congestion. Hugh Ferriss's 1929 Metropolis of Tomorrow was the first. Two others from the 1939 World's Fair in New York were marveled at by millions of viewers: Henry Dreyfus's Democracity in the Theme Center Building and Norman Bel Geddes's Intersection of the Future, created for the General Motors Pavilion. In far less dramatic form the notion influenced the building of American public housing, such as two projects in New York City jointly designed by William Lescaze and Albert

160

Frey—the Chrystie-Forsythe Houses, planned in December 1931, and River Garden Housing, planned in 1932 and 1933. Private housing developments followed similar lines.[20]

This agitation for dispersal or decongestion seems to have affected the design of the tall buildings by promoting structures in which the base was open, the tower or slab arranged with ample free space around it, and greenery incorporated into the scheme. Two crucial instances are projects from the 1940s by Pietro Belluschi and Nathaniel Owings. Belluschi's 1943 Office Building Project located a twelve-story slab in the middle of a block in order to "preserve air, light and space for all time to come." Parking, public transportation, and the road were found behind the building; the front contained a community area with shops, restaurant, health and exercise facilities, club, and theater. A pedestrian walkway through this zone enabled "leisurely promenades, gardens, trees and flowers for a civilized community to enjoy. . .without the tension caused by the dangers, noises and smells of present-day traffic."[21] Owings's 1947 Office Building Project for the Building Managers Association contained a three-story base of stores and parking. The top of the base was treated as a park, with grass, trees, pool, and restaurant. "A man can't live where a tree won't grow," maintained Owings. The forty-story slab of offices was set open and free by the base, permitting "in perpetuity, light, air and view."[22]

Belief in the positive, beneficial qualities of science and industry also left its mark on the high-rise.[23] During the first decades of the twentieth century, America experienced a staggering increase in industrial production and the growth of business. Even the devastating economic reversals of the 1930s did not erode the pervasive belief that science and industry could create a prosperous and brave new world. Industry and technology began to assume symbolic importance, as interest in TVA projects and the 1939 fair demonstrates.

Industry became increasingly involved in things architectural, as for example in the development of aluminum, adopting the new architecture as a symbol of progress.[24] The design profession reciprocated by embracing industrial materials and processes for building. Vividly demonstrating this are designs such as Belluschi's and Owings's, which specifically promoted the use of aluminum, stainless steel, and plastic. The ideal cladding for a building, it was maintained, would be "a curtain wall pre-assembled in panels capable of lasting a hundred years, no more than two inches thick, light, insulating, fire-resistant, withstanding winds up to 150 miles per hour, weather-

American Skyscrapers and Weimar Modern

proof and vaporproof, ventilated and drained, and allowing flexibility of application. Such a hung wall would have to be made of glass and metal or possibly of new materials like plastics."[25]

The combination of slab and new technological materials marked many important projects by American designers during the late 1940s: Harrison and Abramovitz's proposed commercial development in 1946 of the site that was used the next year by the United Nations; the United Nations Secretariat of 1947; several Skidmore, Owings and Merrill undertakings, such as New York University–Bellevue Medical Center, begun in 1945; Lake Meadow Housing in Chicago, first designed in 1948; the partially built Chicago Bus Terminal of 1949; and the Ford Motor Company headquarters in Dearborn, Michigan. In short, before Mies began to build skyscrapers in America, American designers had already met, absorbed, and realized similar dicta for a high-rise architecture based on structure, technological materials, and industrialized processes. This was the result of indigenous events, as well as of cultural transactions with Europe.

Mies had the good fortune to immigrate into a setup—a congenial, supportive context for his architectural ideas had been established in America, and the authority of European modernism strengthened this tradition. A provocative but difficult question follows: How do we account for the prevalent assumption that the metal and glass high-rise is a Miesian product that proliferated in America once the master arrived on these shores?

Presumably, a consideration of this question would take several factors into account, chief among them the character of popular press reports on the built environment, professional and popular criticism, the writing of contemporary architectural history, and the nature of instruction in American schools of architecture. No review of these materials has ever been pursued, thus preventing any purposeful response for the moment. On the other hand, the matter of popular assumptions, though fascinating and curious, does not seem as important as the questions with which we began, concerns with indigenous architectural tradition and its relationship to European attitudes toward design. Such concerns explore the actual making of architecture, rather than generalized notions about it, and deal with the reality of built architecture, of existing cities, of our working perceptions about form and space.

162

If this last question must remain unanswered for the interim, one suggestive event may nevertheless serve as a concluding set piece. In 1947 Mies was given a major retrospective at the Museum of Modern Art, the same year that Wallace Harrison, Nathaniel Owings, Gordon Bunshaft, Pietro Belluschi, and others began to hit their stride. These architects have never had Museum of Modern Art retrospectives. For the 1947 exhibition Philip Johnson published his monograph on Mies, the first full-scale treatment of the architect. In the third revised edition of the book (1978), Johnson, in an Epilogue, admitted his initial intent in writing: "I thought of it as hagiography, exegesis, propaganda—I just wanted to show that Mies was the greatest architect in the world."[26] He succeeded with remarkable thoroughness.

Notes

This paper derives from my present research on Ludwig Mies van der Rohe and from the work of my student, Mark Reinberger, who has explored the pre– and post–World War II history of the skyscraper in America.

1. A telling instance is William H. Jordy, *American Buildings and Their Architects: The Impact of European Modernism in the Mid-Twentieth Century* (New York, 1976); chap. 4 discusses Mies.

2. Philip C. Johnson, *Mies Van Der Rohe*, 3rd rev. ed. (New York, 1978), is the basic source of information on Mies's life and architecture.

3. Ludwig Glaeser, Introduction and Notes, *Ludwig Mies Van Der Rohe* (New York, 1969), pls. 1, 2, 3 and corresponding notes, and Johnson, *Mies*, pp. 23–29, are the best presentations of these skyscrapers. The surviving drawings of these proposals are housed in the Ludwig Mies van der Rohe Archive in the Museum of Modern Art, New York.

4. See, for example: Martin Mächler, "Zum Problem des Wolkenkratzers," *Wasmuths Monatshefte für Baukunst* 5 (1920–21): 191–205, 260–73; Bruno Möhring, "Über die Vorzüge der Turmhäuser und die Voraussetzungen, unter denen sie in Berlin gebaut werden können," *Der Zirkel* (Berlin, 1921); Paul Wittig, *Studie über die Ausnahmsweise Zulassung einzelner Turmhäuser in Berlin* (Berlin, 1918).

5. See the magazine *Frühlicht*, ed. Bruno Taut (Berlin, 1920), especially numbers 1, 3, and 7. In 1921–22, Mies published his glass skyscraper projects in this magazine (see below, n.).

6. Ludwig Mies van der Rohe, "Hochhäuser," *Frühlicht* 4 (1921–22):122–24; trans. in Johnson, *Mies*, p. 187.

7. Jordy, *American Buildings*, chap. 4, and Vincent Scully, *American Architecture and Urbanism* (New York, 1969), p. 186, employ these terms to characterize the "Miesian" skyscraper.

163

8. See Johnson, *Mies*, pp. 58–61, 188.

9. See "The Vertical Style," *Architectural Forum* 83 (July 1954): 104; *The International Competition for a New Administrative Building for the Chicago Tribune* (Chicago, 1923); Louis Sullivan, "The *Chicago Tribune* Competition," *Architectural Record* 53 (February 1923):151–57; Cervin Robinson and Rosemarie Haag Bletter, *Skyscraper Style* (New York, 1975), p. 22 and pl. 35.

10. Sullivan, "The *Chicago Tribune* Competition."

11. Robinson and Bletter, *Skyscraper Style*, pp. 35ff.

12. Claude Bragdon, *The Frozen Fountain* (New York, 1932), p. 25.

13. Norbert Huse, *"Neues Bauen" 1918 bis 1933: Moderne Architektur in der Weimarer Republik* (Munich, 1975), is an excellent history of Modern Movement architecture in Germany during the 1920s, where and when building according to these principles was common.

14. The quotation is reported in the *New Yorker* 17 (June 7, 1941): 60. Also see *What Is Modern Architecture?* (New York, 1942), and Elizabeth Mock, ed., *Built in USA, 1932–44* (New York, 1944).

15. Henry-Russell Hitchcock and Philip Johnson, *The International Style* (New York, 1932), illustrates the work of some early practitioners; also see the *Built in USA* catalogue.

16. Jordy, *American Buildings*, pp. 68–70.

17. Ibid., chap. 2.

18. Criticism of the city has a long history in America: See Morton and Lucia White, *The Intellectual and the City*, new ed. (New York, 1977), and Leo Marx, *The Machine in the Garden* (New York, 1964). But during the 1920s, this criticism shifted from addressing specific problems to criticism of the city per se.
   On Henry Wright and Clarence Stein, see Stein, *Toward New Towns for America* (Cambridge, Mass., 1966), and Lewis Mumford, *From the Ground Up* (New York, 1956). On the United States Resettlement Administration, see O. Kline Fulmer, *Greenbelt* (Washington, D.C., 1941); Albert Mayer, *Greenbelt, Towns Revisited* (Washington, D.C., 1968); United States Resettlement Administration, *Greenbelt Towns* (Washington, D.C., 1936); and George A. Warner, *Greenbelt: A Cooperative Community* (New York, 1954).
   On Frank Lloyd Wright's Broadacre City, see Robert Fishman, *Urban Utopias of the Twentieth Century* (New York, 1977); Henry-Russell Hitchcock, *In the Nature of Materials* (New York, 1942); and Norris Kelly Smith, *Frank Lloyd Wright* (Englewood Cliffs, N.J., 1966).
   On Lewis Mumford, see his articles: "Social Purposes and New Plans," *Survey Graphic* 29 (Feb. 1940):119ff; "How Can Our Cities Survive?" *New Republic* 108 (Feb. 8, 1943):186ff; and "Cities Fit to Live In," *Nation* 166 (May 15, 1948):530ff (quotation from this source).

19. On Le Corbusier, see Le Corbusier, *The City of Tomorrow*, trans. Frederick Etchells (New York, 1929), and Norma Evenson, *Le Corbusier: The Machine and the*

Grand Design (New York, 1969).

On Hugh Ferriss, see his *The Metropolis of Tomorrow* (New York, 1929).

On the World's Fair, see *Architectural Forum* 70 (June 1939), which is devoted entirely to the fair; "The City of Tomorrow," *House and Garden* 74 (Nov. 1938): 28ff; and *Official Guide Book of the New York World's Fair* (New York, 1939).

On public housing, see Richard Pommer, "The Architecture of Urban Housing in the United States During the Early 1930s," *Journal of the Society of Architectural Historians* 37 (Dec. 1978):235ff.

On private housing developments, see Lewis Mumford, *New Yorker* 25 (Nov. 12, 1949):73ff; and "Parkchester," *Architectural Forum* 71 (Dec. 1939):412ff.

20. Other indicators of decentralizing or decongesting the city are slum clearance, urban renewal, the interstate highway program, and population and business shifts to the suburbs.

21. *Architectural Forum* 78 (May 1943):108ff.

22. *Architectural Forum* 91 (Aug. 1949):70.

23. Indications of this attitude toward science and industry can be found in the *Official Guide Book of the Fair* (Chicago, 1933) for the Century of Progress Exposition, and in the *Official Guide Book of the New York World's Fair.*

24. For example, see "Dreams That Will Live in Steel," American Institute of Steel Construction advertisement using a Ferriss drawing, *Architectural Forum* 52 (May 1930):146.

25. John Burchard and Albert Bush-Brown, *The Architecture of America: A Social and Cultural History* (Boston, 1961), p. 472.

26. Johnson, *Mies*, p. 209.

American Skyscrapers and Weimar Modern

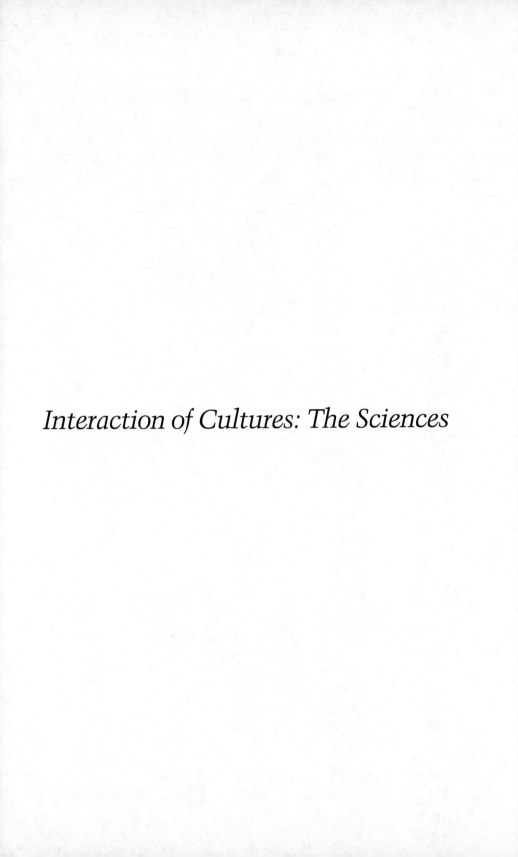

Interaction of Cultures: The Sciences

The Migration of Physicists to the United States

GERALD HOLTON

I One might think that when a nation undergoes a revolutionary upheaval against its own political system and even against reason itself,
the sons and daughters of Urania, the muse representing science,
would be among the last to be touched. For it is generally agreed
that research into the behavior of nature is as free from local political
overtones as intellectual work can be, and that the achievements of
a nation's major scientists—more than those of its poets or statesmen—are embedded in an international and intercultural system of
recognition that is guaranteed by the consensual nature of scientific
proof itself.

During the rise of some authoritarian regimes, such hopes for
leniency in the treatment of scientists were indeed fulfilled. But
during the ascent of fascism in Germany (and later in Austria), the
world witnessed the enthusiastic persecution of scientists from the
very start of the political upheaval. For Albert Einstein—who will
furnish a convenient window for this study, made more appropriate
by the fact that this colloquium has been called in honor of his
centenary—the clouds began to gather on the horizon even earlier.[1]
Largely because of the outpouring of international acclaim after the

November 1919 announcement of experimental support for the predictions of general relativity theory, Einstein came under vicious attack by both political and scientific extremists in Germany. The German ambassador in London even felt constrained in 1920 to warn his Foreign Office privately in a report that "Professor Einstein is just at this time for Germany a cultural factor of first rank. . . . We should not drive such a man out of Germany with whom we can carry on real culture propaganda *(Kulturpropaganda)*."[2] In 1922, following the political assassination of the foreign minister, Walter Rathenau, the news spread that Einstein also was on the list of intended victims. Einstein felt it wise to make a long journey to the Far East and to Palestine, writing from Japan on December 20, 1922, that he had "greatly welcomed" the opportunity for a lengthy absence from Germany so he could "escape the increasing danger."[3]

Ten years later, the power of the state was placed in the hands of Hitler, and the long pent-up floodwaters of hatred finally broke through the dam, washing equally over everyone. Almost overnight, Jewish scientists were dismissed from their posts at the universities and stricken from the rolls of honorific institutions, with virtually no audible protest being raised by their colleagues.

Of the lucky ones who escaped, about one hundred physicists found refuge and a new productive life in the United States between 1933 and 1941.[4] It has often been remarked that their flight turned the personal tragedy, and the tragedy for Germany itself, into an unexpected boon for the intellectual and artistic life of their host country. More than that, in the physical sciences, so the story goes, the influx of refugees from Germany, and later from fascist tyranny in Italy and Austria, provided the necessary critical infusion of high talent that helped to turn the United States rather suddenly into the world's pre-eminent country for the pursuit of frontier research. Indeed, when it became known in 1933 that Einstein was moving to America, rather than to any of the other countries offering him a haven, the prominent French physicist Paul Langevin was quoted as having announced that the United States would now become "the center of the natural sciences."[5] Lord Rutherford, among others, expressed himself similarly.

These perceptions were not wholly mistaken. But they hid a more interesting and more complex truth that, through the work of a number of scholars, has recently become more evident.[6] It is a truth that I wish to illustrate in these remarks today and that may be put succinctly in the following way. At least with respect to the physicists who escaped Hitler's henchmen and fled to the United States, a remarkable symbiosis occurred. While the United States gave European physicists a new life, they in turn provided a new source of energy and a new style of research. This symbiosis would have been impossible without the prior development of a high level of scientific accomplishment in the host country. Einstein did not come to a scientific backwater. On the contrary, he chose to come to the United States chiefly because he was impressed with the achievements already made there (what Robert Oppenheimer later called, with simple understatement, "a rather sturdy indigenous effort"[7]), with the quality of the colleagues, with the conditions of work, and with the bright promise for the future of science in the country. In short, the United States was, in 1933, a country of natural choice for a physicist whose first loyalty was the pursuit of science.

II   Albert Einstein's search for a country of refuge and his eventual decision to settle in the United States form a good lens with which to study the migration of physicists to the United States during the 1930s. When Hitler came to power, Einstein was fifty-four years old and intensely occupied with his work in general relativity theory and cosmology. As it happened, in January 1933 he was away from Berlin on a visit to the United States. He vowed that he would not return to his positions at the university in Berlin and the Kaiser Wilhelm Gesellschaft as long as the Nazis were in charge. Suddenly, he was a man without a home, spending the first uncertain months in Belgium and England. His apartment in Berlin and his summer cottage had been raided and sealed, and he had renounced his German citizenship.

In September 1933 he found himself in England, shortly before having to journey back to the United States to spend a few months at the California Institute of Technology (where R.A. Millikan had arranged for Einstein's periodic visits). Einstein did not know that these were to be his last few weeks in Europe. It was by no means clear where he might settle or which of the many options he would choose. One attractive possibility was England. In the preamble to his Herbert Spencer lecture at Oxford in June, Einstein had clearly expressed the hope that this would be the beginning of a closer association.[8] A bill was then pending in the House of Commons to give him the status of a naturalized citizen. Frederick A. Lindemann   171 at Oxford was hard at work arranging for an appointment there.

But offers came to Einstein from many other directions, and in a certain spirit of absent-mindedness, he seems to have accepted quite a few of them. Chairs were waiting for Einstein, or were being arranged for him, in Belgium, Spain, and France, at the Hebrew University in Jerusalem and the newly formed Princeton Institute for Advanced Study. To Langevin, who begged him to consider a post being created for him at the Collège de France, he wrote with characteristic perception, "I find myself in an embarrassing situation, exactly the opposite of that of my compatriots who were chased out of Germany."[9]

In an interview Einstein gave on September 11, 1933, to a reporter from the *Daily Express,* he provided a further glimpse of his unsettled state of mind at the time. Einstein told of Millikan's proposal that he make his home at the California Institute of Technology in Pasadena, then significantly added:

They have there the finest observatory in the world. That is a temptation. But although I try to be universal in thought, I am European by instinct and inclination. I shall want to return here.

He never did.

The first indication of the trail that would take him, later in 1933, once and for all to the United States can be found in Einstein's correspondence 20 years earlier. In the splendid Smithsonian exhibit of Einstein documents, there is a letter Einstein wrote on October 14, 1913, to George Ellery Hale, the astronomer at Mount Wilson Observatory. Working in Zurich on his first version of general relativity theory, Einstein was at that time by no means a world celebrity. (On the contrary, appended to Einstein's inquiry is a plea from one of his colleagues, Julius Maurer, whom Hale knew, asking the privilege of "a friendly reply to Mr. Professor Dr. Einstein, my honorable colleague at the Polytechnical school.") Einstein was asking the American astronomer's advice on whether one might observe the bending of light from stars near the rim of the sun, when observed against the background of the sun (without an eclipse). Although Einstein's project was not realistic, he was right to consult Hale, whose "rich experience in these matters" Einstein said he valued. Hale was only one of a whole galaxy of American scientists who had demonstrated their experimental prowess. The work of Henry Rowland, Albert Michelson, Theodore Lyman, and R.A. Millikan (not to mention the research of Benjamin Franklin and Joseph Henry) was known to every physicist.

172

Nor should one overlook the early signs of excellence in theoretical contributions of the Americans. Einstein's own work became the focus of theoretical studies soon after his seminal 1905 publications—e.g., by G.N. Lewis at MIT, working alone as well as with his student R.C. Tolman, and in collaboration with Edwin Bidwell Wilson; and by H.A. Bumstead at Yale. As Stanley Goldberg has pointed out in his case study of the American response to Einstein's relativity theory, this work by Americans showed a serious understanding of relativity long before the same could be said of some more prominent European scientists, and it exhibited in addition a characteristic "brashness or boldness" of spirit.[10] For example, the Americans accepted the principles of relativity theory as *experimentally proven* (which Einstein himself, aware of the postulational content of his theory, did not claim), and most of them accepted the need to abandon the ether, which many French and British scientists did not do for a long time. The pragmatism of these American theorists, which seems to me part of the antimetaphysical approach that characterized the American style (and which later so upset the social scientists arriving from Europe, as Professor H. Stuart Hughes indicates in his essay elsewhere in this colloquium), was an additional early indicator of the vigorous growth of science in America during the early decades of this century.

Einstein himself had noticed this much during his first visit to the United States in the spring of 1921. He had seen a number of universities and was impressed by the promise of the young Americans there, with their unselfconscious manners and their uninhibited urge to do research. As Philipp Frank reported Einstein to have said about the trip, "much is to be expected from American youth: a pipe as yet unsmoked, young and fresh."[11]

When he returned from that visit, Einstein published an essay, "My First Impression of the U.S.A.," in which he made six perceptive, rather Tocquevillian points:

1. Contrary to the widespread stereotype, there is in the United States, not a preoccupation with materialistic things, but an "idealistic outlook"; "knowledge and justice are ranked above wealth and power by a large section." (The tumultuous welcome that Einstein was forced to suffer made this point obvious to him.)

2. The superiority of the United States "in matters of technology and organization" has consequences at the everyday level; objects are more solid, houses more practically designed.

173

3. What "strikes a visitor is the joyous, positive attitude to life." The American is "friendly, self-confident, optimistic—and without envy. The European finds intercourse with Americans easy and agreeable." The American lives for the future: "life for him is always becoming, never being." (Einstein chose not to remark on the occasional evidence of xenophobia.)

4. The American is less an individualist than the European is; he lays "more emphasis on the *we* than the *I*." Therefore, there is more uniformity of outlook on life and in moral and aesthetic ideas. But, therefore, one can also find more cooperation and division of labor, essential factors in America's economic superiority.

5. The well-to-do in America have impressive social consciences, shown, for example, in the energy they throw into works of charity.

6. Last but not least, "I have warm admiration for the achievements of American institutes of scientific research. We are unjust in attempting to ascribe the increasing superiority of American research work exclusively to superior wealth; devotion, patience, and the spirit of comradeship, and a talent for cooperation play an important part in its success."[12]

The Germany to which Einstein had returned in June 1921 offered a bleak contrast. He found the campaign against him progressing more viciously than ever. The very same attitudes that had assured him a good reception in the United States seemed to outrage his opponents in Germany. They saw him as a pacifist, an internationalist who had visited the former "enemy country" less than three years after the end of World War I, a "formalistic" theoretician whose work challenged common sense, a nonconformist, a stubborn and vocal defender of human rights, skeptical of the religious establishment, a Zionist, and a Jew. Einstein himself must have seen in which direction history was lurching: Philipp Frank recalls Einstein telling him in 1921 that he would not likely remain in Germany longer than another ten years.[13] The prediction was close to the mark.

III Another indication of the "rather sturdy indigenous effort" and the rapid growth of physics in the United States, even before the refugees arrived in force in the 1930s, is the fact that fully thirteen hundred new Ph.D.s in physics were awarded in the United States in that difficult decade. As if in preparation for this growth, the previous decade had seen a lively exchange across the Atlantic, in both directions. More European postdoctoral physicists chose to go to the United States than anywhere else; conversely, many young Americans went to European centers for a year or two, not as untutored beginners but, as I.I. Rabi was recently quoted by Fritz Stern, "knowing the libretto but learning the tune."[14] Rabi recalls that while traveling through Europe between 1925 and 1927, he encountered other young American physicists such as E.C. Kemble, E.U. Condon, H.P. Robertson, F. Wheeler Loomis, Robert Oppenheimer, W.V. Houston, Linus Pauling, Julius Stratton, J.C. Slater, and W.W. Watson. In her study of the American physics community, Katherine Sopka lists thirty-two Americans studying at European centers of quantum physics between 1926 and 1929.[15] Of these visitors, most of whom soon achieved major recognition, about 40 percent were supported by the new Guggenheim Fellowship Program, with the next most frequent support coming from Rockefeller-financed grants made by the International Education Board and the National Research Council. In short, in terms of the quality and number of its young scientists and the scale of institutional backing, the United States, without planning it, was getting ready, in a way no other country was doing, to become the recipient of the "brain drain," when the time for that would come.[16]

To the evidence given of the transatlantic building of mutual compatibility, competence, and colleagueship must also be added the important role of European physicists who traveled to the United States on lecture tours. During the twelve years following Einstein's first visit, many of the foremost physicists of Europe came to give seminars and lectures, including (in chronological order) Marie Curie, Francis W. Aston, Hendrik A. Lorentz, Charles G. Darwin, Arnold Sommerfeld, J.J. Thomson, Niels Bohr, Oskar Klein, Ernest Rutherford, Paul Ehrenfest, Arthur S. Eddington, Peter Debye, Max Born, Arthur Haas, Abram F. Joffe, Erwin Schrödinger, E.A. Milne, W.L. Bragg, Leon Brillouin, James Franck, H.A. Kramers, Hermann Weyl, Werner Heisenberg, P.A.M. Dirac, Enrico Fermi, Max von Laue, Otto Stern, Gregor Wentzel, Jakov Frenkel, R.H. Fowler, and Wolfgang Pauli.[17] Some of them visited more than once or served as guest professors for a term or a year.

Moreover, there was a relatively small but very significant influx of European scientific immigrants who settled in the United States before the upheaval of 1933, thereby further strengthening the foundation that was being laid. The list includes such distinguished

175

names as W.F.G. Swann (1913), L. Silberstein (1920), P. Epstein (1921), A.L. Hughes (1923), H. Mueller and F. Zwicky (1925), K.F. Herzfeld (1926), S.A. Goudsmit and G.E. Uhlenbeck (1927), L.H. Thomas (1929), G.H. Dieke, Maria Goeppert, J. von Neumann, O. Oldenberg, and E.P. Wigner (1930), and R. A. Ladenburg, C. Lanczos, and A. Landé (1931).[18] Afterwards, the storm in Europe brought to these shores within the next five years such well-established or younger physicist-immigrants as O. Stern, H. Weyl, F. Bloch, G. Gamow, H.A. Bethe, J. Franck, V. Weisskopf, and E. Teller. They came to a country that was by no means unacquainted with or unprepared for their scientific interests or tastes.

IV In 1921, Einstein had remarked in passing on the custom of private philanthropy in the United States. He could not then have known how greatly it would aid the intellectual development of his future country of asylum, and its story still merits much detailed research. One example was the role that the grants and policies of the Rockefeller Foundation played in helping physics in the United States to come of age, particularly with respect to the rise of quantum mechanics in the 1920s and to the emergence and growth of nuclear physics in the 1930s. Rockefeller-financed agencies also helped greatly in the internationalization of physics. The foundation's aid to physicists involved at least seven factors:

1. Supported by Rockefeller funds, National Research Council (NRC) Fellowships to study physics had been given to 190 U.S. citizens by World War II. The list of young awardees contained a large proportion of later world leaders in their profession.

2. Moreover, they studied at U.S. research centers that, in many cases, had been transformed in the late 1920s through the (Rockefeller) General Education Board's carefully placed gifts of about twenty million dollars for the development of science teaching and research (e.g., at Caltech, Princeton, Berkeley, Chicago, Harvard).

3. The International Education Board and the Rockefeller Fellowships encouraged the circulation of physicists among laboratories and institutes throughout the world precisely when the new quantum mechanics and nuclear physics were coming into being. The fellowships could not have been timed better.

4. Nor was physics the only concern of this philanthropy. After its initiation in 1919, the NRC's Fellowships were awarded to over one thousand scientists in fields ranging from astronomy and anthropology to psychology and zoology, and to over 350 medical scientists, at a total cost to the Rockefeller Foundation of about five million dollars. The scientists studied in nearly 150 universities and research institutions, with some 20 percent going to foreign countries.

5. In contrast to the NRC Fellowships, which were awarded largely to U.S. citizens, the Rockefeller Fellowships in the natural sciences, beginning in 1924, were usually awarded to persons from outside the United States. Of the nearly one thousand fellowships distributed before World War II, 187 were in physics; the research was carried out in thirteen different countries, with one-third of the recipients doing their work in the United States.[19]

6. In addition to the fellowships, monies of the Rockefeller Foundation also supported small grants in aid of individual scientific research. Between 1929 and 1937, ninety-three such grants were made in physics.

7. One must add the foundation's gifts specifically for the pioneering of large-scale scientific instruments, including the particle accelerators that opened a new era in both atomic physics and the application of physics to biology and medicine and, from 1928 on, the construction of the 200-inch telescope on Palomar Mountain, later named after its moving spirit, George Ellery Hale.

This brief sketch of some dull figures barely hints at the remarkable institutional achievement and the individual perspicacity of a few key officers in philanthropic foundations (e.g., Wickliffe Rose and Warren Weaver) who, quietly and with efficiency and economy, helped build the scientific potential of the nation between the wars.

V   When those young physicists from Europe came to the United States on a visit, perhaps on a Rockefeller Fellowship in the 1920s, what did they find? The testimony of Werner Heisenberg is illuminating. He came in 1929, a brilliant and personable young man whom the ironies of history would destine to head Germany's effort a dozen years later to make a nuclear weapon (which, but for a series of   177 blunders, might have succeeded, as Leo Szilard, Albert Einstein, and others came to fear in 1939). During Heisenberg's visit at the University of Chicago, he gave a series of lectures on the principles of quantum theory, and also spoke on many other American campuses, including Berkeley, MIT, Oberlin, and Ohio State University. The young man had just come from his new post at the University of Leipzig. There he had, in his first seminar on atomic theory, only a single student! His experience in the United States was quite different, as he noted in his autobiographical account, *Physics and Beyond*.[20] In words that are very reminiscent of Einstein's account of his own first impression eight years earlier, Heisenberg wrote:

The new world cast its spell on me right from the start. The carefree attitude of the young, their straightforward warmth and hospitality, their gay optimism—all this made me feel as if a great weight had been lifted from my shoulders. Interest in the new atomic theory was keen.

Heisenberg added an account of an exchange with a physicist from Chicago, revealing how the American style of research at that time enabled young scientists here to forge ahead with remarkable speed on new territory:

I told him of the strange feeling I had acquired during this lecture tour. While Europeans were generally averse and often overtly hostile to the abstract, nonrepresentational aspects of the new atomic theory, to the wave-corpuscle duality and purely statistical character of natural laws, most American physicists seemed prepared to accept the novel approach without too many reservations. I asked Barton how he explained the difference and this is what he said: "You Europeans, and particularly you Germans, are inclined to treat such new ideas as matters of principle. We take a much simpler view. . . . Perhaps you make the mistake of treating the laws of nature as absolutes, and you are therefore surprised when they have to be changed. . . . I believe that once all absolutist claims are dropped, the difficulties will disappear by themselves."

"Then you are not at all surprised," I asked, "that an electron should appear as a particle on one occasion and as a wave on another? As far as you are concerned, the whole thing is merely an extension of the older physics, perhaps in unexpected form?"

"Oh, no, I am surprised; but, after all, I can feel that it happens in nature, and that's that."

Unlike Heisenberg's friends and opponents in Germany, nobody in the United States seemed to be caught up in those quasi-metaphysical debates on *Anschaulichkeit*. What he encountered here was a pragmatic attitude that brought with it a hospitality to new ideas

178

and to those who could convincingly present them. (Another aspect of the same antimetaphysical approach to the new physics was the essentially American philosophy of P.W. Bridgman, as expressed, for example, in his widely circulating book, *The Logic of Modern Physics*, published about a year earlier.)

Heisenberg may well have noted yet another institutional difference: in the United States, young scientists were allowed to follow their own ideas to a remarkable degree. In the 1920s, when many of them pounced on the new quantum physics, they evidently did not have to worry about the incredulity or displeasure their older mentors may have felt toward those strange new ideas. Since the older generation was trained not only in classical physics but predominantly in experimental physics, young physicists who wanted to do their Ph.D. theses on theoretical quantum physics were pretty much on their own. But emotional and financial support was made available to them in a way that would have been difficult to imagine in a more hierarchic system. Those who wished to take the risk were allowed to set their own agenda. When the wave of forced immigrants began to arrive, just four years after Heisenberg's visit, the welcome that awaited them was based in large measure on the same intellectual and institutional factors that had made Heisenberg feel as if a great weight had been lifted from his shoulders.

VI We return now to Einstein. We left him in England in September 1933, pondering where to go. Ever since his first, stimulating visit to America a dozen years earlier, that country must have remained in the back of his mind as a possible future residence, if worse came to worst. That feeling would have been reinforced soon by the campaign of the far-seeing, energetic R.A. Millikan to bring Einstein to America as part of his grand strategy to make the new California Institute of Technology into a supreme research university. This, too, is a very American story. As Millikan recalled in his autobiography, he himself was persuaded in late 1920 or early 1921 by his "Pasadena friends," including George Ellery Hale and Arthur Fleming, to consider coming from the University of Chicago on a full-time basis to the newly organized Caltech. They

laid siege to me to persuade me to change my allegiance and accept full-time appointment in Caltech. . . . Dr. Hale was my most ardent wooer. He did not quite tell me that he would shoot himself if I did

179

not yield to his suit, but I did actually have some misgivings about his health if I turned him down.[21]

By the late summer of 1921, when Millikan decided to make the transfer to Pasadena, there was in place a fine new laboratory of physics with an adequate budget, and the beginnings of an excellent staff. The next thing to do was to attract the promising young recipients of the newly established National Research Fellowships and those who were supported by the Rockefeller International Board. Another aim was to put Caltech on the map as a place that could attract distinguished foreign scientists.

Some of these ambitions show up in Millikan's own account of his first shopping spree, immediately after agreeing to join Caltech:

In September of the year 1921 I went to Europe in response to an invitation to participate in the so-called Solvay Congress. . . . I used this visit to Europe to persuade Dr. H.A. Lorentz to spend the winters of 1921–1922 and 1922–23 at the Norman Bridge Laboratory [at Caltech]. I also brought back with me from Leiden, as a new member of our physics staff, Dr. P.S. Epstein, an altogether outstanding theoretical physicist, and I further went to Cambridge and arranged to have Charles Darwin join us for the following year. Paul Ehrenfest, Arnold Sommerfeld of Munich, and Albert Einstein later came on similar temporary appointments, each, for at least two successive winters.[22]

As the archives of Millikan's papers at Caltech and of Einstein's papers in Princeton show, Millikan's attempts to bring Einstein at least for winter visits started in the early 1920s and continued with increasing energy and prospect of success. Finally, Einstein agreed to come during the winter of 1930–31, after receiving in Berlin a persuasive visit from Arthur Fleming, the chairman of the Board of Trustees of Caltech. Fleming met Einstein probably at the suggestion of R.C. Tolman, who was working at the Mt. Wilson Observatory on just the kind of cosmological problems that interested Einstein.

When Einstein set out for his first California journey on December 2, 1930, he left behind a country that was more and more obviously losing its grip on its own destiny. By contrast, southern California must have looked like a sunny and strange El Dorado, but even more remarkable were the quality of the people and the work they were doing at Caltech, the atmosphere of collaboration, and the excellent state of the research equipment. The travel diary that Einstein kept on this trip gave a very personal glimpse of his reactions:

180

January 2, 1931: at Institute [with] Karman, Epstein, and colleagues. . . .

January 3: Work at Institute. Doubt about correctness of Tolman's work on cosmological problem, but Tolman turned out to be right. . . .

January 7: It is very interesting here. Last night with Millikan, who plays here the role of God. . . . Today astronomical colloquia, rotation of the sun, by St. John. Very sympathetic tone. I have found the probable cause of the variability of the sun's rotation in the circulatory movement on the [surface]. . . . Today I lectured about a thought experiment in the theoretical physics colloquium. Yesterday was a physics colloquium on the effect of the magnetic field during crystallization of the properties of bismuth crystals.

For January 15, 1931, Millikan arranged a spectacular dinner at the new Athenaeum, with Einstein as the central attraction, seated next to Millikan and Michelson. The gathering also included the physicists and astronomers C.E. St. John, W.W. Campbell, W.S. Adams, R.C. Tolman, G.E. Hale, and E.P. Hubbell, as well as Mrs. Einstein, and two hundred members of the California Institute Associates. The latter group was from Millikan's point of view the central target, for he had founded it in 1924 as an organization that would pledge large sums of money to Caltech for a ten-year period— "men most able, interested, and active in promoting Southern California. . . . [who would] put Caltech on their list of foremost Southern California assets."[23]

When Einstein's turn came to speak to the assembly, he could express his genuine friendship and pleasure at being in that company.[24] Addressing them as "Liebe Freunde!" and referring to his own general theory for relativity and gravitation, he said, "Without your work, this theory would today be scarcely more than an interesting speculation; it was your verifications which first set the theory on a real basis." He added an acknowledgement of each of the experimental contributions by Campbell, St. John, Adams, and Hubbell that had been an essential support for the acceptance of his work. While this meeting may not have been on quite the level of the brilliant colloquia Einstein was used to at Berlin, the company of scientists showed that America had come an immense distance scientifically since Ludwig Boltzmann's tongue-in-cheek account of his visit to California, *Die Reise eines deutschen Professors ins Eldorado,* just 25 years earlier.

By mid-March 1931, Einstein was back in Berlin. Two months   181 later, he left the troubled city again to give the Rhodes lectures at Oxford, where Christ Church College made him a senior member ("research student") for eight weeks per year for five years.[25] Here, too, Einstein found himself happy and in good company, with Frederick Lindemann playing the role of Millikan, although on a much smaller scale. The bonds here went back some years as well—to the first Solvay Conference of 1911, where Einstein and Lindemann had met. And, of course, England had had a special place in Einstein's heart ever since November 1919, when the announcement had been made at the Royal Society in London that observations by a British eclipse expedition under Arthur S. Eddington had confirmed Einstein's prediction on the bending of star light near the edge of the sun. As Einstein had confessed to Lindemann (in a letter written on August 28, 1927), he was very aware that in England "my researches have found more recognition than anywhere else in the world."

As we now approach the moment of Einstein's decision, his oscillation between the German- and English-speaking countries and the vast differences in atmosphere that he found in them takes on a special poignancy. Not long after his Oxford Rhodes lectures, Einstein was invited to go to Vienna for the first time in nine years and gave a lecture at the Physical Institute of the university on October 14, 1931. Providing a view of how things stood was a confidential report from the German Embassy in Vienna to the Foreign Office in Berlin—one in a constant flow of reports by the nervous German Einstein-watchers.[26] There is a measure of classic irony here, as the German Embassy, still intent on using Einstein in its mission of *Kulturpropaganda*, noted how the good Viennese behaved, even though seven more years were to elapse before *they* would throw themselves officially into the abyss of Nazism: "It is typical of the manner in which in Vienna all things are dealt with from a party-political point of view that the official Austrian authorities observed special reserve with respect to Professor Einstein, because he is a Jew, and considered oriented to the political left." Since neither the education ministry nor the rector of the universities came to the lecture, and the distinguished visitor was not received or even invited by any official state authority (no doubt to Einstein's own great delight), the ambassador described his frantic efforts to invite some officials at least to have breakfast with him and Einstein. It was a moment for the stage.

Less than two months later, in December, Einstein was again on his way westward, for his second visit to Pasadena. At home, the drum beat was steadily getting more ominous. The National Socialists had become the second largest group in the Reichstag. In July, the banks had collapsed, and in October the National Socialists, the German National Party, and the Stahlhelm had consolidated as the National Opposition for the avowed purpose of forcing Chancellor Heinrich Brüning's resignation.

The travel diary in the Einstein Archives shows that, for Einstein, the process of crystallizing his decision had begun in earnest:

December 6 [1931]: Yesterday we left the Channel. It is becoming definitely warmer, with rainy weather and considerable agitation of the sea. . . .

I have started to read Fridell's spirited *Kulturgeschichte*, Volume III, and Grünberg's Fairy Tales. In addition, I also read Born's Quantum Mechanics.

Today, I decided in essence to give up my position in Berlin. Well, then, a bird of passage for the rest of life. Seagulls accompany our ship, constantly in flight. They will come with us to the Azores. They are my new colleagues, although God knows they are happier than I. How dependent man is on external matters, compared with the mere animal . . . !

I am learning English, but it doesn't want to stay in my old brain.[27]

VII As this sketch has tried to indicate, by the beginning of the 1930s the process through which physics in the United States was coming of age had reached a satisfactory stage. There was now an adequate balance, such as had been achieved in chemistry a decade earlier, between experimental and theoretical work, adequate provision for undergraduate and graduate training, a strong professional society, a wide range of well-run research publications. Despite the worldwide economic depression, the intellectual, institutional, and financial base was sound. The laboratory facilities in several key places were remarkably good, and the opportunities for study and colleagueship on the national and international level excellent. Also, the interplay between academic and industrial ("pure" and "applied") science research that characterizes the modern United States was well launched. Even that uncertain indicator, the proportion of Nobel prizes awarded to U.S. nationals in physics, was impressive. The country was well on its way to fulfilling the brash prophecy Millikan had made in 1919: "In a few years we shall be in a new

183

place as a scientific nation and shall see men coming from the ends of the earth to catch the inspiration of our leaders and to share in the results [of] our developments."[28]

Thus, even before the major influx of European physicists in the 1930s, the center of gravity of international activity had been shifting westward to the United States, preparing the country to be not only a physical refuge but also an intellectual attraction for the émigrés. And side by side with the professional preparation to receive and put to good use the influx of talent, there was, of course, the special, human quality of American life and spirit that Einstein had described after his first visit. As Victor Weisskopf said of the newly arrived European physicists in the 1930s, "Within the shortest time, one was in the midst of a society that was extremely appealing and interesting and active; and in fact, we felt much more as refugees in Europe than here."[29]

Indeed, the new arrivals, fleeing Hitler's world, came just in time to complete a transition that, at least for the physical sciences, had begun in the mid-1920s, the period Oppenheimer once called the

Einstein with Hungarian physicist Leo Szilard re-enacting the drafting of a letter sent to President Roosevelt in 1939 informing him of the importance of securing an adequate supply of uranium and of the possibility of building a bomb of great destructive power. (G. W. Szilard.)

"heroic time." It was therefore both symbolically and historically appropriate that the new, enlarged community of scientists soon was put to work on tasks that not only shaped modern science but also preserved modern life itself. For it is well to remember that these "graduates" of the transformation, and their students, were destined shortly to play a major role in the fight for survival of the civilized world against the war machine of the totalitarian Axis nations.[30]

In contrast to some of the other fields and to the tragic stories we heard discussed in this colloquium, the interaction of the refugees with the growing field of physics in the United States in the 1930s was a story of mutual benefit. Physics today in the United States is to a large degree the offspring of the happy union of the work of the new and older Americans. Einstein's move to the Western Hemisphere was, therefore, not a cause but a symbol of a historic process.

This, I believe, is what further scientific and scholarly analysis of the migration of scientists will bear out in detail. But in a meeting called to honor Einstein's contributions, at least a few words more must be said to stress again the plain human meaning of the rescue of many scientists through the exertion of Americans—often, as we have heard here, against great obstacles set up by officials within American political institutions themselves. Hence, we must also think of the much greater number who did not find a haven anywhere and who perished in the Holocaust. And, alas, we must not forget, as recent events in Indochina and elsewhere have been indicating insistently, that man's propensity for periodically committing genocide has by no means been conquered. Therefore, it is appropriate to recall a few lines that Einstein wrote soon after World War II, in support of a meeting to memorialize the millions of victims of the Nazis.

Few years separate us from the most horrible mass crime that modern history has to relate, a crime committed not by a fanaticized mob, but in cold calculation by the government of a powerful nation. . . . Today's meeting showed that not all men are prepared to accept the horror in silence. This meeting is inspired by the will to secure the dignity and the natural rights of the individual. . . . For this stand, I wish to express my appreciation and thanks, as a human being and as a Jew.[31]

185

The very existence of this colloquium will undoubtedly greatly energize research in that dark and transforming period of modern intellectual history to which the papers in this volume are dedicated. For that, interested scholars everywhere will be grateful.

Notes

1. See, for example, Philipp Frank, *Einstein, His Life and Times* (New York, 1947), and Alan Beyerchen, *Scientists under Hitler: Politics and the Physics Community in the Third Reich* (New Haven, 1977).

2. Letter of Sept. 9, 1920, quoted in Siegfried Grundmann, "Die Auslandsreisen Albert Einsteins," *NTM, Schriftenreihe für Geschichte der Naturwissenschaften, Technik und Medizin* 2, no. 6 (1965):4.

3. Letter of Einstein to the German Embassy in Tokyo; quoted in report of the embassy to its Ministry of Exterior, Berlin, Jan. 3, 1923; quoted in Grundmann, "Die Auslandsreisen Einsteins," p. 9.

4. Charles Weiner, "A New Site for the Seminar: The Refugees and American Physics in the 1930s," in Donald H. Fleming and Bernard Bailyn, eds., *The Intellectual Migration: Europe and America, 1930–1960* (Cambridge, Mass., 1969), pp. 190-91.

5 Daniel J. Kevles, *The Physicists: The History of a Scientific Community in Modern America* (New York, 1978), p. 221.

6. For example, the scholars listed in nn. 1, 4, and 5 above; and also Armin Hermann, *The New Physics: The Route into the Atomic Age* (Munich, 1979), chap. 11, "The Mass Migration from Under"; Laura Fermi, *Illustrious Immigrants*, 2d ed. (Chicago, 1971); J.H. Van Vleck, "American Physics Comes of Age," *Physics Today* 17 (June 1964): 21–26; Katherine Sopka, *Quantum Physics in America, 1920–1935* (New York, 1981); Stanley Coben, "Scientific Establishment and the Transmission of Quantum Mechanics to the United States, 1919–1932," *American Historical Review* 76 (1971): 442–66; Stanley Coben, "Foundation Officials and Fellowships: Innovation in the Patronage of Science," *Minerva* 14 (Summer 1976): 225–40; Spencer R. Weart, "The Physics Business in America, 1919–1940: A Statistical Reconnaissance," in Nathan Reingold, ed., *The Sciences in the United States: A Bicentennial Perspective* (Princeton, 1979). In Kevles's book, see particularly chapters 14–16 and his bibliographical essay on Resources, pp. 450–57, for further primary sources.

7. J. Robert Oppenheimer, in a filmed interview conducted Nov. 1, 1966, by Charles Weiner for Harvard Project Physics; transcript at American Institute of Physics, Center for the History of Physics, New York; see n. 4, p. 191.

8. "May I say that the invitation [to give the lecture] makes me feel that the links between this University and myself are becoming professionally stronger?" Trans. from Albert Einstein manuscript; cf. *Mein Weltbild* (Frankfurt am Main, 1977), pp. 113–19.

9. Luce Langevin, "Paul Langevin et Albert Einstein d'après une Correspondance et des Documents inédits," *La Pensée*, No. 161 (Feb. 1972): 29.

10. Stanley Goldberg, "The Early Response to Einstein's Special Theory of Relativity, 1905–1911: A Case Study in National Differences" (Ph.D. diss., Harvard University, 1968).

11. Frank, *Einstein*, p. 186.

12. Albert Einstein, "My First Impressions of the U.S.A.," in *Ideas and Opinions* (New York, 1954), pp. 16–19.

13. Frank, *Einstein*, p. 178.

14. Fritz Stern, "Einstein's Germany," in Gerald Holton and Yehuda Elkana, eds., *Albert Einstein: Historical and Cultural Perspectives* (Princeton, 1982).

15. Sopka, *Quantum Physics*, pp. 3.40–3.42.

16. See Weiner, "A New Site," p. 226.

17. Sopka, *Quantum Physics*, pp. A.17–A.26.

18. Ibid., p. A.29.

19. Figures derived from the *Rockefeller Foundation Directory of Fellowship Awards, 1917–1950* (New York, 1951); Myron Rand, "The National Research Council Fellowships," *The Scientific Monthly* 58, no. 2 (August 1921); and *NRC Check List of Grants-in-Aid for May 1929–December 1937*. I thank Professor Weiner for making many of these data available to me.

20. Werner Heisenberg, *Physics and Beyond* (New York, 1971), chap. 8, p. 94.

21. R.A. Millikan, *The Autobiography of Robert A. Millikan* (New York, 1950), pp. 215, 217.

22. Ibid. p. 221.

23. Ibid., p. 239.

24. See Gerald Holton, *Thematic Origins of Scientific Thought: Kepler to Einstein* (Cambridge, 1973), p. 320.

25. Letter of Oct. 23, 1931, from the Dean of Christ Church, announcing Einstein's election to a "Research Studentship" in the College. Einstein Archive at the Institute for Advanced Study, Princeton, N.J. I thank Professor John Stachel for having drawn my attention to the letter.

26. Reprinted as Document 160 in C. Kirsten and H.-J. Treder, eds., *Albert Einstein in Berlin 1913–1933* (Berlin, 1979), 1:239–40.

27. Travel Diary no. 5, Dec. 1931–Feb. 1932.

28. R.A. Millikan, "The New Opportunities in Science," *Science* 50 (1919):297, quoted in Kevles, *The Physicists*, p. 169.

The Migration of Physicists to the United States

29. Victor Weisskopf, quoted in Fleming and Bailyn, *The Intellectual Migration,* p. 222. It is also significant that Einstein's own scientific publications, from 1935 on, refer more frequently than before to work going on in America and to articles published in American scientific journals.

30. Ironically, Einstein was barred (without his knowledge) at the highest level from participating in sensitive U.S. war research—again for fear of his internationalist tendencies. See Bernard T. Feld, "Einstein and the Politics of Nuclear Weapons," in Holton and Elkana, *Albert Einstein.*

31. Quoted in Helen Dukas and Banesh Hoffmann, eds. *Albert Einstein, the Human Side* (Princeton, 1979), pp. 96–97. I also wish to express my indebtedness to Miss Dukas and to the Estate of Albert Einstein for permission to cite from Einstein's writings and to the National Science Foundation and the National Endowment for the Humanities for support for research in this field.

188

Immigrants in American Chemistry

P. THOMAS CARROLL

I cannot pass up this opportunity to repay a debt. I was born on March 14, 1949, in Princeton, New Jersey. At the moment of my birth, a mile from my birthplace, Albert Einstein was celebrating his seventieth birthday. The symbolism of this coincidence was not lost on my parents and teachers. Consequently, more than most American youngsters during the Sputnik era, I grew up admiring the great physicist and wanting to follow his chosen profession. Somewhere along the way, my ambitions were redirected, most notably when my performance as an undergraduate at Caltech showed just how little my scientific talents resembled Einstein's. In default, my curiosity about the father of relativity was a good starting point for an interest in the history of science and technology. I therefore dedicate this paper to Einstein for the unwitting role he played in shaping my professional life.

The United States has relied consistently over the years upon chemical contributions from abroad. We depended heavily upon foreign supplies of chemicals and apparatus until World War I disrupted importations. In institutions American chemists borrowed freely from European colleagues, most particularly the Germans: the American Chemical Society, founded in 1876, was patterned in part after the Deutsche Chemische Gesellschaft zu Berlin, established a decade earlier, and when Ira Remsen inaugurated the *American Chemical Journal* in 1879, he hoped it would provide as good a forum for the researches of his laboratory as the *Annalen der Chemie* had for Justus Liebig's. In the realm of education, American chemistry owes a special debt to foreign influence. In the late eighteenth and early nineteenth centuries, Americans learned chemistry largely from European texts, and journals such as the *Annalen* were read avidly by those in the field. While our universities were only approaching maturity, at least two generations of Americans went to Germany to receive Ph.D.s or do postdoctoral research in chemistry. The first generation, with such central figures in the history of American chemical education as Eben Horsford and Evan Pugh, brought back the spirit of the research orientation; the next and much larger group—including such notables as T.W. Richards, the first American Nobel laureate in chemistry, and Irving Langmuir, the second—brought that orientation to fruition.[1]

These various means of importing foreign chemistry have received more than passing attention in the historical literature; however, with the exception of two brief notes, totaling eight pages between them, and two paragraphs in a survey article, there are no studies specifically devoted to foreign-born American chemists.[2] Refugee chemists from Nazism, who were by far the most important group in this discipline ever to come to the United States, have not been omitted from general studies of the intellectual migration, but they are overshadowed in these accounts by the atomic physicists—this despite the fact that most estimates show chemists to be the largest disciplinary group among the scientists who fled Hitler. For instance, chemists constitute nearly one-fifth of the 424 scientists and other scholars identified by discipline in Maurice R. Davie's *Refugees in America*. The population of refugee chemists during the 1930s numbers at least in the hundreds and may exceed a thousand.[3] While some may quibble with this assertion—it is universally conceded that the available statistics are not too reliable—there is no arguing that America's immigrant chemists in general, and her chemist refugees from fascism in particular, have been relatively large groups with a relatively small press. Based on a sample of 754 chemists and chemical engineers from all periods (Table 1), this paper will survey a number of foreign-born chemists who came to America before the 1930s and compare them to refugee chemists who arrived in this country during the Nazi period.[4]

190

Table 1
Foreign-Born Chemists, by Period of Immigration

	Chemists in Sample	
Period of Immigration	*Number*	*Percent of Total*
Before 1848	32	4%
1848–65	20	3
1866–1918	167	22
1919–32	266	35
1933–37	100	13
1938–50	142	19
Uncertain	27	4
TOTAL	754	100%

SOURCE: Author's tabulations.

It is not surprising that the first people to practice chemistry in what would later become the United States were refugees, since a significant proportion of the Europeans who came here early did so to escape persecution at home. John Winthrop, Jr., the well-known early colonist, was by many accounts the first chemist in America, although such an appellation is anachronistic to an age of virtuosos and natural philosophers. A Fellow of the Royal Society, he equipped the first chemical laboratory in the English colonies so that he could conduct his own philosophical inquiries. His migration in 1631, at the age of twenty-six, was an escape from religious persecution. That year is as good as any to date the start of American chemistry.

Far better known as a chemist per se was Joseph Priestley, discoverer of dephlogisticated air (oxygen), who journeyed to America in 1794 after an angry mob had burned his Birmingham, England, home to protest his support for the French Revolution. Although offered the chair of chemistry in the University of Pennsylvania Medical School, Priestley refused a formal post, and his advanced age—sixty-one upon arrival—meant that his impact on American chemistry was more symbolic than real. As the chemical world grew increasingly disenchanted with his phlogiston theory, Priestley lived out his last ten years in peace and relative obscurity in Northumberland, Pennsylvania, in a home that would later provide a site for the founding meeting of the American Chemical Society.

191

The arrivals of Winthrop and Priestley bracket an era that saw few other immigrants interested in chemistry. The New World offered scant occupational inducement to the chemically adept from the Old, and there was little or no sense of a domestic American chemical community. Those who did come were apt to have a philosophical frame of mind, which simultaneously sparked a curiosity about things chemical and generated controversial political and religious positions likely to force them to seek refuge across the Atlantic.

Opportunities for chemical employment in America appear to have increased somewhat in the early nineteenth century, and the pace of chemical immigration quickened accordingly. Like most immigrants during this period, the chemists tended to be from Britain, Ireland, or France. Many found posts as professors in America's few medical schools. Others applied their chemical knowledge in the investigation or analysis of the young nation's unusual biological or mineralogical compounds. A few eked out a living translating and editing European texts, delivering public lectures, or both, while some went into business and managed to succeed. Still, the relative dearth of inducements for foreign chemists meant that many of those who came did so, as had been the case before, because they had been driven out of their homelands; they were, in a word, refugees. Thomas Antisell, for example, arrived in 1848 at the age of thirty-one after political imprisonment in Ireland. Somewhat of a transition figure, Antisell had medical training like most of his predecessors, but he chose employment outside academe after he landed here. He was the first chemist of the U.S. Department of Agriculture, and he held many other posts in and out of government.

The European revolutions of 1848 combined with the Irish potato famine to produce a spurt of migration to the United States, which reached nearly a half million in the peak year of 1854. Chemists among these emigrants tended to come from the German states and brought a new sense of professionalism. For example, Frederick Augustus Genth, who was working in Robert Bunsen's laboratory at Heidelberg when the revolution occurred, became one of the first German Ph.D.s to migrate to America; he also differed from his predecessors in that he became an American academic with no responsibilities to medical education, pursuing instead private consulting activities for commercial concerns that specialized in mineralogical chemistry. Genth's career presaged two important trends in further chemical immigration: the increasing appearance of research-

192

oriented holders of doctorates and the increasing attraction of foreign chemists to commercial possiblities in the rapidly developing American industrial landscape.[5]

Many doctorate chemists trained in Europe came to take advantage of these improved prospects. Leo Baekeland arrived here in 1889, having received a Ph.D. five years earlier at the University of Ghent. His successes in the photographic industry made him wealthy, and his invention of Bakelite plastic immortalized his name. Baekeland, like Genth, retained his ties with the academic elite in American chemistry; as Genth had done in 1880, Baekeland served as president of the American Chemical Society (ACS) in 1924. In fact, the founding of the ACS in 1876 signaled the emergence of the chemist as a professional interested in both academic research and practical pursuits of benefit to society at large. During this era, Baekeland and other Ph.D.-level chemist-practitioners from abroad took advantage of the failure of American academe to produce their counterparts in sufficient numbers to meet commercial and regulatory needs.

Until the 1890s those chemists not forced to flee their homelands had been attracted to the United States primarily by the promise of lucrative employment. With the emergence of the American graduate school, however, immigrants—Canadians especially—began to come here to obtain higher degrees in chemistry. The American system of graduate education might have been second-rate at this time, as is commonly asserted, but for many unwilling or unable to make the pilgrimage to Germany, it was clearly a solid second choice. Arthur Douglas Chambers, for one, earned a Ph.D. at Johns Hopkins in 1896 after undergraduate work in his native Ontario, then stayed to work in American industry. The success of his long career at Du Pont, where he led the diversification into dye intermediates during World War I, justifies Du Pont's decision to name their Deepwater plant after him. Clarence G. Derick left Canada to take degrees in physical chemistry at MIT and Illinois. He was instrumental in building the latter's ties with the nascent American synthetic organic chemicals industry at the outbreak of the Great War.

One small but important subgroup during this period came to do a very specific kind of work. Eager to maintain his dominance at the turn of the century over the photographic industry, George Eastman sought imaginative chemists to conduct original research in photochemistry for Eastman Kodak. He found what he wanted in C.E. Kenneth Mees, an eccentric young Englishman, and Mees's college friend, Samuel E. Sheppard. Mees and Sheppard had long and   193 distinguished careers at Kodak, during which such innovations as Kodachrome and Kodacolor were made. In 1914 these two were joined by Hans T. Clarke, the son of Eastman's agent in England, who had spent three semesters in Emil Fischer's laboratory in Germany. (This latter association with researchers investigating proteins and other natural substances may have figured in his decision to re-enter academe as a biochemist later in his life.) Clarke supervised Kodak's venture into the production of organic intermediates during and after World War I. Through a sort of Anglo-Kodak pipeline, many more English photochemists found their way to America in the 1920s.[6]

Few of the chemists who seized all these opportunities for a Ph.D. or for commercial employment in America had much impact upon fundamental, academic research; the ones mentioned here are atypical since they did. Indeed, in stark contrast to the many immigrant academicians in America before and just after the Civil War, few among the generation at the end of the nineteenth century found any academic employment whatsoever. This was the era in which, for the first time, Americans in significant numbers were earning their own doctorates in chemistry, often in Germany. The academic jobs, understandably, went largely to the first and second generations of such Americans with Ph.D.s: Ira Remsen, Charles F. Chandler, T.W. Richards, Edgar Fahs Smith, William A. Noyes, and Wilder D. Bancroft, to name several. While it was often advantageous to have a German Ph.D. at this time, it seems to have been equally important to have been native-born. American academic chemistry was becoming a culturally closed institution, in which only a few immigrants such as Moses Gomberg, Alexander Smith, and John Ulric Nef were able to find careers.

The 1920s and early 1930s saw the continuation of many old trends, an increase in the absolute number of immigrant chemists, and a few new developments. The commercial prospects for foreign-born chemists expanded (as they did for native chemists), as the American chemical industry flourished at the expense of German competition, and the burgeoning petroleum industry provided an added stimulus. Canadians in large numbers continued to capitalize upon these opportunities, but Europeans began to rival them. Many of the new arrivals during this period came from the German-speaking countries, even though German immigration generally had peaked before 1900. No doubt part of the reason for this lay in the catastrophic economic conditions in Weimar Germany in the early

194

1920s, reinforced by an increasingly unstable political climate. To exacerbate the situation, relative to the diminished demand of the Depression-plagued economy, Germany was overproducing Ph.D.-level chemists. L.F. Haber claims that by 1931, nearly three thousand of Germany's seventeen thousand graduate chemists either were unemployed or worked altogether outside of chemistry.[7]

However successful these new German immigrants were in relocating to America, the phenomenon of their migration was strictly industrial in nature. No chemist in the sample who left Weimar Germany during the 1920s vacated an academic appointment. There may have been some German academic chemists of the day who decided to take up industrial employment, but if so, they did not come to the United States to do it. Meanwhile, although American industry readily hired the Germans, few foreign-born chemists from any country found a welcome in the nation's colleges and universities during the 1920s.

The examples of those who did are very instructive. Unable to find satisfactory employment in his native Germany following the Great War—in part because he was a Jew—Leonor Michaelis took a professorship of biochemistry in Japan, coming to the United States only when his work there caught the attention of Americans. Carl and Gerty Cori, as well as Erwin Brand, managed to land academic positions here only through interim employment in clinical medicine. Their ability to enter American colleges and universities at all reflects their then-unusual field of specialization, molecular biochemistry. In Germany, the institutional conjunction of medical school and university had encouraged a cross-fertilization between organic chemistry and scientific medicine, while this was a rare orientation in America. As late as 1936, Warren Weaver of the Rockefeller Foundation could still decry "the relative weakness in this country of those fields of chemistry which should contribute most directly to biological studies," a complaint that applied "mildly to physical chemical studies" but "with full force to the organic structural chemistry of natural substances," a field "notably developed in Europe."[8]

By the time the Nazis came to power, the pattern of chemical immigration to America was clear. Chemists from central Europe were arriving in record numbers, joining a significant population from nations that had been supplying the United States with chemists for a long time. Opportunities for industrial employment were abundant, but the academic possibilities stopped at graduate or per-   195 haps postdoctoral education. Academics from overseas were not particularly welcome on American campuses unless, by dint of unusual specialization, they faced no domestic competition. North central Europeans, blessed with an excellent domestic higher education system in chemistry, tended not to avail themselves of the American degree, and those chemists who procured academic posts at home after graduation showed minimal desire to emigrate. While the attractions and limitations on this side of the Atlantic remained consistent through the 1930s, the pattern of migratory response, as we shall see, was transformed by Hitler's rise to power.

To be sure, not all the chemical immigration to America between 1933 and 1945 can be laid at Hitler's door. In particular, except during the war years themselves, Canadians and Englishmen continued to stream in. William Robson Conn, for example, arrived in 1933 to add a Ph.D. from New York University to his master's degree from Queens University, Kingston; he stayed to conduct research at Rohm & Haas, for which he was rewarded in 1948 with the headship of his own laboratory. Robert Henry White-Stevens attended Cornell graduate school between 1935 and 1942, taking various posts in agricultural chemistry and nutrition after receiving his Ph.D. in the latter year. Clearly, the Nazi phenomenon was but an overlay upon existing patterns.

But what an overlay. Perhaps the most significant professional difference between the refugees from Hitler and the other immigrant chemists was that so many of the former were academics; what is more, many clearly were first-rate scientists. Ernst Berl, Peter Debye, Kasimir Fajans, James Franck, Walter S. Loewe, Otto Loewi, Otto Meyerhof, and Carl Neuberg, to name only a few, held professorships or their equivalent at the time of their departure. Franck and Meyerhof had won Nobel prizes in the 1920s. All these refugees, plus many more, had been making fundamental contributions to science before their arrival, and they continued to do so in the United States. It seems unlikely that most of them would have forsaken their careers in their homelands and enriched American science had it not been for the Nazi persecutions.

The prominent refugee chemists fell into two specialty categories. The larger of the two, and the one most mentioned in existing accounts of the intellectual migration, was biochemistry and molecular biology. Included among this group were Konrad Bloch, Henrik Dam, Fritz A. Lipmann, Otto Meyerhof, David Nachmansohn, Carl Neuberg, and Severo Ochoa. They are the best known of all immigrant chemists, and their work is covered in detail in many sources. Unlike most contemporary biochemists in America, and unlike all but a few from previous generations of foreign biochemists, these scientists did not approach biochemistry from an agricultural or industrial (especially brewing) perspective or from a clinical perspective. Instead, they applied the techniques of the physical sciences to the investigation of vital processes. Their work on the structures of amino acids and proteins and on metabolic pathways and molecular genetics has materially advanced our understanding of the chemistry of life. In 1958, Hans Clarke assessed the situation with respect to his own program as follows:

Among the many benefits which accrued to Columbia University from the racial policy adopted by the Germans under the Third Reich was the arrival in our laboratory of various European-trained biochemists, notably Erwin Chargaff, Zacharias Dische, Karl Meyer, Rudolf Schoenheimer, and Heinrich Waelsch. Erwin Brand, who joined our group during the same period, reached this country somewhat earlier. The scientific achievements subsequently made by these men are so well known that their enumeration is unnecessary.[9]

The second prominent specialty group among the refugees again involved those who approached their work from an interdisciplinary perspective. These scientists married chemistry not to medicine or biology but rather to physics. Peter Debye won the Nobel Prize in chemistry in 1936 for his contributions toward the understanding of molecular structure, chiefly his work on dipole moments and the x-ray diffraction of gases. James Franck was awarded his Nobel Prize in physics in 1925 for elucidating the laws governing the impact of the electron upon the atom. In fact, he and Peter Pringsheim were not even physical chemists until after their migration: while in his homeland, Franck showed no signs of identifying himself as anything other than a physicist, and his first employment here was as a physicist; Peter Pringsheim left behind a German career in physics to become senior chemist at the Argonne National Laboratory in Illinois in 1947. The small size of this immigrant specialty group should not blind us to its historical significance. Émigré physicists-turned-chemists played key roles in the development of the American atomic bomb, for example.

Both the biochemists and the physical chemists could be accommodated relatively painlessly in American universities, in large measure because Americans had not developed those areas of research as fully as had Europeans; there was less resistance to employing

197

James Franck (left) won a Nobel Prize in physics before emigrating to America. Konrad Bloch (right) was awarded his Nobel Prize in chemistry after his arrival here. (Franck photo courtesy of The Photographic Files of The University of Chicago Archives. Bloch photo courtesy of Konrad Bloch.)

those who did not constitute disciplinary competition. Even so, this still left many hardships to be overcome. An unusually large number of the émigrés came at a relatively late stage in their careers, and many had to spend more or less protracted interim periods in stopover countries. Many faced prejudice; James Franck, for example, was driven out of Johns Hopkins by the anti-Semitism of its president, Isaiah Bowman.[10] (Anti-Semitism was nothing new, of course. Thirty years earlier, Ira Remsen had suggested that Illinois might not want to hire Moses Gomberg because "he is, to be sure, a Hebrew, as you may judge from his name."[11]) The strain of relocation also took its toll, contributing to Schoenheimer's suicide in 1941. Despite the hardships, a number of the refugees, including eight Nobel laureates and future Nobel laureates (Table 2), did manage to penetrate the longstanding barrier built on American campuses to exclude foreign chemists.[12] These scientists found in America a nurturing academic environment in which to continue their professions, and like the academic immigrants who arrived before the Civil War, they brought with them expertise that their adopted nation lacked.

198

Table 2
Nobel Laureates among Refugee Chemists

Name	Year of Award	Field
Meyerhof, Otto	1922	Physiology or medicine
Franck, James	1925	Physics
Debye, Peter J.W.	1936	Chemistry
Loewi, Otto	1936	Physiology or medicine
Dam, Henrik	1943	Physiology or medicine
Lipmann, Fritz	1953	Physiology or medicine
Ochoa, Severo	1959	Physiology or medicine
Bloch, Konrad E.	1964	Chemistry

SOURCE: Author's compilation.

Another more obscure group of foreign chemists did not fare so well in this country. These persons were united not so much by their specialty areas as by their junior status on German campuses before they came here. No doubt few readers have heard of these refugees, and there is scant information on them, so some examples are in order. Jacob Joseph Bikerman, a physical chemist, was a research associate at the Kaiser Wilhelm Institute for Physical Chemistry in Berlin until 1933. After a twelve-year stopover in Britain, he became a research chemist for Merck in New Jersey in 1946. Gregoire Gutzeit, a chemical engineer, was associate professor of chemistry and mineralogy in Geneva until 1940, when he moved to The Hague to direct the laboratories of Dorr-Oliver, Inc. He transferred to the Dorr subsidiary in New York the following year and stayed in American industry thereafter. Bernard Lustig, a clinical biochemist, escaped Vienna in 1938 when the medical research foundation in which he conducted his research relocated to London. In 1940 he came to America to conduct research for a pharmaceutical firm in Stamford, Connecticut. Robert Steckler, a polymer chemist, had been Otto Loewi's research assistant at Vienna before getting his Ph.D. in 1938. In all likelihood, he would have had a decent chance of an academic post in his homeland, but he was forced to flee after the *Anschluss*. From 1938 to the end of the war, he was a research manager for the Arco Company in Cleveland, after which he went into business for himself. Lest we conclude too readily that 199 all these chemists were completely undistinguished, consider Adalbert Farkas, the Hungarian physical chemist whose promising academic career at Frankfurt under Fritz Haber was interrupted in 1933. After academic stopovers for eight years in Cambridge and Jerusalem, Farkas went to work as a research chemist for Union Oil. In industry, his advancement proceeded rapidly: he eventually directed research at the Houdry Process and Chemical Company in Marcus Hook, Pennsylvania.

This third class of refugees admittedly contained few eminent scientists. But it clearly contained academics, a type unknown in the migrations of the 1920s. A reasonable speculation is that this group would *not* have left Europe under ordinary circumstances. Many of these refugees had been the postdoctoral assistants of Germany's most prominent academic chemists. When they came to America, they were forced to forego their academic ambitions— sometimes, perhaps, because of their lesser talents, but more often, I suspect, because they were just starting out in their careers or had specialized in fields that had already flourished in the United States. In certain respects, however, they may have been far luckier than still another group of colleagues. The sample of immigrant chemists contained few German industrial chemists after 1933, a startling fact considering the large numbers who came here from German industry in the 1920s. This negative evidence seems to indicate that industrial chemists may have been trapped in Germany during the Third Reich and left to suffer a far worse fate, especially if they were Jewish.[13] The Nazi era, then, was a time when chemists from industry came less frequently than had previously been the case, while their colleagues from academe came more.

In this latter respect, the migration of the Nazi period was not unusual. As we have seen, episodes like the French Revolution, various Irish uprisings, and the revolutions of 1848 also unseated prominent academics and other inquiring research chemists who otherwise might not have fled. What did set apart the 1930s migration was its wholesale nature; it was not a matter of the odd politically active professor managing to escape. Our concentration upon the few dozen refugee chemists now considered distinguished has obscured this feature somewhat.

Such a focus has also distorted our perceptions of the refugee experience. Collective biography of the larger group indicates that most chemists who escaped the Third Reich met a different reception than the celebrated few. The flight from Hitler appears to have com-

200

bined with declining opportunities for foreign chemists on American campuses to cut short the academic careers of an entire generation of promising young central European chemists. We cannot undo the Nazi Holocaust, of course, or the lukewarm welcome we accorded to certain survivors, but perhaps we can take measures to preserve cultural pluralism in American colleges and universities. The hiring of foreign faculty during the academic expansion following World War II may have been just an interlude in a secular trend toward academic chauvinism. If so, failure to make changes will undermine the traditional ideal of higher education as an intellectual meritocracy.

Notes

1. A few representative sources in the institutional history of American chemistry are Margaret W. Rossiter, *The Emergence of Agricultural Science: Justus Liebig and the Americans, 1840–1880* (New Haven, 1975); Owen Hannaway, "The German Model of Chemical Education in America: Ira Remsen at Johns Hopkins (1876–1913)," *Ambix* 23 (1976):145–64; Edward H. Beardsley, *The Rise of the American Chemistry Profession, 1850–1900,* University of Florida Monographs, Social Sciences, no. 23 (Gainesville, 1964); and Arnold Thackray et al., *Chemistry in America, 1876–1976: An Historical Application of Science Indicators* (Dordrecht and Boston, 1982).

2. C.A. Browne, "The Role of Refugees in the History of American Science," *Science* n.s. 91 (1940):203–8; John T. Edsall, "Immigrant Scientists and American Biochemistry," *Trends in Biochemical Science* 2, no. 3 (March 1977): N51–N53; and Kenneth L. Taylor, "Two Centuries of Chemistry," jn Benjamin J. Taylor and Thurman J. White, eds., *Issues and Ideas in America* (Norman, Okla., 1976), pp. 267–84.

3. Donald Fleming and Bernard Bailyn, eds., *The Intellectual Migration: Europe and America, 1930–1960* (Cambridge, Mass., 1969), pp. 675–718. I count 15 chemists and 24 physicists; the list of physicists excludes the biophysicists like Walter Rosenblith. Laura Fermi, *Illustrious Immigrants: The Intellectual Migration from Europe, 1930–1941,* 2d. ed. (Chicago, 1971), pp. 174–214 on atomic physics, pp. 308–15 on molecular biology. The traditional published source on the total number of chemist refugees is Maurice R. Davie, *Refugees in America: Report of the Committee for the Study of Recent Immigration from Europe,* with the collaboration of Sarah W. Cohn and others (New York, 1947); relevant statistics for chemists are on pp. 41, 316, and 321. Davie's estimate of 432 to 507 refugee chemists (p. 41) apparently does not include chemists among his "professors" or his "scientists and literary persons," and it may include apothecaries. One's final total depends upon assumptions made in adjusting for these problems.

4. The chemists in the sample were identified from the following sources: Fleming and Bailyn, *The Intellectual Migration;* Davie, *Refugees in America,* pp. 432–40; John M. Spalek, *Guide to the Archival Materials of the German-speaking Emigration to the United States after 1933,* in collaboration with Adrienne Ash and Sandra H.

201

Hawrylchak (Charlottesville, Va., 1978); Edsall, "Immigrant Scientists and American Biochemistry"; David Nachmansohn, *German-Jewish Pioneers in Science, 1900–1933: Highlights in Atomic Physics, Chemistry, and Biochemistry* (Berlin, 1979); Williams Haynes, ed., *Chemical Who's Who, 1951 (Third Edition): Biography in Dictionary Form of the Leaders in Chemical Industry, Research, and Education,* Winfield Scott Downs, assoc. ed. (New York, 1951); Wyndham D. Miles, ed., *American Chemists and Chemical Engineers* (Washington, D.C., 1976); Browne, "The Role of Refugees in the History of American Science"; and Clark A. Elliott, *Biographical Dictionary of American Science: The Seventeenth through the Nineteenth Centuries* (Westport, Conn., 1979). One name even appeared in an obituary in a weekday issue of the *New York Times* about a year ago. The full listing of the sample will appear as an appendix in my dissertation; I also have the list in machine-readable form.

Biographical information for all but a handful of the people in the sample came from: Miles, *American Chemists and Chemical Engineers;* Jacques Caltell, ed., *American Men of Science,* especially the 8th (1949) ed.; Elliott, *Biographical Dictionary of American Science;* Haynes, *Chemical Who's Who,* especially the 3rd (1951) ed.; *Dictionary of American Biography; Dictionary of Scientific Biography;* and National Academy of Sciences, *Biographical Memoirs.* These provided the material for the portraits sketched below.

5. Apparently the character of central European immigration in general changed in response to this transformation; see, for example, R.H. Billigmeier, *Americans from Germany: A Study in Cultural Diversity* (Belmont, Calif., 1974), pp. 98–99; and John Paul von Grueningen, ed., *The Swiss in the United States* (Madison, Wis., 1940), pp. 69–70.

6. A few of the chemists to arrive through this pipeline were K.C.D. Hickman, who immigrated in 1925; L.G.S. Brooker, who came a year later; J. Russell, who entered from Canada two or three years after that; and a Finn, C.J. Malm, who had come in 1923. For an overview of the developments at Kodak, see Reese V. Jenkins, *Images and Enterprise: Technology and the American Photographic Industry, 1839 to 1925* (Baltimore, 1975).

7. L.F. Haber, *The Chemical Industry, 1900–1930: International Growth and Technological Change* (Oxford, 1971), p. 365.

8. Quoted in Robert E. Kohler, "The Management of Science: The Experience of Warren Weaver and the Rockefeller Foundation Programme in Molecular Biology," *Minerva* 14 (1976):303; see also idem, *From Medical Chemistry to Biochemistry* (Cambridge, 1982).

9. Hans T. Clarke, "Impressions of an Organic Chemist in Biochemistry," *Annual Review of Biochemistry* 27 (1958); reprinted in *The Excitement and Fascination of Science: A Collection of Autobiographical and Philosophical Essays by Contemporary Scientists* (Palo Alto, 1965), 1:57–62.

10. Daniel J. Kevles, *The Physicists: The History of a Scientific Community in Modern America* (New York, 1978), p. 281.

11. Ira Remsen to S.A. Forbes, Feb. 29, 1904, Records of the Dean of the College of Liberal Arts and Sciences, College of Science Correspondence, 1900–13, record series 15/1/3, box 1, "1904 R-T" folder, University of Illinois Archives, Urbana, Ill.

12. On other American barriers to the émigrés, see David S. Wyman, *Paper Walls: America and the Refugee Crisis, 1938–1941* (Amherst, Mass., 1968).

13. The Nazi government, it appears, tended to treat chemists in industry differently from those in academe, demanding less support for "Aryan" chemistry in the industrial sector, for example. See Martin Bechstedt, "'Gestalhafte Atomlehre'—Zur 'Deutschen Chemie' im NS-Staat," in Herbert Mehrtens and Steffen Richter, eds., *Naturwissenschaft, Technik und NS-Ideologie: Beiträge zur Wissenschaftsgeschichte des Dritten Reichs* (Frankfurt am Main, 1980), pp. 142–65.

A great many people contributed to the completion of this paper. I am especially indebted to: Pnina Abir-Am, Michele Aldrich, Ronald Calinger, Paul Forman, Robert E. Kohler, Lewis Pyenson, Nathan Reingold, Jeffrey L. Sturchio, Arnold Thackray, and Edward Woodhouse.

203

Refugee Mathematicians in the United States, 1933–1941: Reception and Reaction

NATHAN REINGOLD

Immediately after the Nazis moved in April 1933 to expel non-Aryans and the politically tainted from German universities, concerned American institutions and individuals reacted by organizing efforts to aid these individuals. They were facilitated by the specific exemption of university teachers from immigration quotas in Section (4)d of the Immigration Act of 1924. The clause represented an unintended exception to the nativist, if not racist, character of that legislation. To take advantage of the exemption, a refugee needed the assurance of a post. The newly formed Institute for Advanced Study at Princeton and a few universities directly hired refugee mathematicians; many other refugees came for temporary employment under the aegis of the Emergency Committee for Displaced German Scholars (later Displaced Foreign Scholars), often with the aid of the Rockefeller Foundation.[1] Although the number of mathematicians involved was not very large, the migration was significant both for its consequences and for what it disclosed about historical processes of human and intellectual transfer. By the end of 1935, 44 mathematicians had been discharged by the Nazis from their posts; additional dismissals followed.[2] Through 1939, the number reaching America from the German language world totaled 51, and they were joined by others from elsewhere as Hitler's sway expanded. By the end of the war, the total migration was somewhere between 120 and 150.[3]

The programs of the Emergency Committee and the Rockefeller Foundation, designed as a mechanism leading to permanent posts, are important here because mathematics loomed very large in both. In the absence of a governmental position, these organizations formulated a de facto official policy. Of the 277 individuals aided by the committee, 26 were mathematicians, more than were in any other scientific field. Most were aided early in the period, before efforts focused on other disciplines. The foundation supported 20 (with some being aided by both).[4] What is most striking is that mathematicians were singled out for rescue early for three reasons: (1) scientists and others recognized the intellectual importance of the field for modern culture, as evidenced by the composition of the Institute for Advanced Study; (2) mathematicians were influential in both organizations—for example, the president of the foundation, Max Mason, and the head of its natural science program, Warren Weaver, were mathematicians; and (3) leading U.S. mathematicians and their organizations became active participants in the reactions to Nazism.

II In April 1933, officials in the Rockefeller Foundation became concerned over the fate of displaced German scholars. Many, such as the mathematician Richard Courant (1888-1972) and his colleagues at Göttingen, were known to them because of prior contacts and support. The Rockefeller Foundation officials were appalled to see a great European nation rejecting the ideal of the universality of learning and lapsing into barbarism. They encouraged the formation of the Emergency Committee in May with funds from other private sources.[5]

Both the foundation and the committee were conscious of the effects of the Depression. In October 1933, Edward R. Murrow, the second-in-command of the committee, penned a memo on "displaced American scholars," noting that more than two thousand of a total twenty-seven thousand teachers had been dropped from the faculties of 240 institutions.[6] The two organizations decided that universities could not use their refugee funds to displace existing faculty; that they had to avoid a nationalistic reaction to the coming of foreigners; and that, at all costs, the program had to avoid the danger of arousing anti-Semitism.

206

Specifically, the two bodies decided that they would aid scholarship, not provide relief to suffering. The selection of individuals was based on merit as measured on a worldwide scale, meaning that those chosen for help were principally mature or, at least, recognized scholars. Some younger mathematicians received fellowships from the Institute for Advanced Study. A later writer characterized the programs of the committee and the foundation as dealing with the "few, often well-off and well connected."[7] In practice, the distinctions were sometimes overlooked even at the start. The committee negotiated with individual universities requesting a particular scholar. Like the Rockefeller Foundation, it wanted to find positions for scholars in research settings, perhaps involving an occasional graduate course, but hopefully leading to permanent placement—a principal difference from the British program.[8] Grants were often only made for two-year periods, with local matching funds or a Rockefeller donation, to reduce the perils of nationalism and anti-Semitism by avoiding regular posts and limiting calls on university funds.

These policies sometimes had a different effect. Some faculty members greatly resented giving special privileges to foreigners at a time when money for research was hard to obtain and when others were forced to carry heavy teaching loads. These Americans viewed the program as a way in which opportunities would be denied to young, promising native-born scholars in favor of top Europeans.

III The two principal agents of the mathematicians in aiding émigrés were Oswald Veblen (1880–1960) and R.G.D. Richardson (1878–1949).[9] The former, a graduate of Chicago and a nephew of Thorstein Veblen, the great social theorist, was a distinguished topologist at the Institute for Advanced Study.

Richardson was chairman of the mathematics department at Brown University and since 1926 had been dean of its graduate school. He was also—most significant in this context—the secretary of the American Mathematical Society (AMS) from 1921 to 1940. He was born in Nova Scotia and had come to Yale to get his Ph.D. Never to my knowledge did he publicly mention in this period that he was an immigrant himself. During World War II, Richardson launched a program that would eventually produce a notable applied mathematics institute at Brown. In contrast to the pure mathematician Veblen, Richardson advocated and promoted the application of mathematics.

207

By the time the Depression began in 1929, a mathematical community that had been expanding modestly in the United States from the start of the century was undergoing a great period of growth partly due to an infusion of money, which was in turn largely due to Veblen's fund-raising activities. Richardson, writing to the Rockefeller Foundation in 1929, ascribed all of this to the AMS: "The atmosphere of scholarly devotion which has raised the sciences and arts of the European countries to a lofty plain is being cultivated by the SOCIETY."[10]

After 1929, this promising expansion was imperiled. In 1932, Richardson estimated that, at a minimum, two hundred of the members of the AMS were out of work. Greatly concerned about them, the society passed a resolution readmitting members who had had to drop out because of economic stringencies without asking them to pay a new initiation fee.[11]

Although Richardson and Veblen operated through the American Mathematical Society, it did not represent the entire formal institutional structure of mathematics in the United States. There was another group, the Mathematical Association of America (MAA). The MAA was quite different in character and purpose. Founded in 1915 when the AMS had refused to take on a concern for teaching at the undergraduate level and below, MAA was largely concerned with teaching. There was a great overlap in membership, and the two organizations quite frequently met together.[12]

The split was very important because most of the jobs that might have been available for mathematicians were for teaching undergraduates, not for research and graduate education. Veblen, of course, decried the over-emphasis on teaching;[13] to counter that, he strove to develop the research-oriented Institute for Advanced Study. Richardson, as an academic administrator, had a greater sympathy for the problem of undergraduate education. Academic administrators hesitated about hiring foreigners for undergraduate teaching. Even more than any language difficulties, many émigrés were startled and troubled by the different methods and attitudes in teaching in American colleges. Very few realized, as one émigré later wrote:

It takes a long time for anyone not born or brought up in this country to realize ... that ... the primary aim of a college ... is to educate members of a democratic society, that it includes among its functions the training of mind and character, of social attitude and political behavior.[14]

208   A 1935 survey of the job market for mathematicians concluded

that, given the normal demographic turnover, there were more potential teaching positions than the annual estimated production of Ph.D.s. This assumed only a slight relaxation of the economic conditions plus an upgrading of some posts not then occupied by holders of the doctorate.[15] But as late as 1940, the job market had not appreciably improved in the opinion of many mathematicians. In a time of economic distress, the always present conflict between teaching and research could and did become acute.

In 1936, Richardson published a study of doctorate holders in America since 1862, including foreign or native-born and holders of domestic or overseas degrees. He identified 114 holders of foreign degrees (both native- and foreign-born) compared to a total of 1,286 degree holders from U.S. and Canadian universities.[16] The 34 from Göttingen far surpassed any other foreign source. To this indication of impact must be added individuals such as Richardson who had gone to Göttingen, but not to get a degree.

Richardson's analysis of the current situation disclosed forty foreign-born Ph.D.s in the country by 1930, with an estimated twenty new mathematicians arriving as a result of Nazi policies. He observed that, because fewer Americans had gone overseas since 1913, this actually represented a decrease in the percentage of mathematicians holding foreign Ph.D.s in the country. Noting that foreign Ph.D. holders—native and immigrant—tended to be more prolific in research, Richardson feared inbreeding.[17] The American increase in the award of the degree was more a matter of quantity than quality. What he did not say explicitly, but what emerges from his statistics, is the overwhelming preponderance of undergraduate teaching, not the conduct of research, as a source of employment. Like the 1935 survey, Richardson predicted a shortage of mathematicians if the economy permitted hiring and upgrading. Until that occurred, even placing twenty or so leading mathematicians was a problem, considering the hazards of nationalistic and anti-Semitic reactions.

IV There is no doubt that such sentiments existed, separately or together, before Hitler, and that they continued after the start of the migration. Although immigration looms as a basic feature through all U.S. history, newcomers have always attracted a measure of antipathy.

In 1927, for example, Richardson wrote:

With one foreigner Tamarkin in the department, we feel that it might be a considerable risk to take on another one such as Wilson. Englishmen do not adapt themselves very quickly to American ways, and generally they do not wish to do so.[18]

But there were at least thirty-nine others besides Tamarkin in the United States by 1930, if we can trust Richardson. Some must have been very self-conscious about their origins, judging by Tibor Rado's 1932 greeting to his colleagues "as a representative of those born abroad who have adopted this as their country."[19] From 1933 until 1940, Norbert Wiener kept on worrying about the need for assuaging nationalistic sentiments:

Every foreign scholar imported means an American out of a job. . . . Any appointment for more than a year would cause a feeling of resentment that would wreck our hopes of doing anything whatsoever.[20]

His concern surely stemmed from the difficulties of placing young American-Jewish mathematicians in a tight job market. Veblen voiced similar fears.[21]

In 1934 A.B. Coble of the University of Illinois said, despite hostile questions from a state legislator, that he would hire a foreigner who was better than any native prospect.[22] Wiener's reaction to such hostility was a 1934 proposal to raise new money to provide research posts not competitive with regular posts.[23] The Berkeley economist Carl Landauer disagreed with Wiener, asserting that university administrators were giving preference to Germans over Anglo-Saxons. Rather than concentrating the refugees in graduate courses, Landauer wanted them integrated into undergraduate teaching.[24]

In the same year G.A. Bliss of the University of Chicago turned down a refugee:

I must confess also that if we could secure a new man, I should want to try to get a strong American. It is pathetic to see the good young American men, who have received their Ph.D. degrees in recent years, so inadequately placed in many cases.[25]

In 1941 a dean at Yale, writing about a mathematician, Einar Hille, said:

No foreigner should be chairman of a department where undergraduate work is involved. . . . One of the criticisms of these foreign importations is that they are not suited to undergraduate work or do not wish to do it. Hence they take the most desirable positions away from our American product.[26]

210

Although educated at the University of Stockholm, Hille was born in the United States.

As to anti-Semitism, it was ubiquitous, in at least mild forms, in the genteel world of American academia before World War II.[27] To cite a few examples, the mathematician H.E. Slaught of the University of Chicago, writing in 1931 about a mathematical astronomer, said:

He is one of the few men of Jewish decent [sic] who does not get on your nerves and really behaves like a gentile to a satisfactory degree.[28]

In seeking to fill vacancies, administrators sometimes bluntly excluded Jews or asked, as in one case, for "preferably a protestant."[29] Coble stated that Illinois played it safe on appointments, "a policy with which I am not wholly in agreement." He explained that it arose because the graduate work was conducted by men paid through the administration of the undergraduate colleges, noting that "leads to selections of a rather uniform type."[30]

But Illinois and a number of other departments already had Jewish members, typically one per school. This produced a problem for some faculties when presented with the option of hiring a second. As a dean at Kentucky wrote in 1935, "You know that you have to be careful about getting too many Jews together."[31] Or, as the chairman at Indiana noted in 1938, "But there is a question of two Jewish men in the same department, and a somewhat small one."[32] Wiener encountered this problem with the possible placement of one of his students at MIT. In a conversation in 1935, Karl T. Compton noted the

tactical danger of having too large a proportion of the mathematical staff from the Jewish race, emphasizing that this arises not from our own prejudice in the matter, but because of a recognized general situation which might react unfavorably against the staff and the Department unless properly handled.

After agreeing that no one should fail to receive fair consideration because of race, Compton continued:

Other things being approximately equal, it is legitimate to consider the matter of race in case the appointment of an additional member of the Jewish race would increase the proportion of such men in the Department far beyond the proportion of population.[33]

By the standards of his day, Compton was an enlightened administrator, but he responded to and perhaps adapted to the conventions of his milieu.

211

Nor was anti-Semitism wholly absent from the inner workings of the American Mathematical Society. In 1934, the society elected its first Jewish president, Solomon Lefschetz (1884–1972) of Princeton University, Veblen's successor to the Fine Professorship. That prospect bothered one of the elder statesmen of the mathematical community, Professor G.D. Birkhoff of Harvard University (1884–1944), a close friend of Richardson. Birkhoff and Veblen were probably the two most eminent of the senior American mathematicians of that day. From 1935 to 1939, Birkhoff was dean of the Faculty of Arts and Sciences at Harvard.

Lefschetz, a great topologist, was born in Russia and educated in France as an engineer. After coming to the United States in 1905, he lost both hands in an industrial accident. He then received a Ph.D. in mathematics from Clark University and taught at universities in the Midwest. In 1924, Veblen brought him to Princeton. Eventually, the two men would break.

Richardson foresaw troubles ahead, yet managed to survive Lefschetz's two-year incumbency with little apparent damage. Birkhoff's opposition to the election had interesting overtones:

I have a feeling that Lefschetz will be likely to be less pleasant even than he had been, in that from now on he will try to work strongly and positively for his own race. They are exceedingly confident of their own power and influence in the good old USA. The real hope in our mathematical situation is that we will be able to be fair to our own kind. . . .

And Birkhoff went on to say:

He will get very cocky, very racial, and use the Annals [*Annals of Mathematics*] as a good deal of racial perquisite. The racial interests will get deeper as Einstein's and all of them do.

In the same letter Birkhoff also expressed distress that the presidency of the AMS, usually awarded on the basis of research eminence, would probably go to individuals (incidentally, all other than Lefschetz non-Jewish) all of whom, apparently, had different ideas from those he was espousing. He wondered how to arrange for the presidency to be given for service to the society, rather than for eminence in research.[34] Despite Birkhoff's strong feelings and despite Richardson's apprehensions, when the proper moment came, it was Birkhoff who reported the nomination of Lefschetz for the presidency. To Marston Morse, writing to Veblen, the result was better than selecting a weaker man "regardless of politics."[35] Birkhoff's

212

views were apparently fairly well known during his lifetime. In 1936 Wiener's student, the subject of the Compton memo, then at the Institute for Advanced Study, wrote his teacher a letter in which he closed: "P.S. Einstein has been saying around here that Birkhoff is one of the world's greatest academic antisemites."[136]

V Even before Hitler came to power, there were signs of future American sentiments. In 1932, the *Bulletin of the American Mathematical Society* criticized the dismissal of the Italian mathematical physicist Vito Volterra for refusing to take the oath required by the fascist government. The dismissal, the *Bulletin* asserted, was a violation of "correct principles of academic tenure."[137] Perhaps that rather mild criticism influenced the early reaction to the Nazi program, but increasingly, many mathematicians foresaw deeper and more serious consequences of the occurrences in Germany.

In May 1933 Veblen went to the Rockefeller Foundation about Nazi moves and became a member of the Emergency Committee when it was founded. From then until the end of the war, he and his colleague Hermann Weyl ran an informal placement bureau for displaced mathematicians. In Veblen's papers in the Library of Congress are lists of names with headings such as scholarship, personality, adaptability, and teaching ability. When information about a person was incomplete in the United States, Veblen wrote to European colleagues.

In April and May 1933 Richardson saw an opportunity for America and for his Brown University. In a memorandum of May 23, 1933, to the Brown University Graduate Council noting a luncheon discussion on the German-Jewish situation, he wrote: "In 1900 we were flocking to Germany but now more come here than go the other way." Richardson agreed with the Rockefeller Foundation, Veblen, and the Emergency Committee about the peril of bringing in a considerable number of foreign mathematicians with so many young Americans unemployed—the "danger of causing friction and even of fanning the flames of Anti-Semitism in this country." To insure and control a proper distribution, perhaps one to three leading mathematicians in each participating university, the AMS had to take a leading role. Provided that funds were available, Brown could cooperate by taking two to four mathematicians.[38] By early July, the council of the society authorized its president, A.B. Coble of Illinois,   213 to establish a committee of three to cooperate with the Emergency Committee. Naturally, Veblen was one of the three.[39] On July 15, 1933, Richardson could write the president of the American Jewish Congress that "our organization views with dismay and almost incredulity the developments in Germany."[40]

Despite early successes and the strong backing of men such as Veblen and Richardson, the placement program had a built-in catch. It assumed that the universities (or most of them) would absorb the first wave of refugee mathematicians into their regular staffs at the expiration of the two-year grants from the Emergency Committee and the Rockefeller Foundation, roughly in 1935.[41] That depended, in large measure, upon improvements in the economic climate. In turn, such improvements could provide a degree of security against the perceived dangers of nationalism and anti-Semitism. As 1935 approached and the unemployment of mathematicians continued, pessimism developed. Writing to the Danish mathematician Harald Bohr on April 5, 1935, Richardson gloomily predicted that only half of those presently supported (in all fields) were absorbable by the universities. Most of the rest had possibilities for temporary placement pending later absorption. Beyond that—and this presumably meant others in Europe hoping to come over—Richardson, with a few exceptions, could only see the possibility of providing unemployment relief, not aiding scholarship. With seventy-five American mathematicial Ph.D.s out of work, even the small number taken on by the committee or employed directly approached an upper limit.[42]

Let us consider three instances of successful placement by 1935. The fate of the Göttingen group became an immediate concern to the Rockefeller Foundation and individuals like Veblen. Bryn Mawr College provided a post for Emmy Noether (1882–1935). For all his ambitious plans for Brown, Richardson had to content himself with the youngest man in the group, Hans Lewy (b. 1904). Despite sour comments from at least one outside observer,[43] Richardson was very pleased with his new colleague.

Richard Courant presented a more difficult problem. For one thing, Richardson had clashed with him in Göttingen before World War I. Although hostile to Courant's coming, Richardson pledged not to interfere with efforts to place Courant. As late as 1936, Richardson was grumbling about Courant;[44] the two men would clash at the start of World War II when each had ambitions to launch an applied mathematics program. Courant also had a reputation as a promoter, which both helped and hindered his placement.

214

Veblen first thought of the mathematics department in Berkeley, then undergoing a reorganization. Before Hitler's ascension, Veblen had recommended American mathematicians; by May he was pushing Courant and other displaced Germans.[45] California had selected Griffith C. Evans of Rice Institute as the new departmental chairman. Evans strongly opposed Courant, asserting:

To say that there are too many foreigners in American universities is not chauvinism, but merely, that the careers of promising students in America are being cut off at the top. I do not see how this can be anything but an unfavorable situation in which to develop intellectual life. A generation ago we were in need of direct stimulation and there was plenty of room; now we could well interchange.[46]

To this Veblen replied succinctly:

I think I would differ from you only in attaching a little more weight to the importance of placing a few first-class foreigners in positions where they will stimulate our activity. I am inclined to think that doing so will in fact increase the number of positions that are available to the better grade of American Ph.D.s even though it may decrease the total number of positions. . . . [A]lmost any method of strengthening the local scientific group will make it easier to place our scientifically strong products.[47]

In a later letter to Richardson, Evans elaborated his position:

It seems to me that at the present time our own young men should be the first consideration, given the fact that Europe would not reciprocate in appointing Americans in their universities. Of course, they would say 'But look at the difference!' I doubt if there is much, myself, allowing for the difference in teaching programs.[48]

Even before the exchange with Evans, Veblen had moved to place Courant in New York University, arguing that it presented an opportunity for Courant's entrepreneurial skills.

To return to Hans Lewy, he was one of the victims of the 1935 financial situation; Brown could not keep him. Richardson wrote across the country to many departments on his behalf, with the previous references to Coble, Bliss, and Kentucky being examples of some responses. But Evans hired him for Berkeley on a regular appointment without benefit of subsidy from the Emergency Committee or the Rockefeller Foundation.[49] Evans's nationalistic sentiments were not necessarily anti-Semitic. While at Rice, for example, he wrote in 1932 about a young Jewish mathematician: "But emphatically, there should not be a prejudice against him, discounting ability on the ground that he is a Jew."[50]

215

In 1937 the AMS had an opportunity to face up to what was happening in Nazi Germany when it received an invitation to attend the bicentennial of the founding of Göttingen University. Like other Americans, Richardson had been offended by the previous year's celebration at Heidelberg. Writing to Birkhoff, he declared himself against "science as a national tool rather than as an end to itself."[51] Richardson decided that so important a matter had to be laid before all of the almost ninety present and past officers and members of the council. He sent the invitation out with a memorandum written by his colleague, Raymond Clare Archibald, declaring that the invitation was not from the Göttingen known to all from the old days. The university now was a different body and, like the Heidelberg celebration, its bicentennial would provide an opportunity for Nazi propaganda in violation of the universality of science. Archibald suggested simply sending a letter complimenting Göttingen on its past and hoping that the future would be similar.

The returns were overwhelmingly against participation. Simply say no, wrote Eric Temple Bell of the California Institute of Technology. Professor C.A. Noble at Berkeley remembered his happiness at Göttingen (1893–96, 1900–01), his indebtedness to his professors "and to Germany of those days." Nevertheless, he concurred with Archibald, as did fifty-four others. Only ten recommended participation for reasons such as maintaining solidarity with colleagues. One of the ten, W.A. Wilson of Yale, thought the Jews "are largely responsible for their troubles."[52]

Another occasion implicitly to face the consequences of Nazism occurred in the 1938 celebration of the AMS's semicentennial. Its planners foresaw a festive occasion for a small, strong, tightly knit group. Archibald, who was also a historian of mathematics, would write a history of the society, and a dozen or so papers would survey the development of fields of mathematics in the United States. Archibald thought the American emphasis could "open [us] to charges of provincialism." Veblen wanted to avoid a historical review of mathematical subjects, suggesting simply a survey of current knowledge. Others, such as Lefschetz, objected to having "ancients" speak, simply wanting the best in each specialty. The compromise, suggested by John R. Kline, called for contributions from outstanding mathematicians who were to be free to write historical essays, not necessarily concerned with U.S. contributions. He also suggested excluding recent arrivals in the country as authors, even if they were the best persons for a topic. By 1937 E.R. Hedrick noted the apparent

216

exclusion of the foreign-born and those trained abroad. (Although one speaker, Eric Bell, was born overseas, all were products of U.S. universities.) That did not arouse controversy. Kline's other suggestion did: he wanted Birkhoff to have a prominent place in the program.[53]

Birkhoff presented a historical survey of mathematics in the United States during the past fifty years, offering praise and criticism. He then brought up the question of the foreign-born mathematicians. In getting research positions, they did less teaching than the native-born; they lessened the number of positions for American mathematicians who were "forced to become hewers of wood and drawers of water. I believe we have reached the point of saturation. We must definitely avoid the danger." Birkhoff then listed all of the people who had come in the last twenty years. Included in the list were such colleagues of his as Alfred North Whitehead and others who were neither German nor Jewish. Despite the nature of Birkhoff's list, many ascribed his views to anti-Semitism.[54]

The speech and its printed version elicited strong responses. Abraham Flexner of the Institute for Advanced Study eloquently argued against the presumed bad effects.[55] Lefschetz, who was listed, complained that he had been in America for thirty-three years; all of his mathematical work had occurred in the United States. Writing to his old friend, Richardson reported that people, "not all Jews," looking at the semicentennial volumes expressed marked disapproval of the sentiments. Perhaps reflecting feelings about his own immigrant origins, Richardson gave two omitted names, one a Briton whose residence in the United States was nearly as long as his own.[56]

VI Of all the American mathematicians' reactions to Nazism, by far the most significant was the decision in 1939 to found *Mathematical Reviews*. Among American mathematicians the desire for a critical abstracting journal was part of the general drive to develop a well-rounded mathematical community not in a state of colonylike dependence on Europe. In 1922 H. E. Slaught included it in his proposal for increasing funding and activities of mathematics.[57] Oswald Veblen also tried for an abstracting journal during his presidency of the AMS. The Depression halted efforts in this direction.

The situation changed materially in 1931 when the Berlin firm of Springer launched the *Zentralblatt für Mathematik und ihre Grenz-*   217 *gebiete.* It was satisfyingly prompt, critical, and complete in coverage. Its editor, Otto Neugebauer, a member of Courant's group at Göttingen, was not Jewish but was politically suspect to the Nazis. Neugebauer fled to Denmark in 1934. Reputedly, he later said of his exile, "I did not have the honor of having a Jewish grandmother." As early as August 1933, Veblen proposed bringing Neugebauer to America to continue the *Zentralblatt.* Richardson disagreed on financial grounds.[58]

In late 1938 the *Zentralblatt* removed the Italian mathematician Tullio Levi-Civita from its board for racial reasons, presumably under pressure from the regime. Neugebauer resigned, as did many foreigners on the advisory board such as G. H. Hardy, Oswald Veblen, and Harald Bohr. On November 27, 1938, Richardson reported the resignations to Evans, as president-elect of the AMS, adding news of the barring of Russians as collaborators and as referees. Not surprisingly, refugee mathematicians were also excluded from the review process.[59]

Having long prepared for this moment, Veblen drafted a statement urging the founding of an American journal. In it he wrote, referring to his efforts fifteen years earlier, that the United States was then

not yet strong enough to carry the load without much of a strain on its creative elements. Since then the number of productive mathematicians in our country has increased much more rapidly than anticipated and has also been supplemented by an influx of scholars who found it difficult or impossible to continue their work in Europe. As a result the mathematical center of gravity of the world is definitely in America.

Veblen called for a new journal passing judgment on new theories, one "based on the traditional decencies of scientific and human intercourse."[60]

Although outwardly neutral, Richardson's position was now favorable to the proposal. He moved to get Neugebauer a place on the Brown faculty so that the journal would function in Providence. Richardson's actions caused tensions with Veblen, eventually leading to a clash after the periodical was founded.[61] Early in December 1938 Richardson organized a committee of the AMS to consider what should be done and also prepared for what he knew should be a spirited discussion at the society's Christmas meeting in Williamsburg, Virginia. Writing to his counterpart in the MAA, W. D. Cairns, Richardson penned a paragraph whose meaning was instantly clear to the society's insiders who were sent copies:

218

We must avoid any reference to political, religious, or racial questions. We must under no circumstance put ourselves in a position of appearing to kill the Zentralblatt. We must study the question objectively and make up our minds as to what is best to be done for mathematics.

What Richardson meant was that the question of Nazi racial policies should not figure explicitly in the committee's composition or its stated conclusions.[62]

The AMS's council directed the committee to consider three necessary conditions for the launching of an abstracting journal: (1) financial assurance for the first five years of publication, (2) international cooperation, and (3) confirmation that the *Zentralblatt* was not likely "to make its reviews unimpeachable." The first condition reflected considerable hesitation, if not anxiety, about an undertaking large enough to imperil the solvency of the society. Veblen handled that problem by getting a sixty-five thousand dollar grant from the Carnegie Corporation. The second condition generated a spate of letters to organizations and individuals in many nations asking for cooperation and pledging adherence to scientific internationalism.

The existing *Zentralblatt,* warmly regarded by many American mathematicians, provided the thorniest problem for the committee. Richardson observed: "I cannot now see what assurances they [Springer] could give that would be satisfactory to me. . . . " He had recently read in *Science* that German medical abstracting journals now omitted reviews of articles by Jews. As he wrote to Hardy before the matter was decided, Richardson wanted an international journal "independent of the whims of a dictatorship."[63] The society even considered the possibility of purchasing the *Zentralblatt* from Springer. To the purchase offer, Ferdinand Springer later asserted he did not regard the journal as a commercial venture. More importantly, he offered to dispatch an emissary to America, F. K. Schmidt of Jena.[64] The society deferred its decision until Schmidt met with the committee.

In March and April an unexpected event further tipped the balance of opinion. Marshall Stone, then at Harvard, received a letter from Helmut Hasse of Göttingen. Hasse justified splitting the refugees from other possible referees. "Looking at the situation from a practical point of view, one must admit that there is a state of war between the Germans and the Jews." He failed to understand why the Americans withdrew their collaboration with the *Zentralblatt* 219 and referred to "Neugebauer's pro-Jewish policy." C.R. Adams, the chairman of the committee, circulated the Hasse letter to his committee in preparation for the coming meeting at Durham, North Carolina, noting: "Mr. Veblen insists that there is a war by the Germans against *civilization*."[65] The letter made a strongly unfavorable impression on the members of the committee and the society's council.[66] In his May 2 reply to Hasse, Stone said the decision on the journal was

not likely to be taken for the purpose of passing judgment on the past history of the Zentralblatt . . . [but] primarily on the desire to assume for the future of mathematical abstracting a responsibility commensurate with America's great and growing mathematical importance. . . . As for the Americans who withdrew, I feel that they merely acted with true loyalty to their own national traditions and ideals.[67]

Nor did Schmidt's presentation in May convince many American mathematicians. Springer offered a compromise arrangement with two separate editorial boards: one for the United States, Britain and its commonwealth, and the Soviet Union; the other for Germany and nearby countries. To avoid any imputation of racial motivations, Springer now asked that papers by German authors not be reviewed by German emigrants, whether Jew or Gentile. Writing to A.B. Coble about the meeting, Adams said that Schmidt

states that the German idea is that mathematics, like everything else, exists in a real world in which political considerations play a part; and that, like everything else, mathematics must expect to be affected in some measure by political considerations.[68]

Springer's proposal was perceived as a gross affront to the ideal of scientific internationalism. One mathematician, T.C. Fry of Bell Telephone Laboratories, commented that Springer gave no assurance against a future ban against refereeing of Aryans' papers by non-Aryans who were not German refugees.[69]

Unexpectedly, Schmidt found allies among some members of the Harvard mathematics department. Fearing a German boycott of the planned 1940 international congress in Cambridge, Massachusetts, William C. Graustein argued against the proposed journal, "We would, I feel, be denying a principle for which we have long fought—that of the emancipation of science from international politics."[70] It was an ironic obverse of Schmidt's position. Although Graustein sat in on the committee's last session and addressed an open letter to it

220

and to AMS council members, the effect was minimal. Richardson regarded Graustein's letter as playing into the hands of the Germans, who were acting on Harvard advice.[71] Adams told the committee on May 17 that Springer's moves were simply designed to confuse issues.[72]

Not everyone in Harvard (let alone MIT) agreed with Graustein and Birkhoff. Marshall Stone, as a member of the AMS council, convened a meeting of Cambridge, Massachusetts, mathematicians on May 18, 1939, presided over by Saunders MacLane. The meeting unanimously repudiated Graustein's letter and supported the proposed journal with only one abstention.[73] Richardson had taken control of the process from his colleague Adams, who was ill, and he was determined to push the decision through.[74] On May 22 Birkhoff proposed a compromise, a publication of bibliographic entries without any analysis.[75] On May 25 Richardson wrote his old friend that the council had voted twenty-two for the new journal, five against, and four uncertain.[76] Oswald Veblen was named chairman of the committee to launch and supervise the newest publication of the society.[77]

VII   While the leadership of the AMS, the disciplinary establishment, grappled with the impact of the foreign-born already in their ranks, refugees continued to come across the ocean in the closing years of the 1930s, and as Hitler's pressures expanded, still more became potential migrants. The unemployment situation remained discouraging. Richardson thought America had done all it could to absorb refugees. Approvingly, in 1938 he cited to W.D. Cairns the policy of the Emergency Committee (and the Rockefeller Foundation):

I think the principle laid down there [that is, in the committee],
namely that humanitarian considerations must be laid aside, should
be followed and what can be done should be for those of high scientific merit. We want to save the scholar for the sake of scholarship.[78]

After his retirement from the secretaryship, Richardson explained in 1941:

I have been compelled to consider these cases of appointments from
the scientific and monetary point of view. If I should think of the
humanitarian aspects I would get bogged down very quickly.[79]

221

Not everyone adopted that stance. In the 1938 letter to Cairns quoted above, on a "hopeless case," Richardson also wrote: "You might write to Veblen. That would seem the only possibility." Like his colleague Hermann Weyl, who ran a German Mathematicians' Relief Fund during the period, Veblen no longer restricted his efforts to the eminent. Nor were they alone. John R. Kline wrote to Courant in 1938 about an Austrian who

is not an outstanding mathematician and it may be difficult to do anything for him but still the need is extremely desperate and human feeling makes us wish to do anything that is at all possible.[80]

Veblen's actions stemmed from more than humanitarian considerations. Almost at the very time Richardson saw a saturated job market, Veblen asserted to Karl Menger that "our power of assimilation in this country is not yet exhausted."[81] Certainly, the university authorities did not agree with Veblen. Under the leadership of President James B. Conant of Harvard, many joined in a drive to raise an endowment for aiding refugees as the existing funds were so limited.[82]

What Veblen had in mind becomes clear from the refugee files that he and Weyl maintained. Not only were they aiding the non-eminent, but also the two men had long ago stopped limiting placements to institutions with research capabilities. Veblen was now placing refugees in any willing four-year college and even in junior colleges. In these moves Weyl and Veblen had the cooperation of Harlow Shapley, head of the Harvard College Observatory. The matter was sensitive; it was, after all, the upgrading called for in the 1935 article on the job market and in Richardson's 1936 piece.

If teaching posts at these lesser institutions were conspicuously filled by refugees, then the existence of a substantial number of unemployed native-born mathematicians might lead to the feared nationalistic and anti-Semitic backlash. To avoid a clash, Veblen needed the agreement of Birkhoff, whose influence stemmed both from intellectual prominence and the role of Harvard as the leading undergraduate source of American mathematicians. On May 24, 1939, Shapley wrote Weyl:

When Veblen and Birkhoff were in my office the other day, it was agreed that the distribution of these first-rate and second-rate men among smaller American institutions would in the long run be very advantageous, providing at the same time we defended not too feebly the inherent rights of our own graduate students.[83]

222

The meeting occurred just as the AMS decided to found an abstracting journal. The society made another decision in September 1939. It formed a War Preparedness Committee, chaired by Veblen's colleague, Marston Morse. Evans and Richardson at first wanted to bar participation of individuals with German names. Morse smoothly avoided that position by insisting, "It is important that such German names as we have represent the best possible choices."[84] The society now moved, modestly but unequivocally, toward the time in World War II when mathematicians were in short supply and refugee skills could help to free the Old World from the Nazi blight.

VIII Even before the United States joined the conflict, writings appeared appraising the meaning of the transfer of cultural skills across the ocean. To the chemist C.A. Browne in *Science,* the current situation was a rerun of history, recalling the Göttingen seven and the Forty-eighters: "That Germany should now repeat on a vastly greater scale the tyrannical follies of a century ago seems too incredible for belief." Making no mention of anti-Semitism, he noted how well earlier German migrants had assimilated, enriching the country.[85] Like Browne, other writers stressed both Nazi folly and American precedent. In 1942 Arnold Dresden of Swarthmore gave a listing of refugee mathematicians, opening and closing with an account of Joseph Priestley's 1794 arrival and welcome by the American Philosophical Society. The recent migrants became another example of America's traditional role as a haven for the oppressed of Europe.[86] And in 1943, replying to a letter from Weyl about a German refugee mathematician in Chile, Evans expressed interest, noting, "Certainly at Berkeley we are proud of Lewy, Tarski, Wolf and Neyman."[87] It was quite a contrast to his 1934 exchange with Veblen.

The growth of the American mathematical community clearly helped absorb the individuals in the migration. At the same time this growth, coinciding with the Depression, created a problem for the refugees. Insecurity about economic conditions reinforced insecurity about status in the world community of mathematicians. Despite these persisting feelings the statistics disclose a different situation. In the decade of the 1920s, American universities granted a total of 351 doctorates in mathematics. The number rose to 780 in the following decade. Some universities had spectacular expansions in the same period. Princeton went from 14 doctorates granted

223

The Courant Institute of Mathematical Sciences on the campus of
New York University, named after émigré mathematician Richard
Courant. Few in number, most of the refugee mathematicians were
able to find academic positions and in general were well received by
their American colleagues. (Courtesy of Adrienne Ash.)

to 40; MIT from 5 to 32; Michigan from 11 to 59; and Wisconsin
from 8 to 32.[88] Although published figures on mathematics alone do
not exist, the total number of teachers in higher education in the
period 1930–40 rose approximately 77 percent.[89] The job market
problem was largely one of accommodating the increase in home-
grown Ph.D.s. Despite Depression conditions, many mathematicians, including refugees, did somehow get posts, even if their positions did not always match their aspirations. As in the case of
physics in the United States, the Depression period was one of growth
for mathematics in terms of both quality and quantity.[90]

224

At the same time American mathematicians and physicists in 1933–34 were noticeably sensitive about the perils of nationalism and anti-Semitism. Afterwards, in his defense against charges of communism, Veblen described his efforts to place refugees as seriously encountering "the opposition of American anti-Semites."[91] Both perils existed, and the latter certainly affected young Americans born into the wrong faith as they entered learned professions in the interwar years. In retrospect, the fears expressed in 1933 and 1934 were overstated. Recent historical studies have pointed to the New Deal as the period in which the concept of a pluralistic society took root and even as a source for much of the post–World War II expansion of civil rights.[92] Foreign observers in the early 1930s reacted differently than most Americans. From a comparative prospect, they noted the absence of the virulent, pathological nationalism and anti-Semitism of many European countries.[93]

Like all significant historical events, the reception of the émigré mathematicians was filled with ambiguities and contradictions reflecting the complexity of the situation. Like Richardson, many Americans were influenced both by altruism and cool calculations of national and institutional advantage. Precisely disentangling the two motives is impossible. Veblen clearly convinced himself that his course favored both the refugees and the future of mathematics in the United States. Others were not so certain.

Judgments of motives are hazardous. Birkhoff did nominate Lefschetz for the presidency of the AMS and aided individual refugees despite his stated position. Evans refused Courant in strong nationalistic terms and then hired Lewy. Evans and Richardson stood up for internationalism, as they saw it, in the founding of *Mathematical Reviews* but later wanted to bar from the War Preparedness Committee not only refugees but also Americans of German ancestry. Instead of implacable historical forces or clear-cut social processes, the sources disclose troubled, inconsistent humans struggling to do right, however defined, in the face of opposing or indifferent trends. The mathematicians were just like everyone else in this respect.

The successful absorption of the émigré mathematicians was partly a triumph of two ideals, those of scientific internationalism and of the United States as a refuge from tyranny. Of course, neither ideal is literally true historically. Schmidt had a point; there was no way mathematicians could escape from the realities of the world. But faced with Nazism abroad and its victims in the United States, the leaders of the American mathematical community in effect voted

225

for a world in which those ideals were to be realized and even merged. What happened is also describable as a process by which a largely moderate, if not conservative, disciplinary establishment shed a belief in political neutrality and assumed an explicitly hostile stance toward Nazi Germany.

Notes

Many of the notes below cite manuscript sources. They are abbreviated as follows:

AMS   Archives, American Mathematical Society, Lehigh University, Bethlehem, Pa.

BHA   George David Birkhoff Papers, Harvard University Archives, Cambridge, Mass.

CIMS   Archives, Courant Institute of Mathematical Sciences, New York University, New York. N.Y.

GCE   Griffith C. Evans Papers, Bancroft Library, University of California, Berkeley, Calif.

NW   Norbert Wiener Papers, Archives of the Massachusetts Institute of Technology, Cambridge, Mass.

OV   Oswald Veblen Papers, Manuscript Division, Library of Congress, Washington, D.C.

RBA   R.G.D. Richardson Papers, Archives, Brown University, Providence, R.I.

RFA   Archives, Rockefeller Foundation, Rockefeller Archive Center, North Tarrytown, N.Y.

1. For the Emergency Committee, see Stephan Duggan and Betty Drury, *The Rescue of Science and Learning: The Story of the Emergency Committee in Aid of Displaced Scholars* (New York, 1952). For the Rockefeller Foundation, see Thomas B. Appleget, "The Foundation's Experience with Refugee Scholars," Mar. 5, 1946, in RG1/Series 200/Box 47/Folder 545a, RFA.

2. Norman Bentwich, *The Refugees from Germany, April 1933 to December 1935* (London, 1936), p. 174.

3. The 1939 count is from Arnold Dresden, "The Migration of Mathematics," *American Mathematical Monthly*, 49 (1942):415–29. The listing in Dresden is both chronologically incomplete and rather peculiar in some specifics. The range given here is an extrapolation. None of the sources really attempts to identify individuals who were not yet visible as members of a professional community at the time of migration, even though some entered into the field in the United States. An interesting source is Max Pinl and Lux Furtmüller, "Mathematicians under Hitler," Leo Baeck Institute, *Yearbook XVIII* (London, 1973), a revision of Pinl's series in *Jahresbericht der Deutschen*

Mathematiker-Vereinigung under the title "Kollegen in einer dunklen Zeit," 71 (1969): 167–228; 72 (1971):165–89; 73 (1972):153–208; and 75 (1974):166–208.

4. Based on Appleget, "The Foundation's Experience," and Duggan and Drury, *The Rescue of Science and Learning.*

5. As evidenced by many documents in 2/717/91/725 and 726, RFA, and elsewhere in the same collection.

6. In 2/717/92/731, RFA.

7. A.J. Sherman, *Island Refuge: Britain and Refugees from The Third Reich, 1933–1939* (Berkeley and Los Angeles, 1973), p. 259.

8. See Walter Adams, "The Refugee Scholars in the 1930s," *The Political Quarterly* 39 (1968):7–14. For contemporary comments see R.A. Lambert to A. Gregg, May 20, 1933 (2/717/91/726); Lambert memo of Oct. 2, 1933 (2/717/92/729); Lambert diary entry, July 2, 1934 (2/717/109/840), all in RFA. In his reminiscences, the physicist Hans Bethe recalled the distinction between Britain and the United States: "In America, people made me feel at once that I was going to be an American." Jeremy Bernstein, "Master of the Trade," *New Yorker*, Dec. 3, 1979, p. 100. Bethe noted about England: "It was clear there that I was a foreigner and would remain a foreigner."

9. In his autobiography, *I Am a Mathematician* (Cambridge, Mass., 1964), p. 175, Norbert Wiener names Veblen and John R. Kline. The latter shows up in sources known to me but not as significantly as does Richardson. I have not located Kline's papers, which may say more on his role. Kline succeeded Richardson as secretary of the American Mathematical Society in 1941.

10. Richardson to Max Mason, Feb. 20, 1929, 1.1/200/125/154, RFA. Veblen's papers contain charts, graphs, and tables about the improvement in mathematics in this period.

11. Richardson to G.D. Birkhoff, Feb. 25, 1932, BHA; Richardson to O.D. Kellogg, Mar. 1, 1932, RBA; minutes of Board of Trustees, AMS, Jan. 2, 1932, box 20, OV.

12. The specific spur to forming MAA was the AMS refusal to take over the *American Mathematical Monthly*. In 1938, R.C. Archibald of Brown, who favored a research emphasis, took issue with Richardson's ex post facto characterization of MAA as "child of AMS," stressing the distinction. Richardson appealed to his contemporaries for reassurance on the closeness of the two. See Richardson to E.R. Hedrick and T.S. Fiske, Oct. 15, 1938, and Hedrick's reply of Oct. 21, 1938, in Old file, AMS.

13. See Veblen to J.W. Alexander, May 1, 1923, OV.

14. Maurice R. Davie, *Refugees in America: Report of the Committee for the Study of Recent Immigration from Europe* (New York, 1947), p. 307. How this influenced social relations is shown by two anecdotes in S.M. Ulam, *Adventures of a Mathematician* (New York, 1976), pp. 90, 119.

15. E.J. Moulton, "The Unemployment Situation for Ph.D.s in Mathematics," *American Mathematical Monthly* 42 (1935):143–44. See also K.P. Williams and Elizabeth Rutherford, "An Analysis of Undergraduate Schools Attended by Mathematicians,"

School and Society 38 (1933):513–16; and "Report on the Training and Utilization of Advanced Students of Mathematics," prepared for MAA, *American Mathematical Monthly* 42 (1935):263–77.

16. R.G.D. Richardson, "The Ph.D. Degree and Mathematical Research," *American Mathematical Monthly* 43 (1936):199–215.

17. A similar conclusion was voiced by T.C. Fry to Richardson, July 12, 1935, in Semicentennial Correspondence, AMS.

18. Richardson to Birkhoff, May 17, 1927, RBA.

19. *American Mathematical Monthly* 39 (1932):126.

20. Wiener to Otto Szasz, Aug. 13, 1933, NW.

21. For example, Veblen to B.L. van der Waerden, Dec. 18, 1933, OV.

22. Coble to Richardson, June 30, 1934, Old file, AMS.

23. See *Jewish Advocate*, Dec. 14, 1934, pp. 1, 4.

24. Landauer to Wiener, Jan. 7, 1935, NW.

25. Bliss to Richardson, Apr. 10, 1935, in Lewy file, RBA.

26. Charles H. Warren to Richardson, Nov. 28, 1941, RBA.

27. See, for example, the treatment of exclusionary practices in Marcia G. Synnott, *The Half-Opened Door: Discrimination and Admissions at Harvard, Yale, and Princeton, 1900–1970* (Westport, Conn., 1978).

28. Slaught to Richardson, Jan. 23, 1931, RBA.

29. D. Buchanan to Birkhoff, Aug. 18, 1937; W.M. Smith to Birkhoff, Feb. 9, 1937, BHA.

30. Coble to Richardson, Mar. 30, 1935, Old file, AMS.

31. Paul P. Boyd to Richardson, Mar. 18, 1935, Lewy file, RBA. But the president of the university thought otherwise, expressing a desire for more men with European training.

32. K.P. Williams to Veblen, May 6, 1938, OV. Also see S.A. Mitchell to Veblen, Dec. 14, 1935, OV.

33. K.T. Compton, Memorandum of a conversation with Norbert Wiener, May 13, 1935, NW. See Wiener's comments relating to this incident in *I Am a Mathematician*, pp. 180, 211.

34. Birkhoff to Richardson, May 18, 1934, RBA.

35. Morse to Veblen, Sep. 12, 1934, OV.

36. N. Levinson to Wiener, Oct. 1, 1936, NW. For Wiener's view, see *I Am a Mathematician*, pp. 27–28.

37. "Notes," *Bulletin of the American Mathematical Society* 38 (1932): 337.

38. In RBA, T.B. Appleget of the Rockefeller Foundation was a Brown graduate, and RFA has a number of relevant letters between him and Richardson in the spring and summer of 1933.

39. Richardson to Veblen, July 3, 1933, OV. Richardson to committee, July 25, 1933, Old file, AMS.

40. Richardson to B.S. Deutsch, July 15, 1933, RBA.

41. J.R. Kline to Veblen, Nov. 23, 1933, OV.

42. Richardson to Bohr, Apr. 5, 1935, RBA.

43. In his diary entry for June 24, 1934, Warren Weaver reported the critical comments of the physicist F.K. Richtmyer of Cornell, then head of the Division of Physical Sciences of the National Research Council. Richtmyer objected to Lewy's favored treatment while so many were unemployed. 2/717/109/839, RFA.

44. Constance Reid, *Courant in Göttingen and New York* (New York, 1976), p. 227. Richardson to Bohr, Dec. 26, 1933, OV. Richardson to Birkhoff, July 21, 1936, BHA.

45. Veblen to J.H. Hildebrand, Jan. 23 and May 9, 1933, OV.

46. Evans to Veblen, Jan. 16, 1934, OV. As part of the upgrading, two American mathematicians were dismissed and four others placed on notice. Perhaps this influenced Evans. C.A. Noble to Evans, Oct. 23, 1933, carton 1, GCE.

47. Veblen to Evans, Jan. 23, 1934, OV.

48. Evans to Richardson, Apr. 18, 1934, Displaced German Scholars file, RBA.

49. Evans to Richardson, May 1, 1935, Lewy file, RBA.

50. Evans to Birkhoff, Apr. 13, 1932, BHA.

51. July 21, 1936, BHA.

52. Taken from the Göttingen Celebration file in AMS. Noble's letter is dated Apr. 10, 1937; Bell's, Apr. 9; and Wilson's, Apr. 8.

53. Based on the Semicentennial celebration folder in AMS, which is largely from 1935. See also E.R. Hedrick to L.P. Eisenhart, Jan. 30, 1937, AMS.

54. In vol. 2 of AMS, *Semicentennial Publications* (New York, 1938), pp. 276–77. Reid, *Courant*, pp. 211–13.

55. Sep. 30, 1938, BHA.

Refugee Mathematicians in the United States

56. Sep. 20, 1938, BHA.

57. H.E. Slaught, "Subsidy Funds for Mathematical Projects," *Science*, n.s. 5 (1922): 1–3.

58. Veblen to Richardson, Aug. 4, 1933; Richardson to Veblen, Aug. 9, 1933; Veblen to Richardson, Aug. 12, 1933, Displaced Scholars file, RBA.

59. Bohr to Veblen, Mar. 11, 1938; Veblen to J.H.C. Whitehead, Nov. 22, 1938, OV. Richardson to Evans, Nov. 27, 1939, *Mathematical Reviews* file, New file, AMS.

60. Veblen, pencilled draft of "The Abstract Journal Problem, Historical Background," box 17, OV.

61. Richardson to Birkhoff, Jan. 18, 1939, BHA, which also discloses opposition to Neugebauer's entering Richardson's department. The latter clash brought out explicitly the differences between the research-oriented Veblen and the AMS-oriented Richardson: "Veblen is not interested in helping build up the Society. He thinks it is being run by a group of mediocrities and has even suggested that there be a new organization of a limited number of people who are actually doing high grade research . . . [and is a] bit contemptuous of the ordinary way of looking at things." (Richardson to Mark Ingraham, Jan. 24, 1940, RBA).

62. Dec. 4, 1938, OV. Evans to Richardson, telegraph, n.d. [December 1938?], in *Mathematical Reviews* file, New file, AMS. Evans did tell Richardson to go ahead if his suggestion of Lefschetz as a member was not acceptable.

63. Richardson to Veblen, Jan. 11, 1939, box 17, OV. Richardson to Hardy, Apr. 8, 1939, in Richardson file, OV, which also contains other comments about these events.

64. Springer to Veblen, Jan. 12, 1939, in response to Veblen's letter of Dec. 5, 1938, box 17, OV. The refusal to sell is in Springer to Adams, Apr. 24, 1939, filed under F.K. Schmidt in OV.

65. Adams to Committee, Apr. 11, 1939, enclosing translated extract of Hasse to Stone of Mar. 15, 1939, which Stone received on Mar. 29, in box 17, OV. See S.L. Segal, "Helmut Hasse in 1934," *Historia Mathematica* 7 (1980):46–56.

66. For example, see the letter to Hardy cited in n. 63.

67. Copy in box 17, OV.

68. See Adams to Coble, May 3 and 8, 1939; also Schmidt to Richardson, May 15, 1939, all in box 17, OV.

69. Fry to Adams, May 19, 1939, BHA.

70. Graustein to Adams, May 11, 1939, box 17, OV.

71. Richardson to Veblen, May 13, 1939, box 17, OV. Richardson to Evans, June 28, 1939, Evans file, New file, AMS.

72. Adams to Committee, May 17, 1939, box 17, OV.

73. Stone to AMS Committee, May 24, 1939, enclosing minutes of meeting, carton 14, GCE.

74. Richardson to Evans, May 25, 1939, enclosing his letter of May 24 to AMS Committee, carton 14, GCE.

75. Birkhoff to Committee, May 22, 1939, box 17, OV.

76. May 25, 1939, in *Mathematical Reviews* file, New file, AMS. In his obituary of Birkhoff, Veblen noted that he loyally worked for the new publication "after main issues decided against his judgement" (see Birkhoff's *Collected Papers*, vol. 1 [1950], p. xxi).

77. In 1947–48, when F.K. Schmidt and others decided to revive a German abstracting journal for mathematics, both Veblen and Courant were bothered by what Courant described as the "aggressive German nationalistic attitude" (Schmidt to Courant, Dec. 1, 1947; Courant to Schmidt, Jan. 14, 1948; Courant to Veblen, Feb. 3, 1948; all in Master Index File, CIMS. Veblen to Schmidt, Feb. 25, 1948, OV). In 1938–39, Courant stayed out of the discussions because of his relations with the Springer firm.

78. May 23, 1938; in Cairns file, New file, AMS.

79. Richardson to Hermann Weyl, June 25, 1941, RBA.

80. Dec. 12, 1938, General File, CIMS.

81. July 22, 1938, OV.

82. See Duggan and Drury, *The Rescue of Science and Learning*, pp. 96–101; and the comments in David C. Thomson, "The United States and the Academic Exiles," *Queens Quarterly*, Summer 1939, pp. 212–25. This proposal continued the theme of protecting young American scholars while clearly reflecting an impatience with a process in which a nonacademic body exerted pressure.

83. In box 29, OV.

84. Morse to Evans, carton 14, GCE.

85. C.A. Browne, "The Role of Refugees in the History of American Science," *Science*, n.s. 91 (1940):203–8.

86. Arnold Dresden, "The Migration of Mathematics."

87. Feb. 11, 1943, in Frucht file, box 30, OV. The addition of a Czech and two Polish mathematicians indicates the widening effect of Nazism.

88. Lindsay Harmon and Herbert Soldz, *Doctorate Production in United States Universities* (Washington, D.C., 1963), from tables in Appendix 1.

89. U.S. Bureau of the Census, *Historical Statistics of the United States* (Washington, D.C., 1957), p. 210.

231

90. Spencer R. Weart, "The Physics Business in America, 1919–1940: A Statistical Reconnaissance," in Nathan Reingold, ed., *The Sciences in the American Context: New Perspectives* (Washington, D.C., 1979), pp. 295–358.

91. Duggan and Drury, *The Rescue of Science and Learning*, p. 68; Veblen's Summary of Defense, item 11, box 21, OV.

92. See, for example, the recent article by Richard Weiss, "Ethnicity and Reform: Minorities and the Ambience of the Depression Years," *Journal of American History* 66 (1979):566–85.

93. In RFA, 2/717/92/730, is a note of a conversation of Nov. 6, 1933, between A.V. Hill and R.A. Lambert of the Rockefeller Foundation on this point. See Lambert's earlier statement of Oct. 2, 1933 in 2/717/92/729.

232

CULTURAL ADAPTATION
IN WORLDWIDE PERSPECTIVE

The Role of Switzerland for the Refugees

HELMUT F. PFANNER

No other country has given such an open account of its refugee policy as Switzerland, and no other country has been more severely criticized for its response to the refugee problem of the 1930s and 1940s than this small nation of six million people who lived in close proximity to the Nazi war machine. In 1954, when politicians abroad were nurturing the cold war, the Swiss government (Bundesrat) requested a detailed investigation of its country's handling of the European refugee crisis between 1933 and that date. Three years later, Professor Carl Ludwig furnished an objective report containing many historical facts and a critical assessment of Switzerland's refugee policy during the given period.[1] His work prompted several additional studies that tried either to defend or to attack Switzerland's role in the saving of human lives from Nazi persecution.[2] The simile of a small lifeboat on a torrid ocean, coined by the Swiss Federal Councilor Eduard von Steiger in 1942, was reintroduced into the discussion, and, depending on a critic's outlook, it was felt either that the boat had been crowded beyond capacity or that it could have held more people. Both sides are still reflected in two studies that appeared in the last decade, the one contending that, once reliable data on all countries' management of the refugees become available, Switzerland will appear "in the most unfavorable light,"[3] and the other one refuting any such negative generalization against the Swiss nation.[4]

Although the small geographical size and population of Switzerland do not seem to warrant the comparison, the country had a basis for coping with the large influx of unexpected refugees from Nazi Germany similar to the United States's. In each case an established tradition of giving asylum to those who were persecuted elsewhere for political or religious reasons existed, and throughout the years, an open-door policy had long been upheld, though any formalization of this policy had only come about during the past one hundred years. In both countries, the economic crisis of the 1930s deeply affected the general political and social conditions, leaving many people unemployed and encouraging anti-alien sentiments. Nazi agents infiltrated Switzerland and the United States after Hitler's rise to power; the pro-Nazi party in the United States, the German-American Bund, had its equivalent in Switzerland, the so-called Vaterländische Front.[5] German exiles who recounted their experiences with Nazi terror to their Swiss and American hosts generally felt that their words fell on deaf ears. The very fact that they had left their homes was viewed with suspicion, as reflected in this remark by a Swiss citizen to Klaus Mann: "Don't you realize what an awful blunder you make? To give up your home, your friends, your career—everything! On account of what? Because you have an animosity to Herr Hitler's nose."[6] Not until 1943, when several reports about the mass murder of Jews by the Nazis were published in Swiss and American newspapers, did large numbers of the population begin to sympathize with the victims. By then, however, it was already too late for many to be saved, and for others who had escaped death in Germany the democratic state bureaucracy in the United States and in Switzerland moved too slowly to ameliorate their situation noticeably before the Third Reich was defeated.

Despite all these similarities, there were also some obvious differences between the situations in the two countries. Since Switzerland was closer to Germany than the United States, it was also closer to the Nazi threat. On the other hand, the geography helped make it far less expensive to escape to Switzerland than to the Western Hemisphere. But to some refugees the natural obstacle of the Atlantic Ocean may not have appeared any more difficult to overcome than the man-made barrier of the heavily guarded Swiss border.

In 1933 the first wave of German refugees from Hitler arrived in Switzerland, numbering about two thousand persons. These figures gradually increased during the 1930s and quickly jumped to somewhere between ten and twelve thousand in 1938, after the *Anschluss*

HELMUT F. PFANNER

of Austria.[7] While at first many refugees came as legal immigrants, the number of illegal entries into Switzerland rose during the late 1930s and early 1940s, when more and more countries fell under Nazi domination, and the Swiss authorities simultaneously imposed greater restrictions on legal immigration into their country. Because the refugees were also constantly encouraged to proceed to other countries, only seventy-one hundred foreigners (not counting the members of the various diplomatic corps) were living in Switzerland in September 1939, when the war broke out in Europe. But soon afterwards new waves of refugees arrived, especially after the Nazi conquest of France in 1940 and the German occupation of Belgium and Holland in 1942, and during the forced deportation of European Jews from France between the latter part of 1942 and the spring of 1943.

Altogether some 300,000 people fled to Switzerland during the six years of World War II, a figure that included many military refugees and deserters. In mid-1944 the main stream of refugees began to flow in the opposite direction, as they were able to find asylum in other countries, such as Palestine or the United States, or began to return, via France, to their old homes in the liberated parts of Europe. Nevertheless, almost 115,000 refugees were still left in Switzerland at the end of the war. How much greater this number might have been if many refugees without legal documents had not been turned back at the Swiss border, and if others had not been deported from the country because they entered illegally or worked without a permit, is not known exactly. The official reports of the Swiss border guards list 9,751 persons turned back at the border between August 1942 and May 1945.[8] Some of those rejected once may have been able to enter successfully later, while others who might have wanted to go to Switzerland may never have dared to make an attempt, knowing the danger of being handed over to the Gestapo if they were caught at the border.

One specific facet of Swiss refugee policy merits special attention because of its detrimental consequences for many German and Austrian Jews. During the first five years of the Third Reich, anyone with a legal passport was able to enter Switzerland; however, in the summer of 1938, after the arrival of a large number of Austrian refugees, the Swiss government adopted two measures that reflected their fear that the country's population might undergo a process of "alienation" if it admitted all the Jews who wanted to escape Hitler.[9] First, they suggested that the Germans mark all passports of Jews

237

living in the Third Reich with the letter *J*, which the Nazis actually began to do in October of that year. At the same time, the Foreign Office in Bern instructed all of its consular officers abroad to require a visa of anyone wanting to immigrate to Switzerland. The Swiss consuls, then, just like the Nazis, were able to discriminate between "Aryan" and "non-Aryan" applicants.

The devastating effects of this policy soon became apparent, for even while Germany and Switzerland were still exchanging diplomatic notes about the letter *J*, many of the thousands of German Jews who had to leave their homes and businesses during the *Kristallnacht* of November 1938 headed for the Swiss border, where, if they lacked a visa, they were not allowed to pass. During the following years many *Schriftenlose* (as the Swiss called foreigners without the proper papers) were sent back across the border. To see the anti-Semitic intention behind the Swiss refugee policy in its full light, one only needs to read the confidential bulletin that Heinrich Rothmund, the chief of the Swiss Alien Police Office in Bern, sent to all his subordinate departments on August 4, 1942: "Refugees in flight solely because of racial reasons—Jews, for example—do not qualify as political refugees."[10] That this definition of a "political" refugee clearly contradicted events in Germany and in all Nazi-occupied countries did not seem to bother Rothmund, whom the Swiss sometimes ironically called their "eighth Federal Council."[11] But even those refugees who could, by Rothmund's definition, qualify as political refugees were to be treated "in such a way that they themselves would prefer to be sent back and that the others still waiting on the other side of the border would be discouraged from making any attempt to flee into Switzerland."[12]

If such statements reflected the official Swiss attitude toward the refugees, it would be wrong to assume that the average Swiss citizen felt the same. Actually, a large part of the population seems to have favored a different position, expressed in verbal and written protests by Swiss from all walks of life, including writers, journalists, publishers, actors, cabaret satirists, lawyers, physicians, politicians, teachers, clergymen, soldiers, workers, and housemaids.[13] Perhaps the most prestigious Swiss voice supporting the cause of the refugees was that of the theologian Karl Barth, who appealed to his government on their behalf in a speech before a large religious meeting in Zurich in 1941. His words must have been very effective, since the planned publication of the speech was officially stopped.[14] On a more personal level Gertrud Kurz, who headed the Christian Peace Center

238

in Bern, and who was widely looked upon as "the mother of the refugees," pleaded with Councilman von Steiger to rescind, or at least to mitigate, the terms under which refugees without visas and passports were to be turned back at the border; her appeal caused von Steiger to send a memorandum to the Swiss border personnel allowing them to make certain exceptions.[15] In contrast to these sympathetic voices, the "Frontists" and other nationalistic organizations made loud propaganda against the alleged "submersion" of Switzerland by alien elements.[16] Eventually, but not until July 12, 1944, when the defeat of Nazi Germany was clearly foreseeable, the Swiss doves in the refugee question won a clear victory. On that date the Police Section of the Helvetic government formally rescinded the racial restriction in their refugee policy, thereby granting asylum to any "foreigners who for political *or other* reasons are in actual peril of life and limb and who have no way of avoiding this danger other than that of flight to Switzerland."[17] Although the new ruling came too late for those millions of people who had already been killed in Auschwitz and other Nazi extermination camps, it helped to save many others under equal danger—for example, several thousand Hungarian Jews whom the Nazis were willing to trade for money and scarce raw materials.

What sort of life did the people who found asylum in Switzerland face? Many of those who had left Germany during the early years of Nazi power had been able to transfer sufficient funds to support themselves and their families in small Swiss hotels until they found a new source of livelihood or immigrated to another country. Some could live with Swiss friends or relatives. Private groups, supported by religious and professional organizations, cared for those without sufficient means of their own. In 1939, all Swiss relief efforts were consolidated by the Central Swiss Refugee Relief Office, which, at first, received only moderate government funding, primarily to relocate the refugees in other countries. But in the summer of 1942, with the great increase in the number of new refugees, the need arose for the government in Bern to bear a larger portion of the financial support for the refugees living in Switzerland. Already in existence was a law that taxed all refugees in possession of more than twenty thousand Swiss franks on a graded scale, for the purpose of caring for those others in need. In 1940 the first labor camps were established. Physically able men were employed in road building, civic improvement, or farming; women were assigned to tasks such as mending and laundry work. In March 1943, when the number of

239

refugees in Switzerland reached its peak, an entire system of refugee camps was established by the Federal Council: collection camps for newly arrived refugees; quarantine camps where they were examined by the Swiss Army's Health Service; reception camps for those people whose status could not be sufficiently clarified during their stay in the collection and quarantine camps; labor camps for the able-bodied between the ages of twenty and sixty; training camps for the young refugees between the ages of seventeen and nineteen.[18] Students could continue studies begun in their home countries as long as they or a relief organization provided for their financial support.[19] All other refugees who did not fall into any of the above groups, such as children under seventeen years of age, mothers with children under six, and old people, were assembled in special boarding houses. Only those with substantial financial means were "privately interned."

Life in the Swiss camps has been severely criticized by German exile writers. Max Brusto, for example, complained about the insufficient quantity and poor quality of the food, the lack of warm bedding, and the unfriendly treatment by the camp guards. He also criticized his camp physician and other Swiss camp employees for having made anti-Semitic statements.[20] Lee van Dovski had similar experiences in another camp, but his report reflected more the psychological pain that resulted from the refugees' awareness of their "unfree" state in "the country of freedom."[21] Both authors, however, dealt repeatedly with the special problems of the intellectual refugees, a consequence of their greater-than-average psychological sensitivity and also their limited ability to cope with physical hardship. What the camp guards sometimes saw as an expression of the refugee intellectuals' asocial character may, in fact, have been provoked by the Swiss trying to impose their idea of "democratic coordination" upon them: intellectuals were expected to perform the same kinds of duties in the labor camps as refugee farm laborers.[22]

To German and Austrian intellectuals fleeing the Third Reich, Switzerland had seemed to be an especially attractive place of asylum because of the country's major language, German. Many refugee intellectuals, therefore, came to Switzerland hoping to be able to continue in their old professions and, at the same time, to take part in the political battle against the Nazi dictators in their homelands. What a false expectation! Aiming at neutrality, the Swiss authorities prohibited political activities among the refugees and also tried to suppress verbal and written attacks against their strong German neighbors. In addition, Switzerland had seriously hindered the exiles' prospects for work by passing a law that forbade foreigners from engaging in any kind of profitable occupation. But like most laws, this one had its loopholes, and exceptions were made for different groups and individuals. As far as the German and Austrian writers were concerned, the Swiss Writers' Union acted on a case-by-case basis to advise the Swiss government whether an author should be allowed to publish or not. The members of the union were anxious about their own diminished possibilities for publication in the German-speaking countries and, even more so, about the competition that they saw in the large number of foreign writers in their own country. Consequently, when they were asked for evaluations, they clearly favored those German and Austrian authors who, in the themes and genres of their works, concentrated on specialities other than their own.[23] Their lack of interest in lyrical poetry, for example, was reflected in the positive recommendations they gave to the two German-language exile poets Alfred Ehrenstein and Else Lasker-Schüler. Writers of prose literature with travel themes, a rather neglected area of Swiss writing, also had a better chance. Thus, Wilhelm Hoegner and Ernst Preczang, both of whom fell in this category, received the union's stamp of endorsement. On the other hand, many excellent German-language refugee journalists and fiction authors were not allowed to publish. Although the reasons were quite obvious, they were not always directly expressed. In the case of Alexander Roda Roda, the union claimed that his work "had very little to do with Switzerland" and could therefore not contribute to the country's intellectual life;[24] and Victoria Wolff was not able to renew her Swiss residence permit after the Swiss Writers' Union had bluntly stated that the country "will lose nothing by this."[25] Both of these authors ended up in American exile. So did Thomas Mann, although the Swiss authorities saw no need to solicit the Writers' Union's endorsement in his case: the Nobel-Prize-winning author was not hindered in any of his literary activities. However, when Mann's German publisher, Gottfried Bermann Fischer, tried to transfer his firm from Berlin to Zurich in 1935, he encountered closed doors. To be sure, the Swiss publishers would have been happy to incorporate the famous Samuel Fischer Company's publication rights, but they did not want to allow the German publisher to get a foothold in Switzerland.[26]

As were the Swiss immigration rules in general, so was the country's official handling of the refugee intellectuals challenged and secretly contradicted by individual Swiss citizens. Many German and Austrian men of letters found a close friend in the Swiss publisher Emil Oprecht, who specialized in the publication of anti-Fascist and anti-Nazi literature. In 1937, the Swiss government, under pressure from the German Embassy in Bern, asked Oprecht to curtail his publication of books that were critical of Nazi ideology and events in Germany, but Oprecht successfully defended his right to objective reporting and criticism. The Nazis then took steps against Oprecht directly by excluding him from the worldwide German Book Dealers' Association in Leipzig and also by publishing a series of anti-Semitic booklets under the name of Europa Verlag, which was also the name of one of Oprecht's two publishing houses in Zurich.[27] Despite these attacks and the resulting losses, Oprecht remained loyal to the refugees. The only major literary exile periodical in Switzerland, Thomas Mann's *Mass und Wert* (co-edited by Mann and Konrad Falke, and after Mann's immigration to the United States carried on by his son Golo Mann and Ferdinand Lion), was also published by Oprecht. Another exile periodical of more political than literary content was published by the Ähren-Verlag under the title *Über die Grenzen* (Across the Borders); the German communist Michael Tschesno-Hell served as the journal's chief editor during the one year (1944–45) in which all its fourteen issues were printed. A number of Swiss journals and newspapers carried contributions by German and Austrian refugees who used pseudonyms to protect themselves from the Swiss Alien Police.

Individual Swiss citizens provided shelter and meeting space in their homes for German-language intellectuals. For instance, the Swiss writer R.H. Humm opened his Zurich home to many German theater people, among them: Ernst Ginsberg, Wolfgang Heinz, Kurt Horwitz, Erwin Kalser, Wolfgang Langhoff, Leopold Lindtberg, Teo Otto, and Leonard Steckel.[28] Also in Zurich, the lawyer Wladimir Rosenbaum and his artist-wife Aline were hosts to the writer Hans Marchwitza, the composer Wladimir Vogel, and the painter Spepude.[29] Marcel Fleischmann, a grain salesman, Alis Guggenheim, a pictorial artist, and Hermann Hesse, the German writer who had become a Swiss citizen in 1932, were frequently visited by refugee intellectuals. Certain well-to-do exiles played important roles for their less fortunate German or Austrian compatriots: The industrialist and writer Julius Marx was a close friend of the German dramatist Georg Kaiser; and Thomas Mann stood in the center of a circle of friends including the German novelist Bruno Frank, the composer

242

Bruno Walter, and his own brother Heinrich Mann. Without the help of a newly found Swiss friend, Robert Lejeune, the now famous Austrian writer Robert Musil might not have been able to complete his master work, *Der Mann ohne Eigenschaften* (The Man without Qualities). Lejeune was a Zurich clergyman who provided Musil with financial support and also prevented his deportation from Switzerland.

The fear of deportation had a very strong effect upon the refugees and was closely connected to the emotional frustration caused by the Swiss law against their engaging in any profitable occupation. Occasional acts of, and (more frequently) thoughts of, suicide among the refugees in Switzerland must be understood as the consequence of these fears and frustrations.[30] But the long periods of idleness and depression could also generate visions of their own grandeur and a certain amount of self-pity for the lack of recognition by their Swiss hosts. "There are many among us," Lee van Dovski proclaimed, "who could be the same for Switzerland what Spinoza is for Holland, what Marie Curie, van Gogh, Von Dongen and Picasso are for France; foreigners who will some day be called the pride and glory of the country."[31] Future historians will have to tell us who of the intellectual refugees in Switzerland (among them, 180 writers alone still lived there at the end of the war)[32] belong in that category. There is no doubt, however, that the Swiss law did not encourage the creativity of the German and Austrian intellectuals. When the German journalist Kunz von Kauffungen tried to paint the ceiling of the primitive hut in which he lived with his Dutch wife in the French part of Switzerland, he was stopped by the local policemen, who informed him that his activity was depriving some Swiss painter of a job.[33] The protagonist in the exile novel *Die Steine* (The Stones), written by the German actress Jo Mihaly, is a German physician who is warned by the local policeman, when he gives a hand to a farmer and his foaling horse, that he does not have a work permit.[34]

The largest loophole in the Swiss law against refugee employment was the one for theater people, for they were considered seasonable workers and, as such, could be employed from one season to the next. The Zürcher Schauspielhaus could draw on the many great German actors, stage designers and other theater workers living in Switzerland during this time, and, thus, it developed into a highly renowned center of German stage art. In addition to the persons mentioned earlier, the cast included such German and Austrian stars as Therese Giehse, Karl Paryla, and Mathilde Danegger. Although other Swiss theaters also employed German exile actors, the Zürcher Schauspielhaus, because it was privately owned, could be used more directly by the German directors and actors as a vehicle of anti-Nazi propaganda. Moreover, it provided exile dramatists with the largest German-speaking audience for the performance of their works. Brecht's *Mutter Courage* (Mother Courage), Ferdinand Bruckner's *Die Rassen* (Races), and Friedrich Wolf's *Professor Mannheim* (Professor Mamlock) were performed there with great success as were some works of the classical European tradition, such as Goethe's *Goetz von Berlichingen* and Shakespeare's *Troilus and Cressida*, which bore an unmistakable humanistic and antimilitaristic message. On a different scale, but certainly no less effective, was the anti-Nazi propaganda that the satirical cabaret The Peppermill, under the direction of Erika Mann, generated in Zurich and other Swiss cities. After repeated interference by Nazi hecklers, however, The Peppermill was forced to halt its performances in Switzerland in 1937. Erika Mann and her cast later made an unsuccessful attempt to repeat their European successes in the United States. In Zurich, another cabaret, named Cornichon, was able to continue the fight against political and social evils of the time. Since it had a Swiss director, it was not affected by the new law against foreign cabarets with a political tendency. Cornichon was also able to employ German and Austrian refugee actors, and its program contained some texts by German-language exile writers such as Hans Sahl.

Despite their common goal of fighting the Nazis, German exile intellectuals in Switzerland, as in other countries, were politically quite diversified. Their differing ideas about Germany's future were discussed in secret groups that they formed in Switzerland and that were inspired by similar associations of German-language exiles living in Moscow and in New York. Although at first members of several different parties joined together in these new organizations, the Free Germany Movement clearly followed communist directions, while the Council for a Democratic Germany was modeled after the constitutions of the Western democracies. After the battle of Stalingrad, in 1943, the German political exiles began to make plans for the rebuilding of Germany; in their ideological divisions, they unconsciously foreshadowed the later partition of their country. Many Jewish refugees did not wish to return to their former homes, but a majority of them also did not want to remain in Switzerland: the United States and Palestine (later Israel) became more attractive. At this point, one must guard against idealizing the refugees who,

244

despite their historical plight, were not without the personal short-comings of human nature. As acts of prejudice are not the peculiar feature of any race or religion, confrontations occurred among the newcomers as well as between them and their already established coreligionists.[35] A large part of the exile novel *Liebe deinen Nächsten* (Flotsam) by Erich Maria Remarque takes place in Switzerland, and one of the most pitiful scenes in it occurs when the chief protagonist, after many experiences of unselfish help, loses all his money, forty franks, to a thief, another refugee.[36] Both the positive and the negative side of the exile are expressed in the words with which Remarque's hero confesses his creed: "I believe in the holy egotism! In merci-lessness! In lying! In the indolence of the heart! . . . [but] I also believe in goodwill, in friendship, in love, and in the readiness to help others!"[37]

As this confession mirrors both the good and the bad consequences of exile for the refugees, on a larger scale it also sums up the attitude with which the Swiss nation reacted to the refugee crisis. On the one hand, there were cruel regulations that restricted the free flow of persecuted people across the Swiss border; on the other hand, there were persons who risked their own freedom in order to help others. There were docile border guards who handed defenseless human beings over to their murderers, but there were also anony-mous peasants who hid unknown strangers in their haylofts. Besides the German and Austrian intellectuals already mentioned, many others found either permanent or temporary asylum in Switzerland during this period, among them: Wilhelm Abegg, Theodor Balk, Alfred Bassermann, Johannes R. Becher, Ulrich Becker, Richard Beer-Hofmann, Walter Benjamin, Ernst Bloch, Otto Braun, Bernard von Brentano, Hermann Broch, Eduard Claudius, Alfred Döblin, Julius Epstein, Walter Fabian, Leonhard Frank, Hans Habe, Julius Hay, Konrad Heiden, Stefan Hermlin, Max Hermann-Neisse, Wilhelm Herzog, Rudolf Hilferding, Paul Hindemith, Kurt Hirschfeld, Ödön von Horváth, Hanns Henny Jahn, Erich von Kahler, Bruno Kaiser, Alfred Kerr, Kurt Kersten, Arthur Koestler, Oskar Kokoschka, An-nette Kolb, Heinz Liepman, Hubertus Prinz von Loewenstein, Emil Ludwig, Hans Mayer, Carl Meffert-Moreau, Walter Mehring, Max Ophüls, Hertha Pauli, Alfred Polgar, Hermann Rauschning, Gustav Regler, Hans Richter, Joseph Roth, Hermann Scherschen, Anna Se-ghers, Willi Oscar Somin, Manès Sperber, Karl Spiecker, Herbert Steiner, Ernst Toller, Friedrich Torberg, Kurt Tucholsky, Walther Victor, Jakob Wassermann, Hans Weigel, Erich Weinert, Peter Weiss, Franz Werfel, Joseph Wirth, Karl August Wittfogel, Karl Wolfskehl,   245

Carl Zuckmayer, and Stefan Zweig. Future studies will have to determine to what extent the encounter of these intellectuals with Switzerland has influenced their works or the intellectual life of their Swiss host country.

Most of the refugees who came to Switzerland between 1933 and 1945 left again after a relatively short time, with some of them returning to their old homes after the war. As a result, the country's major role in the handling of the refugee crisis was that of providing a way station for people en route to other countries. It is certainly easy to see the black spot that was caused by its anti-Semitic admission practices during the late 1930s and early 1940s; nevertheless, in the overall picture of refugee migration, Switzerland can stand the test of comparison with other countries. After 1945, when the period of exile had ended, many German and Austrian refugee intellectuals returned to Switzerland in their search for a final home, either as a result of even worse experiences elsewhere or because of their inability to readjust to living in their native countries.

Notes

1. Carl Ludwig, *Die Flüchtlingspolitik der Schweiz seit 1933 bis zur Gegenwart 1957* (Bern, 1966).

2. See especially Alfred A. Häsler, *Das Boot ist voll: Die Schweiz und ihre Flüchtlinge 1933–1945* (Zurich, 1967); Eng. trans. *The Lifeboat Is Full: Switzerland and the Refugees 1933–1945* (New York, 1969); Victor Willi, *Überfremdung: Schlagwort oder bittere Wahrheit?* (Bern, 1970); Oskar Felix Fritschi, *Geistige Landesverteidigung während des Zweiten Weltkrieges* (Dietikon-Zurich, 1972); and Werner Rings, *Schweiz im Krieg. 1933–1945: Ein Bericht* (Zurich, 1974).

3. Werner Mittenzwei, *Exil in der Schweiz* (Leipzig, 1978), p. 16.

4. Ulrich Seelmann-Eggebert, "Die Exilsituation in der Schweiz," in Manfred Durzak, ed., *Die deutsche Exilliteratur* (Stuttgart, 1933), p. 105.

5. There were about three hundred pro-Nazi organizations in Switzerland, according to Willi, *Überfremdung*, p. 57.

6. Klaus Mann, *The Turning Point: Thirty-five Years in This Century* (New York, 1942), p. 267.

7. Cf. Peter Stahlberger, *Der Zürcher Verleger Emil Oprecht und die deutsche politische Emigration 1933–1945* (Zurich, 1970), p. 58; and Häsler, *Lifeboat*, p. 25.

8. Cf. Ludwig, *Die Flüchtlingspolitik*, pp. 245, 271, 309; also Häsler, *Lifeboat*, p. 331.

9. The reality of this fear is clearly suggested by the title of Willi's book (*Überfremdung*).

HELMUT F. PFANNER

10. Häsler, *Lifeboat*, p. 82.

11. Cf. Kurt R. Grossmann, *Emigration: Geschichte der Hitler–Flüchtlinge 1933–1945* (Frankfurt am Main, 1969), p. 242.

12. From the files of JUNA (the Jewish Overseas News Agency) in Geneva, as quoted by Häsler, *Lifeboat*, p. 103.

13. Cf. Häsler, *Lifeboat*, p. 116.

14. Cf. Alice Meyer, *Anpassung oder Widerstand: Die Schweiz zur Zeit des deutschen Nationalsozialismus* (Frauenfeld, 1966), p. 182.

15. Cf. Häsler, *Lifeboat*, p. 131.

16. Ibid., p. 207.

17. Ibid., p. 285.

18. Cf. ibid., p. 339.

19. Cf. Ludwig, *Die Flüchtlingspolitik*, pp. 276–79.

20. Max Brusto, *Im Schweizer Rettungsboot: Dokumentation* (Munich, 1967), pp. 17ff.

21. Lee van Dovski, *Schweizer Tagebuch eines Internierten* (Utrecht, 1946), p. 93.

22. Häsler, *Lifeboat*, p. 264.

23. Cf. ibid., pp. 279–80.

24. Ibid., p. 280.

25. Ibid., p. 275.

26. Cf. Gottfried Bermann Fischer, *Bedroht–bewahrt: Weg eines Verlegers* (Frankfurt am Main, 1967), pp. 118–20.

27. Cf. Stahlberger, *Der Zürcher Verleger Emil Oprecht*, pp. 121–23, 134, 274.

28. Cf. Mittenzwei, *Exil in der Schweiz*, p. 72.

29. Cf. ibid., pp. 75–79.

30. An exile's suicide in Switzerland has been documented in Wilhelm Hoegner, *Der schwierige Außenseiter: Erinnerungen eines Abgeordneten, Emigranten und Ministerpräsidenten* (Munich, 1959), p. 146; more frequently only the *temptation* to commit suicide is reflected in the exiles' memoirs—e.g., with reference to the German dramatist Georg Kaiser, in Julius Marx, *Georg Kaiser, ich und die anderen: Alles in einem Leben. Ein Bericht in Tagebuchform* (Gütersloh, West Germany, 1970), pp. 107–8, 111.

31. Van Dovski, *Schweizer Tagebuch*, p. 53.

247

The Role of Switzerland for the Refugees

32. Cf. Mittenzwei, *Exil in der Schweiz*, p. 11.

33. Cf. Kunz von Kauffungen, *Ohne Maulkorb: Erlebnisse eines Nonkonformisten* (Bern, Stuttgart, and Vienna 1964), p. 257.

34. Jo Mihaly, *Die Steine: Roman* (Stuttgart, 1946), p. 112.

35. Cf. Erich Maria Remarque, *Liebe deinen Nächsten: Roman* (Munich, 1953), p. 214, Eng. trans. *Flotsam* (Boston, 1941); the tension that existed between Eastern and Western Jews in the United States during the same period is described in "Immigranten und jüdische Umwelt," *Aufbau* (New York), Feb. 5, 1943, p. 14.

36. Remarque, *Liebe*, p. 241.

37. Ibid., pp. 267–68.

Intellectual Émigrés in Britain, 1933–1939

BERNARD WASSERSTEIN

One refugee is a novelty, ten refugees are boring, and a hundred refugees are a menace.

This is the epigraph to A.J. Sherman's book, *Island Refuge: Britain and Refugees from the Third Reich 1933–1939* (1973), which was the first work on the subject to draw on the newly released official documents at the Public Record Office. Sherman's conclusions aroused surprise and criticism, especially among some Americans. Yet they have, I believe, withstood attack, and the book remains the best all-around consideration of British official policy towards refugees in the 1930s.

Sherman's central conclusion was expressed as follows:

The standard charges, based on a narrow view of the Palestine problem, of British Government lack of generosity or indeed of indifference to the fate of refugees from the Nazi regime must receive the verdict of "not proven".... Despite confusion, hesitations, and often a lack of appreciation that time could literally mean life or death, a relatively large number of refugees did manage to find sanctuary within Great Britain and her dependencies, and a comparison with other countries yields a not unimpressive record.[1]

Of the fifty-six thousand refugees who reached Britain from Germany, Austria, and Czechoslovakia between 1933 and 1939, only a

249

small fraction fell into the category of "intellectual émigrés." But this category included, of course, several names of international eminence, and as a whole the group made a quite disproportionate impact on the host society. The story of this intellectual migration can, in many ways, be regarded as a litmus test for the reaction of British society in general to the refugee phenomenon. It also provides us with a case study against which to test the general argument of Sherman's book.

From the very outset of the refugee crisis in 1933, it was clearly recognized in government circles that intellectuals among the potential refugees were a group who were both specially endangered and specially gifted in ways that might benefit Great Britain. In the course of a cabinet discussion on April 12, 1933, it was pointed out that it would be in the public interest to

> try to secure for this country prominent Jews who were being expelled from Germany and who had achieved distinction whether in pure science, applied science, such as medicine or technical industry, music or art. This would not only obtain for this country the advantage of their knowledge and experience, but would also create a very favorable impression in the world, particularly if our hospitality were offered with some warmth.[2]

Broadly speaking, that expression of hospitality based on enlightened self-interest remained an accurate description of British policy until the outbreak of the war. It was particularly apparent during the last frenzied rush out of the Third Reich in the period after the Anschluss in 1938, when guidelines were issued to British consuls and passport control officers for special favorable treatment to be accorded prominent intellectuals who applied for British entry visas.

However, some caveats must be entered to somewhat cloud this generally rosy picture. With few exceptions, the British government did not make public funds available for the reception or absorption of intellectual émigrés. In general, the refugee migration (some 90 percent of which was Jewish) proceeded on the basis of a guarantee given in 1933 by the representative leaders of the Anglo-Jewish community that no refugee who entered England under their auspices would become a public charge. The most extravagant estimate then of the potential number of arrivals was four thousand. Yet the guarantee was maintained until after the outbreak of the war, by which time over fifty thousand Jewish refugees had arrived and over five million pounds had been raised from Jewish sources (plus more from non-Jews) to prevent their falling on the public purse. (We have to

250

remember that this was from a community of some 350,000 people and at a time when the pound was a real pound.)

The government, therefore, restricted its role in regard to intellectual émigrés to one of benevolent laissez-faire rather than vigorous direction. Occasionally one encounters in the official documents a tendency toward complacency or myopia. For example, in April 1936, Lord Cranborne, at that time a junior minister at the Foreign Office, recorded his irritation at Professor Lewis Namier for his approach favoring refugees. (Namier, of course, was himself an intellectual émigré of an earlier vintage. He was highly active on behalf of German refugee academics but often "put the backs up" of the ministers and officials he lobbied.) Cranborne wrote on this occasion:

I am glad no encouragement was given to Professor Namier. He is a most tiresome person, and we already know he is not to be trusted. We cannot say often enough to Jews of this type that people do not become refugees until they leave their country of origin. While they are still there, their treatment is a question of internal policy.[3]

Given the self-effacing role of the government, the chief task of organization and reception of intellectual refugees devolved on unofficial bodies. Here the Anglo-Saxon genius for voluntary association for public works found its fullest expression. In April 1933 the Academic Assistance Council (later known as the Society for the Protection of Science and Learning) was formed. The president was the most eminent scientist of the day, Lord Rutherford, and the leading members constituted a galaxy of British intellectual life, among them Sir Frederick Kenyon, Professor A.V. Hill, Lord Cecil of Chelwood, and H.A.L. Fisher. The only Jewish member was Samuel Alexander, professor of philosophy at Manchester, and the very energetic general secretary was Walter Adams (later head of University College of Rhodesia and still later of the London School of Economics).

The Academic Assistance Council's aims were formally defined as "the relief of suffering and the defence of learning and science [and] assisting university teachers and other investigators of whatever country who on grounds of religion, political opinion, or 'race' are unable to carry on their work in their own country."[4] Parallel to the general council there was a Jewish Academic Committee (later the Professional Committee), of which the first chairman was Sir Philip Hartog, ex-registrar of London University.

The AAC was launched at a mass meeting in the Royal Albert

251

Hall presided over by Lord Rutherford and addressed by Albert Einstein. It soon gathered two thousand subscribing members (drawn in particular from universities), and it provided "life belts" for several hundred refugee academics. The AAC secured the blessing both of the government and of broad segments of educated public opinion as expressed in such papers as the *Times, Manchester Guardian, New Statesman,* and *Observer.* Overall, the AAC was a striking example of British generosity and voluntary organization.

There were, however, certain less heartening occurrences that should be mentioned. Professor Selig Brodetsky of Leeds University, who served on the executive committee of the AAC, recorded in his memoirs a conversation with the vice-chairman, Professor A.V. Hill, who "said that he did not like Jewish academic refugees being admitted to British academic life because Jews had a habit of filling their departments with Jews. I asked him to give an example. He did not refer to it again."

Brodetsky continued:

But the same trouble came up at the meeting of the Council of the Association of University Teachers when it met at Exeter. I moved a resolution from the Leeds branch welcoming academic refugees at the British universities. Some members of the Association saw that as a danger to themselves. They were afraid of sacrificing their own chances of promotion out of charity to others. I said that I agreed with their fears, and suggested that our resolution should be amended accordingly. This was done, and the following resolution was adopted almost unanimously:

"That the AUT is ready to cooperate with a view to the temporary accommodation and provision of special facilities at the British universities for teachers deprived of their posts in German and other universities . . . it being understood that such facilities be provided out of moneys made specially available and that the usual channels of promotion in the profession be not thereby affected."[5]

Similar attitudes, often based on a mixture of fear of the impact on the labor market of a large refugee influx and on ignorance of or blindness to the reality of the terror in Nazi Germany, can be discerned if we look briefly at some of the specific academic groups involved.

First, refugees in the sciences included some of the most outstanding figures to come to Britain, and they made an immense contribution to British intellectual life and, of course, to the British war effort. Among them were Hermann Bondi, Nicholas Kurti, Rudolf Peierls, Ernst Chain, and (the non-Jewish) Klaus Fuchs (who later defected to the Soviet Union). Here was the most obvious and immediate area of advantage to the host country, and there was indeed little hostility to the immigration of such men. Nevertheless, the attitude in some important quarters was half-hearted rather than open-hearted. Lord Snow recorded the example of Professor Frederick A. Lindemann (later Lord Chewell), who managed to combine what Snow termed "a rather silly anti-semitism" with help to refugee scientists.[6] There was an ambivalence also in the attitude of Sir William Bragg, president of the Royal Society, who was approached by Rutherford for support for the AAC and who responded, "It is possible, I suppose, to do more harm than good by angering the people in charge in Germany." Yet Bragg *did* give help to refugee scientists.[7]

A rather different, and less favorable, picture emerges if the medical profession is examined. Here there was a considerable degree of professional jealousy and hostility to refugee doctors together with some remarkable examples of island xenophobia. For example, in November 1933 Lord Dawson of Penn, president of the Royal College of Physicians, told the home secretary, Sir John Gilmour, that while there might be room in Britain for a few refugee doctors of special distinction, "the number that could usefully be absorbed or teach us anything could be counted on the fingers of one hand."[8]

The truth was, of course, that there was an anxiety in the profession that those trained in Heidelberg, Berlin, or Vienna might have only too much to teach their professional colleagues in England and that they might well prove to be successful competitors. In December 1933 and January 1934, the *British Medical Journal* printed an acrimonious correspondence on refugee doctors, and as the refugee crisis worsened, the issue found its way into the opinion columns of the popular press. On June 14, 1938, the *Sunday Express* editorialized:

In Britain half a million Jews find their home. They are never persecuted and indeed in many respects the Jews are given favoured treatment here. But just now there is a big influx of foreign Jews into Britain. They are overrunning the country. They are trying to enter the medical profession in great numbers. They wish to practise as dentists. Worst of all, many of them are holding themselves out to the public as psycho-analysts. A psycho-analyst needs no medical training, but arrogates to himself the functions of a doctor. And he often obtains an ascendancy over the patient of which he makes base use if he is a bad man.

The case of Sigmund Freud was not only the most notable example, but also in many ways the most revealing one, of both immigrant   253 and host attitudes. Freud was long reluctant to leave Vienna in spite of the urgings of his English disciple Ernest Jones, and he eventually did so only after the arrest of members of his family. When Sir William Bragg was approached for help in Freud's case, he gave it, then added, "Do you really think the Germans are unkind to the Jews?"[9] The government, and especially the home secretary Sir Samuel Hoare, was willing to admit Freud with no difficulty, though the official procedures took some time. Freud's famous first words when he reached London were (a presumably ironical) "Heil Hitler." He was by this time suffering from cancer. He said his only remaining ambition was to die a British citizen—but, having been deprived of Austrian citizenship and not yet naturalized, he died the following year (perhaps appropriately) stateless.

How successfully were the émigrés integrated into British society and intellectual life? Here again, the answer is generally positive, with occasional dark patches. By and large the refugees were quickly absorbed into the mainstream of British academic and artistic life. The careers of a few representative figures testify to this: Sir Ernst Gombrich in art history; Freddy Fisher, who became editor of the *Financial Times*, in journalism; the terrible twins of Keynesian economics, Lords Balogh and Kaldor; Eduard Fraenkel in classics; Karl Popper in philosophy (first in New Zealand, then in England).

There was a rise in chauvinism and antiforeigner sentiment after the outbreak of the war, culminating in the absurd scandal of the mass internment of enemy aliens (mostly refugees) in 1940 and the deportation of several thousand of them, often in conditions of brutality and larceny, to Canada and Australia. The internment nevertheless had some tragicomic aspects. The Hampstead Public Library was raided by the police in the course of a roundup of aliens (presumably on the basis of the "known haunts" theory of criminal behavior). Hermann Bondi was arrested in Cambridge, interned, and later deported; after some months in exile, he was permitted to return to England to resume work on the perfection of radar. Ernst Kitzinger, a young art historian from Germany, was entrusted with work of national security importance when he helped organize the transfer of some of the treasures of the National Gallery to their secret wartime hiding-place in Wales. Shortly afterwards, he was arrested, interned, and deported as an enemy alien. He recently retired as professor of the history of art at Harvard University.

But most of the refugees accepted that total war inevitably brought about such anomalies. Notwithstanding occasional resentment at official obtuseness during the alien roundups, the common feeling remained similar to that expressed by an émigré of an earlier generation, Alexander Herzen, who wrote in 1857:

Until I came to England the appearance of a police officer in a house where I was living always produced an indefinable disagreeable feeling, and I was morally on guard against an enemy. In England a policeman at your door merely adds to your sense of security.[10]

The internment camps on the Isle of Man became popular universities and concert halls. Indeed, the nucleus of what later became the greatest string quartet of our generation, the Amadeus, was formed after a chance meeting in one of the Manx camps. The intellectuals among the refugees, of course, made a notable contribution to the war effort. Their role in the development of nuclear weapons is well known. One might also mention the vital role played by refugees in the BBC's foreign broadcasts during the war, in the service established at Caversham to monitor overseas broadcasts, and in the special contribution of the Wiener Library to the understanding and analysis of Nazism during and after the war.

In general, the refugees settled down happily in England. But not all could feel at home, particularly those who were more elderly and settled in their ways. Those such as Stefan Zweig who were deeply rooted in German and Austrian culture found it hard to adapt to a profoundly alien intellectual environment. In *The World of Yesterday*, Zweig left a poignant memoir of such a failure to integrate into Anglo-Saxon society with all its philistinism and insularity. The forthcoming work of Reinhard Bendix, recording his and his father's emigration from Germany (the former to the United States, the latter to Palestine), leaves (in the case of the father) a similarly sad impression of failure in cultural adaptation. It is noteworthy that several of the intellectuals who came to England, though a minority, left during or after the war: Zweig went to Brazil, which (remarkably) he fixed on as the promised land, there to commit suicide. Stefan Lorant, Hungarian journalist, editor of the highly successful news magazine, *Picture Post*, was subject to petty official persecution in 1940 until, his friendship with Churchill not availing any relief, he went to the United States. Ernst Cassirer also immigrated to the United States. After the war there was a further trickle of westward intellectual migration, a recent example being the legal scholar, David Daube. Some of these later emigrants departed echoing the feelings of Herzen who said, upon leaving England after twelve and

255

one-half years' residence, that there was nothing much he missed there save "Colman's mustard, English pickles and mushroom ketchup."[11]

Perhaps the bittersweet flavor of exile in England was best expressed by John Plamenatz, son of a Montenegrin politician who became professor of political thought in Oxford (and whose former rooms in Nuffield College I was privileged to occupy). Isaiah Berlin in his new book, *Personal Impressions*, says of Plamenatz that he felt rooted in a remote culture and that the sudden break of immigration (in Plamenatz's case as a child) to an alien environment had forced him to turn in to some degree upon himself. That was why, although he had made personal friends among individual English people, and although he could feel at home with two or three at a time, when larger numbers were gathered in a room, he would become aware of a relationship between them from which he felt excluded.[12]

Notes

1. A.J. Sherman, *Island Refuge: Britain and Refugees from the Third Reich 1933–1939* (London, 1973), p. 264.

2. Ibid., p. 32.

3. Ibid., p. 70.

4. Austin Stevens, *The Dispossessed* (London, 1975), p. 125.

5. Selig Brodetsky, *Memoirs: From Ghetto to Israel* (London, 1960), p. 161.

6. Stevens, *The Dispossessed*, p. 126.

7. Ronald W. Clark, *Freud: The Man and the Cause* (New York, 1980), p. 509.

8. Sherman, *Island Refuge*, p. 48.

9. Clark, *Freud*, p. 514.

10. E.H. Carr, *The Romantic Exiles* (New York, 1933), p. 136.

11. Ibid., p. 255.

12. Isaiah Berlin, *Personal Impressions* (New York, 1981), p. 116.

Canada and the Refugee Intellectual, 1933–1939

IRVING ABELLA
HAROLD TROPER

To observers both within its borders and elsewhere who have written about Canada, authors as varied as Graham Greene and H.L. Mencken, Winston Churchill and Mordechai Richler, Marshall McLuhan and Walter Lippmann, there is a Canadian stereotype. These men as well as countless others have universally portrayed Canadians as a capable but dull, plodding, unimaginative people who make excellent soldiers but frightful generals, who are competent in their work but somewhat dim in everything else, and who on the whole are neither very bright nor very creative—otherwise they would have, as one wag put it, been smart enough to migrate across the border long ago.

Though Canadians naturally—and with good reason—reject these generalizations, they probably contain some validity. And a major reason has been Canada's extraordinarily restrictive immigration policy. From the outset Canadian governments have had unabashed ethnic priorities. We knew who we wanted and how to keep out those we did not. British and American immigrants were always welcome; we encouraged them to come, recruited them, made them great promises, and even subsidized their journeys. When for economic reasons we needed more immigrants, we gave preference to northern and central Europeans. In periods of great boom, we allowed in southern Europeans. Finally, at the bottom of the list—and this was explicitly written into our immigration legislation—were Jews,

257

Asians, and blacks.[1] These we only let in when we had to, that is, when we needed a large and cheap pool of unskilled labor to work in the mines, forests, and sweatshops of the nation.[2] In addition, we always knew exactly what type of immigrant we wanted. When given a choice between artist and agriculturist, "littérateur" or lumberjack, muse or miner, scholar or stonemason, Canada inevitably chose the latter. After all, our government believed that a young, developing country had more use for farmers, miners, and construction- and woodworkers than it did for philosophers, musicians, writers, or savants. The emphasis of our immigration policy has always been on brawn over brain, of lowbrow over highbrow, of muscle over mind.

And at no time was this preference more apparent than in the 1930s, when the immigration market was suddenly flooded with the cream of the European intelligentsia. With the establishment of the Nazi government in Germany, Canadian immigration offices as well as those of various Jewish organizations were deluged with letters from terrified German intellectuals begging to be allowed into Canada. Requests also poured in from Canadians pleading for the entry of some of these displaced scholars. There were applications from, and on behalf of, some of the great names of German science. They also came from judges, bankers, artists, professors, surgeons, lawyers, and merchants. Most of these refugees were Jews, who needed special permits to be allowed into Canada in these years. Unfortunately, special permits for Jews were rarely issued.

To each of the letters asking for permission to immigrate, the response from both government and Jewish groups was the same: "Unfortunately, though we greatly sympathize with your circumstance, at present Canada is not admitting Jews. Please try some other country."[3] For most of these people, there was no other country to immigrate to. Symbolic of our constant choice of strong backs over strong minds, the only immigrants allowed into Canada in these years were farmers with capital.

The tragedy, of course, lay not only in the fate of those who did not survive, but in the impact on Canada of turning these people away. Allowed into the country, these men and women would have given us the best of European culture and society. They would have been immigrants unlike any who had arrived in Canada before, and we needed them desperately. Even by the standards of the Depression, Canada was still a country of great wealth, potential, and, above all, empty space. Yet in the 1930s, when they most needed to be

258

open, our doors were firmly shut.

Even the lobbying of some prominent Canadians could not alter our government's policy. It was obstinate and unyielding. As one leading industrialist entreated Prime Minister Mackenzie King: "How can we turn our backs on these people? Think of what they can contribute. . . . Think of what they can do for us."[4]

The Canadian government, however, was thinking of other matters; it had no time for the plight of the muses and the other refugees of Nazi terror. Of all the immigration countries in the world, Canada had by far the worst record toward Jewish refugees. From 1933 to 1939, in response to undoubtedly the greatest crisis of morality of our time, Canada accepted a grand total of some five thousand refugees, of whom just over thirty-five hundred were Jews.[5] Even such smaller and poorer nations as Mexico, Brazil, Colombia, Australia, South Africa, and Uruguay accepted far more. And since most of those permitted into Canada were either farmers or close relatives of Canadian residents, there was little possibility of many refugee intellectuals finding a haven in Canada.

Our miserliness toward the muses of Europe is, in hindsight, unbelievable. Of the thousands of scholars, teachers, scientists, artists, musicians, and writers driven from German schools, universities, research centers, and conservatories, only six found full-time jobs in Canadian universities. According to a report by the League of Nations's High Commission on Refugees, only seven others were admitted to Canada on temporary work permits. Most incredible, from the middle of 1936 to September 1939, as the anguish of German scholars grew increasingly unbearable, only one refugee scholar was hired by a Canadian university.[6] Yet throughout these years both the Canadian government and universities were being regularly circularized by various refugee organizations, including the Emergency Society for German Scholars Abroad and the Carnegie Foundation, informing them of the large numbers of academics, scientists, and researchers wishing to come to Canada.

The attitude of Canadian universities was not surprising. In the 1930s they were clearly bastions of Anglo conformity. Since most hired no native-born Jews, they could hardly be expected willingly to hire those born elsewhere. They were determined to keep their faculties as *Judenrein* as possible. Shortages of funds, they argued, made it impossible for them to provide work for any of the refugees. However, even when these German academics were to be funded by the Carnegie Foundation, Canadian universities could still find

259

no room for them. Meanwhile the Canadian government refused to issue an entry permit to anyone who might take a job away from a Canadian applicant. For example, when the University of Saskatchewan pleaded with the Department of Immigration to admit Professor Gerhard Herzberg, who would later become our most eminent scientist and Canada's only Nobel laureate in any of the sciences, government authorities replied, "Unfortunately, Dr. Herzberg does not come within the classes ordinarily admittable to Canada under existing regulations."[7]

The university persevered, however, and immigration officials finally relented when Herzberg promised to stay for only two years and to have his salary paid by the Carnegie Foundation. Two years later, when Herzberg, already recognized as one of the world's leading molecular physicists, applied to remain, the immigration department insisted that he leave; in its words, "he has taken a job for which a Canadian might qualify." The president of the university was warned by the government that to permit Herzberg to stay would set an appalling precedent since "there are any number of well qualified persons in Europe who might benefit Canada, but would do so only at the detriment of some Canadian resident with similar qualifications whose job they might take."[8] Nonetheless, after a long series of letters and meetings, Herzberg was permitted to remain. He was forbidden, however, from taking out citizenship until 1945, fully ten years after he had arrived in Canada.

Though there were some Canadian academics who supported the movement of German scholars to Canada, most were either apathetic or hostile. One leading Canadian historian praised the government for its restrictionist policy and warned that if it became more flexible Canadian universities would be flooded with refugees. What would happen, he asked the leader of the opposition in Ottawa, to the country's graduate students if Canada allowed in European Jewish academics? There would be no jobs for them, he charged, since the Jews would have taken them all.[9] At the annual Conference of Canadian Universities, a session was held to discuss the plight of the refugee intellectual. The chairman of the meeting, one of the nation's most distinguished intellectuals, reassured his audience that although they had ostensibly been called together to examine the problem of refugee scholars, this problem *would not* be solved at the expense of Canadian academics. They would have to make no sacrifices, he added. At the conclusion of a short discussion, a resolution was unanimously passed calling on the government not to

Gerhard Herzberg. In 1935 Canadian authorities resisted admitting Herzberg, a Jewish refugee, into the country, even though he was one of the leading molecular physicists in the world. He would later become Canada's first and only Nobel laureate in the sciences. (Courtesy of Gerhard Herzberg.)

admit any of these refugees unless it guaranteed that no Canadian teacher, professor, scientist, mathematician, or musician would lose his job. Further, the resolution demanded that the immigration authorities deport all those refugees with temporary entry permits who could only find jobs "for which other Canadians might be qualified."[10] This resolution was passed in May 1939, just three months before the Nazis marched into Poland.

In the 1930s, wrote Chaim Weizmann, the first president of the State of Israel, the world was divided into two parts: those places where Jews could not live and those places where they could not enter. Canada clearly fell into the latter category.

There were various reasons for Canada's obsession with keeping her shores clear of refugees. Obviously, in the 1930s, in the midst of a terrible depression, the government saw little reason to allow in any job-hungry immigrants. But other countries suffering far worse than Canada still found room for appreciably more refugees than did we.

261

The country in the 1930s was permeated with xenophobia and anti-Semitism. These were most apparent in the staunchly Catholic province of Quebec, where the Roman Catholic Church, having hived itself off long before from the more worldly influences that had buffeted Catholicism in other Western countries, remained impervious to any liberal doctrines. From the pulpit and through various fiats from the province's bishops, the faithful were warned against alien doctrines. A new French-Canadian nationalism, based on the purity of the faith and of the French-Canadian race, was being nurtured. Quebec was turning inward and insular, hunkering down for the battle against foreign influences. Jews were regularly denounced in sermons and in Catholic newspapers as "demons," "Christ-killers," and "exploiters" who "cheat and rob the innocent habitant."[11] Many church and nationalist leaders supported a movement to boycott Jewish businesses and to keep Jews out of public life. European pogroms, from Kishinev to *Kristallnacht*, were applauded by segments of the French-Canadian press and leadership. In popular journals Jews were constantly portrayed as "scoundrels," "cheaters," "untrustworthy," and "evil." Even the most prestigious French language newspaper, *Le Devoir*, joined in the anti-Jewish crusade and pleaded with federal authorities to keep these "aliens" as far away as possible from Canada's shores. Most Quebec politicians, including Premier Maurice Duplessis and his cabinet, and almost every newspaper took part in this anti-Jewish campaign. While spreading the most vile anti-Semitic canards about Jews already in Canada, they were also vigorously lobbying against the admission of any more.

Since the Liberal party, which governed Canada in these years, had the base of its support—as it still does today—in Quebec (fully 40 percent of its seats in Parliament were from that province), few government officials were foolhardy enough to publicly embrace the refugee cause. Any policy, the party felt, that would allow in substantial numbers of Jews—or any other immigrants for that matter—would corrode Liberal support within the province and strengthen forces of separation.

But anti-Jewish feeling was not restricted to Quebec; it was also strong—although less vocal—in English-speaking Canada. Quotas against Jews existed in most universities, professions, and industries. Almost no Jews taught in schools or colleges, worked in anything but the most menial positions in large companies or banks, or played any important role in the legal, medical, or business community of the country. Jews were also legally forbidden by restrictive covenants

262

from buying land or homes in many areas, from vacationing in certain resorts, or from joining various organizations. Anti-Semitic sentiments were voiced regularly—and with impunity—by leading Canadian political, church, business, and labor leaders. There was even some violence as Jew and anti-Semite confronted one another on the streets of the nation's cities.[12]

The federal cabinet, fully aware of the extent of anti-Jewish feeling throughout the country and of the hostility that would greet any program to admit refugees, did have the power through orders-in-council to allow anyone it wished into the country. Occasionally, when the pressure was severe enough, as it was in the case of Herzberg, it did. Most often, however, it left the choice to the Department of Immigration.

And this was most unfortunate for the European refugee, since the director of immigration was a rabid anti-Semite. A devout elder of the Baptist church, Frederick Charles Blair was, in effect, in charge of Canada's immigration policy from 1936 to 1943, the key years for those attempting to escape Nazi terror. Blair saw it as his job to keep refugees out of Canada.

To Blair the term *refugee* was a code word for *Jew*. Unless "safeguards" were adopted, he warned, Canada was in danger of being "flooded with Jewish people." His task, as he perceived it, was to make sure that the "safeguards" did not fail. Indeed, he was inordinately proud of his success in keeping out Jews. As he put it, "Pressure on the part of Jewish people to get into Canada has never been greater than it is now and I am glad to be able to add, after 35 years experience here, that it was never so well controlled." Blair expressed a strong personal distaste for Jews and especially for "certain of their habits." He saw them as unassimilable, as people apart "who can organize [their] affairs better than other people" and therefore accomplish more.

It seems that Blair's contempt for the Jews was boundless. Only a short time after the outbreak of hostilities in Europe in 1939, Blair confided to his immigration commissioner in London, "Someone has facetiously said that numbers of our Jewish refugees lustfully sing 'Onward *Christian* Soldiers' but are very content to stay here and grab up all opportunities." And in a revealing letter to a strong opponent of Jewish immigration Blair wrote:

I suggested recently to three Jewish gentlemen with whom I am well acquainted, that it might be a very good thing if they would call a conference and have a day of humiliation and prayer which might

263

profitably be extended for a week or more where they would honestly try to answer the question of why they are so unpopular almost everywhere. . . . I often think that instead of persecution it would be far better if we more often told them frankly why many of them are unpopular. If they would divest themselves of certain of their habits I am sure they could be just as popular in Canada as our Scandinavians.[13]

That a man who displayed such anti-Semitic tendencies should be in charge of Canadian immigration at any period was a disgrace; that he should be in charge in the 1930s was, for the Jews of Europe at least, a tragedy. It was Blair who gave the ultimate and final interpretation of government regulations and who acted as the de facto judge and jury on individual requests for admission. Yet to blame Blair alone for Canada's response to the refugee crisis would be both overly simplistic and incorrect; after all, he was only a civil servant, albeit a powerful one. As a functionary he merely reflected the wishes of his superiors; it was they who were ultimately responsible for government policy. Refusing to accept refugees was not a bureaucratic decision but a political one made by Prime Minister Mackenzie King and his cabinet.

The prime minister of Canada was obsessed with Jews. He dreamed of them often and filled his diary with his thoughts about them. While he saw Jews as "the people of the Book" and as somewhat "mystical," he was also capable of repeating—and believing—the most bilious anti-Semitic slander. He either truly felt or convinced himself that permitting Jewish refugees of "even the best type" into Canada would destroy the country. As he wrote in his diary, "We must seek to keep Canada free from unrest and too great an intermixture of foreign strains of blood."[14] Jews, he feared, would not only pollute Canada's bloodstream, but worse, allowing them in would also cause riots and worsen relations between the federal government and the provinces. Accepting Jewish refugees, he told his sympathetic cabinet, would undermine Canadian unity, alienate many Canadians, strengthen the forces of Quebec separatism, and bring about bloodshed in the streets.

King's—and Canada's—policy was symbolized by the instructions he gave the Canadian delegate to the Evian Conference, Hume Wrong. The prime minister told Wrong that his job was simply to listen and make notes, to say as little as possible, and to "make no commitments." Canada, King said, was at Evian just for information, and actually only for cosmetic reasons. In fact, it was the last country to accept President Roosevelt's invitation and did so only when the

264

cabinet was told that it would look peculiar if Canada were the sole nation aside from Mussolini's Italy not to attend.[15] Should any delegation make any concrete suggestions to solve the refugee problem, Wrong was ordered to "oppose" them while trying not to be patently "obstructionist." The Canadian government, King said, would do everything possible to find these refugees a home—"in some other country," since most of the refugees were "likely to be Communists and Jews."[16]

King was obviously being influenced by his Quebec lieutenant, Ernest Lapointe, who kept the bug in his ear about the dangers of alienating his province should the government open up Canada's doors to Jewish immigration, no matter how limited. King, however, was a consummate politician, the most successful in Canadian history. He prided himself on his ability to gauge the pulse of the nation. Instinctively he seemed to know what the Canadian people wanted, and he gave it to them. How else can one explain why this colorless, uninspiring, inarticulate man could serve a full quarter of a century as Canada's prime minister? Had he believed there were votes to be won by admitting refugees he would likely have done so; but he was convinced that there were not, so he did not.

Another key figure in this drama was the country's senior diplomat at the time, one of Canada's leading patrons of the arts, and later the nation's first native-born governor-general. In the 1930s, the wealthy Vincent Massey, scion of the farm implement family, was Canada's high commissioner in London and responsible for advising the government on its refugee policy. Massey was a fringe member of the Cliveden Set, which centered around the pro-German Astors, and was certainly no partisan of Jewish immigration. If a way could be found to keep out the Jews and allow in other refugees, he would be delighted. And in fact, he helped devise just such a scheme. He successfully urged the government to ignore Jewish refugees and to accept in their stead the several thousand Sudeten Germans displaced by the Munich Agreement. Would it not be a wonderful tactic, he recommended to the prime minister, to take in as many as possible of these "Aryans" who he claimed were "more desirable" than the Jews and certainly "of a superior quality." Having done this, he pointed out to a receptive King, "would put us in a much stronger position in relation to later appeals from and on behalf of non-Aryans."[17] He also informed his colleagues in Ottawa that they should move quickly to admit a large number of central European refugees "of means and education" who would enrich Canada. Perhaps gra-

265

tuitously, he added that he did not have in mind Jews, but rather "the numerous non-Jewish people who find life quite intolerable under the Nazi regime."

By the onset of 1939, an unofficial unholy triumvirate had been forged in the Immigration Service, the cabinet, and the Department of External Affairs against refugees in general and Jewish refugees in particular. In Immigration, the intransigent and morally obtuse Blair gave vent to his anti-Semitism by placing every possible bureaucratic encumbrance in the path of refugees. In the Cabinet, Lapointe, King's trusted Quebec lieutenant, scuttled any backsliding—including by the prime minister—on the refugee issue. In External Affairs, Massey flirted with the protofascist aristocratic crowd in London, while doing what he could to keep Jews out of Canada. Individually, each had immense power; collectively, they were beyond challenge. Each had his own sphere of influence, but on the refugee issue these spheres overlapped. Though there is no evidence that they consulted on this issue—and they likely did not—what united them was a common conviction: Canada did not need any more Jews.

While the prime minister was not a prisoner of this anti-Jewish coterie, he could not help but be influenced by it. When the foremost immigration authority, the leading French-Canadian politician in the country, and the nation's senior foreign diplomat spoke, he listened, especially since they were all saying the same thing. King himself vacillated. At times his humanitarian and religious instincts led him to argue the refugee case; yet always his political instincts prevailed. His sympathy for the refugees was genuine. He sincerely wanted to find them a home—anywhere but in Canada.

In the face of this, the Jewish community could do little. Making up about 1 percent of the population, Canadian Jewry had little political or economic clout. And most Jews themselves were recent immigrants feeling somewhat marginal and frightened. Until the wealthy industrialist, Samuel Bronfman, became active in the latter part of 1938, the representative voice of the community, the Canadian Jewish Congress, was a weak, underfinanced, divided body.

From the onset of the crisis, Jewish leadership saw quiet diplomacy as the only tactic that might convince the government to open its doors to a handful of refugees. Regularly and unobtrusively, Jewish emissaries tramped off to Ottawa cap in hand to lobby with immigration officials and members of Parliament. They were made promises that were never kept. In order to keep the Jews quiet, some

266

prominent members of the community were rewarded with special immigration permits they could distribute to a fortunate few in the community. It was a cynical gesture but it worked. For the most part, though restive, Canadian Jews remained loyal to the Liberal party. After all, on immigration matters, the Conservative opposition was even worse.

Jewish leaders entreated such Jewish organizations as the trade unions, the Zionists, and the fraternal societies to avoid mass meetings, protest marches, and demonstrations, because they feared such activities would alienate the government and create an anti-Semitic backlash throughout the country. It was no time, the leaders argued, for what we today would call the "politics of the street." Helpless, the Jews of Canada followed orders; they remained silent. To the very end the Jewish community put its faith in its own leadership and in the Liberal government; neither delivered. But even if Canadian Jewry had been more forceful, it would have made little difference. The Canadian government was committed to keeping Jews out of Canada, and it was not to be deterred in its objective by the tiny Jewish community, whether it was noisy or silent. So long as the churches remained passive (and they did) and the provinces did not say anything (and they did not), there was little domestic pressure on the government to force a change in policy.

Hence, there were only a few thousand refugees who managed to break through the Canadian barricade, and of these only a handful could be classified as muses. Indeed, so complete was the Canadian success in keeping out refugees that it is almost possible to count the number of Jewish intellectuals who took up permanent residence and academic jobs in this country before 1939 on the fingers of one hand. What Canada missed became evident after the war, when the population of several thousand refugee internees shipped over from Britain during the war produced many of Canada's leading intellectuals, writers, philosophers, and scientists.[18]

How much different Canada would have been had we taken a significant number of these muses in the 1930s is difficult to say. Perhaps, it would have somewhat altered the perception Canadians—and others—have of themselves. One thing, however, can be said: Canadians must forever live with the consequences of their government's abject refusal to help save the refugee intellectuals of Europe. At a time when the consciences of all the Western democracies were tried and found wanting, Canada was no exception. We differed only in that we behaved worse than most.

267

Notes

1. Canada, Sessional Papers, Immigration Statutes, 1896–1947. See also, for example, *Canada Year Book* (Ottawa, 1937).

2. For a useful study of Canadian immigration policy, see Irving Abella and Harold Troper, *None Is Too Many: Canada and the Jews of Europe, 1933–1948* (Toronto, 1982), and Gerald Dirks, *Canada's Refugee Policy: Indifference or Opportunism?* (Montreal, 1977).

3. For example, see M. Solkin to J. Braun, Sep. 17, 1938; manuscript in Jewish Immigration Aid Society archives, Montreal.

4. J.S. MacLean (president, Canada Packers) to King, Apr. 7, 1938; manuscript in King Papers, Public Archives of Canada, Ottawa (cited as PAC).

5. For a more detailed study of the Canadian record, see Irving Abella and Harold Troper, "The Line Must Be Drawn Somewhere: Canada and Jewish Refugees 1933–39," *Canadian Historical Review* 60, no. 2 (1979):178–209.

6. Saul Hayes to Joint Distribution Committee, New York, Nov. 8, 1939, National Archives, Canadian Jewish Congress, Montreal (cited as CJC); see also Lawrence D. Stokes, "Canada and an Academic Refugee from Nazi Germany: The Case of Gerhard Herzberg," *Canadian Historical Review* 57, no. 2 (1976):150-51, and Edward Y. Hartshorne, Jr., *The German Universities and National Socialism* (London, 1937), p. 97.

7. Stokes, "Canada and an Academic Refuge," p. 162.

8. Ibid., pp. 163–65.

9. George Stanley to Robert Manion, Dec. 22, 1938; manuscript in Manion Papers, PAC.

10. Constance Hayward, Report of meeting of National Conference of Canadian Universities, May 1939, CJC.

11. For a survey of anti-Semitism in Quebec, see David Rome, *Clouds in the Thirties: On Anti-Semitism in Canada,* 12 vols. (Montreal, 1977–81).

12. For anti-Semitism in English Canada, see Lita-Rose Betcherman, *The Swastika and the Maple Leaf* (Toronto, 1975).

13. Quoted in Abella and Troper, "The Line Must Be Drawn Somewhere," pp. 183–85.

14. King Diary, Mar. 29, 1938, PAC.

15. O.D. Skelton (undersecretary of state) to King, Apr. 21, 1938; manuscript in King Papers, PAC.

16. King to Wrong, June 11, 1938; reprinted in John Munro, ed., *Documents on Canadian External Relations VI: 1936–1939* (Ottawa, 1972), pp. 801-5.

17. Massey to King, Nov. 29, 1938; reprinted in ibid.

18. See Erich Koch, *Deemed Suspect: A Wartime Blunder* (Toronto, 1980), and Paula Draper, "The Accidental Immigrants," *Canadian Jewish Historical Society Journal* 2, pts. 1 and 2 (1978).

Muses behind Barbed Wire: Canada and the Interned Refugees

PAULA JEAN DRAPER

The article in the *Toronto Star* of June 3, 1942, read:

INTERNED 12 MONTHS, GETS B.A. IN EIGHT
  "Lack of Aryan ancestry," which forced Ulrich Goldschmidt to
leave his native Germany in 1940, did not hinder his ability to obtain a Bachelor of Arts degree in 8 months at the University of Toronto. . . . Goldschmidt studied law, commerce and political science
. . . in Berlin, Hamburg and London. He holds several other university degrees besides the one in modern languages which he will obtain tomorrow. He hopes to obtain a job teaching in Canada which
he says he "likes very much." . . . [His] father, Dr. Hans Goldschmidt, noted German scholar, fled to England just before the war
and was killed by a Nazi bomb there during the blitz.[1]

Two years later the same newspaper reported on the activities of
two young musicians who had also been interned in Canada. Under
the title "Recital by Refugees Thrills Music Fans," the resident
music critic wrote:

One of the few excuses for Hitler being born, is such refugees as Helmut Blume and Gerhard Kander, whose recital at Eaton's last night
for Refugee Agencies was one of the music thrillers of the season.[2]

Yet another interned refugee was in the news in 1944. Dr. Johanns
Holtfreter, an embryologist supported by a grant from the Rockefeller

Foundation, had been working in the McGill University Laboratories since his release. The *Toronto Star* reported that Holtfreter had received a Guggenheim Foundation Fellowship for 1944–45, one of only five persons in Canada to be so honored.[3]

Since early 1942 articles such as these had begun to appear regularly in local Canadian newspapers, and they heralded the first evidence of the remarkable character of a group of young male refugees from Austria and Germany. Incarcerated since the summer of 1940 in Canadian internment camps, by 1942 many of the younger refugees had been released to attend various educational institutions; they would go on to make significant contributions to the cultural and intellectual climate of Canada. The irony was that in 1940, and even in 1944, Canada did not welcome immigrants, particularly Jewish ones. The interned refugees arrived by accident and remained only by sufferance.

The collective tale of the interned refugees began in Great Britain.[4] Living peacefully there until the declaration of war, foreigners categorized as enemy aliens were then brought before tribunals to be classified into one of three groups: Class "A" aliens were termed "dangerous enemy aliens" and immediately interned. Class "B," or "friendly enemy aliens," were under suspicion and were given restrictions such as curfews and five-mile travel limits. The third group, and the largest, was Class "C," "friendly aliens and refugees from Nazi oppression." Most of the Jewish refugees fell into the "B" and "C" categories, although some were unjustly imprisoned as "A"s.

As fear of invasion mounted, rumors of fifth column activities spread throughout the country. The British military especially came increasingly to believe that there could be subversive elements among the refugees residing in England, and some type of police action was urged. Beginning in mid-May, "B" and then "C" categories of enemy aliens living in the eastern coastal areas of England and Scotland were interned by the Home Office. All were German and Austrian nationals between the ages of sixteen and sixty, totaling twenty-three thousand men and three thousand women. Internment was only intended to be a temporary measure, yet for thousands of those affected freedom was to be regained not in a few weeks or months, but in one, two, or even three years.

The drain on manpower required to administer and guard twenty-six thousand people led to a decision to send male internees to Commonwealth countries. Canada and Australia concurred, as a

272

means of aiding the war effort. Britain let it be assumed that only Class "A"—dangerous Nazi sympathizers—would be sent. But the War Office felt there was no time to make such fine distinctions, and over twenty-two hundred "B" and "C" male refugees were loaded onto ships that also transfered prisoners of war and Nazis to Canada in June and July 1940.

The sinking of one of the ships bound for Canada, the *Arandora Star*, led to a public outcry in England for an end to the deportations. This tragedy, in which many innocent lives were lost, combined with pressure from the Canadian government to effectively discontinue the deportations. Canada had been horrified to discover that the supposedly dangerous men it had agreed to accept included orthodox Jews as well as sixteen-year-old boys in short pants. The embarrassed British government reevaluated its refugee policy and set upon a program of release. By the end of July 1940, opportunities for release were made available to "C" internees in England. The regulations regarding release were duly transmitted to the Canadian authorities along with the recommendation that similar chances be given to the internees for release into Canada. Meanwhile, the deported refugees languished in internment camps scattered throughout eastern Canada. In some, they shared facilities with hard-core Nazis.[5]

Who were these men? In many ways they were a select group. Most had come to England alone. In many families, only the children had escaped; the war had trapped parents who were desperately trying to join them. England had been especially receptive to refugee children. By September 1939 the Movement for the Care of Children from Germany had rescued 9,354 children selected by Jewish and Christian organizations in Germany and Austria;[6] permits had been issued by the Home Office, with priority given to those whose emigration was urgent because their fathers were in concentration camps or because they were homeless or in danger themselves. Thus, many were the offspring of intellectuals, anti-Nazis, and wealthy Jews. Other refugees had escaped because they had the money to set up businesses in England, or at least could support themselves and their families in exile. After November 1938 England permitted large numbers of refugees who had quota numbers for the United States to enter the country on temporary transit visas while awaiting their emigration. Many of these people were penniless. Single men, released from concentration camps and forced to emigrate without their families, found themselves in Canadian internment camps as   273 well. Teenagers and young adults entered England on Children's Transports, with work permits, or, often, on student visas. Universities, schools, and yeshivas welcomed the refugees, who formed a heterogeneous group yet had many common characteristics. Except for a minority of non-Jews who had left for political reasons, the émigrés had fled Germany because of Nazi racial laws. Some were orthodox Jews, but the majority shared an assimilated background in which their Judaism had played a minimal role. Typically they came from wealthy or middle-class homes. Of the approximately one thousand men who remained in Canada after their release, over half were under thirty years of age in 1940, and a large number were between thirty and thirty-five. About one-third had been businessmen, bankers, professionals, and some had been trained in skilled trades. Finally there was a substantial group of intellectuals: professors, artists, musicians, journalists, and scientists.

Indeed, the refugees were the most unusual batch of potential immigrants Canada had ever seen. Ambitious, well educated, and highly motivated, they brought with them knowledge and a sense of culture that were sorely lacking in prewar Canada. The optimistic among them believed that as soon as the Canadian government became aware of their harmless nature, they would be liberated and welcomed to a new home. The more realistic prayed that they would at least be allowed to live as free men until they could complete their journeys to the United States. But, by 1942, over half the internees had taken their lives into their own hands and made the dangerous Atlantic crossing once again. These were the pragmatic ones. Canada did not want Jewish refugees—whether they came in the front door or sneaked in the back—and these men harbored no illusions of early release on this side of the ocean.

The Canadian authorities would have been quite content to have seen all the refugees returned to England. But they could not be sent back against their will. So the government had to resign itself to a constant barrage of complaints, appeals, and pressures to deal leniently with these men and, ultimately, to release them. The refugees, on the other hand, had to resign themselves to life in internment camps. Almost a year after the camps were created, they were redesignated as "Refugee Camps," and the slow trickle of releases finally began. The reasons for this long delay were twofold. Government officials had vociferously protested that the treatment of the internees could not be altered until it was sufficiently proven, to their satisfaction, that not one of them was an enemy agent. The

274

British had therefore sent a high-ranking representative to interview and report on each man, and his work was not completed until June 1941. Secondly, the hope of refugees that they might gain access to the United States was shared by Canadian immigration authorities, but in the spring of 1941 these hopes were dashed.

The American government had been aware of the interned refugees from the very beginning. In October 1940 five internees, one whose mother was dying of cancer in an American hospital, received permission from the British government to immigrate to the United States. The American consul in Montreal, acting on the instructions of his superiors in Washington, refused to see any of them.[7] Four days later the consul did interview one internee and granted him a visa; his name was Hermann Bondi. The American Department of Immigration immediately stepped in, decreeing that since the internee "had not arrived at a port in the United States, he was not eligible for entry."[8] In December the Canadian government was informed that no internee would be interviewed unless he was first released from internment. The Americans knew Canada would not release any refugee without a guarantee of a U.S. visa.

The Bondi case was decided in February 1940.[9] Influenced by widespread xenophobia and anti-immigrant sentiment in the United States, Attorney General Robert H. Jackson's decision was a negative one. By preventing this one refugee's admission, he effectively obstructed the admission of the whole group.* Meanwhile the American Legion's Washington lobbyist had succeeded in introducing a bill that was specifically designed to prevent internees from applying for visas. The Bondi ruling was meant to forestall any decision on the Allen Bill.[10] Eventually it was presumed by Canadian government officials that a small stream of internees would be permitted into the United States. But the situation did not improve, and by June the Americans had clamped down tightly on refugee immigration from all parts of the globe.[11] The new visa directives refused admittance to refugees with close relatives resident in Nazi-occupied territories, as well as those whose presence might possibly be interpreted as endangering public safety. This effectively ended any chances the internees had of entering the United States.

The Canadian government was stuck. Fifteen hundred men, who would not return to the United Kingdom, and who could not cross

---

* Bondi returned to England where his work in radar and space research eventually earned him a knighthood.

the border to the south, were begging to be given a chance in Canada. They were legitimate refugees. They could not be kept behind barbed wire forever.

Selected refugees were released as temporary residents in Canada from February 1941 until the camps were closed in December 1943. The average length of imprisonment for those who had remained in Canada was between one and a half and two years. It was not long before they realized that their captivity was to be an extended one, and many were determined to make the best of it. From the moment the internees had settled into the first camps, they embarked upon an active intellectual life. Together, refugees built an environment that was not only livable but intense and stimulating. Particularly for the youths, many of whom had suffered drastic interruptions in their education through exclusion from German schools and forced migration, the camps offered an opportunity to learn from some of the best minds in Europe. The intellectual climate of the camps was utterly unique, in terms of the expertise available and the strong motivation of the students.

Education was both informal and organized. Camp schools were established on three levels: academic, technical, and spiritual. Schools catering to the needs of the teenagers were created in every camp. By 1941 permission had been granted for the writing of McGill University matriculation examinations, which would qualify them for university entrance. Most organized educational efforts were therefore directed toward enabling the "camp boys" to pass the McGill examinations. There were many difficulties to overcome, but finding willing pupils was not one of them. The refugees were an ambitious lot, having been raised in a tradition that placed tremendous emphasis on scholarship. Despite the hardships most had suffered, their motivations and expectations remained, even in the isolation of a Canadian internment camp. Neither was there any problem finding qualified teachers for matriculation subjects. Along with the professors and scientists who were interned was a large group of university students from Oxford and Cambridge who, unable to properly pursue their studies while incarcerated, gladly helped their younger friends with high school studies. (The majority of these university students returned to England, including Max Perutz, who in 1962 won the Nobel Prize in chemistry.) The highest enrollments of matriculation students were in English, German, and mathematics, but interests ranged from mediaeval history to the study of heat, light, and sound. There was someone qualified to teach almost every course in each camp.

The worst problem the camp schools faced was obtaining books and writing materials. Despite the assistance of organizations such as the YMCA, the European Student Relief Fund, the Canadian Jewish Congress, and the nonsectarian Canadian National Committee for Refugees, educational materials were scarce and books were often out of date. Instructors were occasionally restricted to total reliance on their memories. But they managed. Of the students who wrote the first matriculation examinations, in June 1941, forty-two out of sixty-two passed.[12] Their marks ranged from 63 to 84 percent.[13] Of the three highest-ranking students, two went on to obtain Ph.D.s in physics, with one becoming the dean of graduate studies at McGill University. The third, Gregory Baum, was to become one of Canada's most influential Roman Catholic theologians, and certainly its most controversial one. Thus, the first schooling experience of the interned refugees in Canada became a stepping stone to further studies. Behind the barbed wire there began a search for knowledge that would ultimately blossom into academic careers—careers that would enhance the atmosphere and reputations of Canadian universities.

A second institution of camp life was the "popular university." Less structured than the camp schools, the universities offered older students, as well as the general camp population, a chance to study a wide spectrum of subjects. The most unique attribute of the popular universities was the teaching staff. Among the educators were two art historians, Otto Demus and Max Stern; Professor Wolfgang Von Einsiedel, an authority on Immanuel Kant who lectured on philosophy; and Johanns Holtfreter, the embryologist. Hans Priester, the former assistant editor of the largest German newspaper (*Berliner Tageblatt*) and author of *The Miracle of German Economics*, taught commerce and finance courses. There were other economists, as well as doctors, dentists, lawyers, a professor of international relations, and two rabbis expert in the history of religion and Semitic languages. One of the latter was Emil Fackenheim, now professor of philosophy at the University of Toronto and renowned for his work in the field of Judaism and the Holocaust. One Canadian Jewish Congress visitor was moved to remark that each of the camps held "enough learned men to staff several universities."[14]

The curriculum of the camp universities was highly diversified, matching the interests of students to the talents of teachers. The only widely shared interest of the internees was the study of the English language. Convinced that their futures lay in the English-speaking world, the refugees made a concerted effort to read English

277

books and to conduct conversations, classes, and entertainments in English. There was also an interest in the academic study of Jewish subjects, including modern Hebrew literature. (Nothing like this was to be found in any Canadian university syllabus.) Then, there was the demand for courses in medicine, engineering, law, music, art, commerce, economics, political science, modern languages, oriental languages, paleography, and divinity. Not even the most ambitious educational program could hope to cope with such a wide range of subjects. Nevertheless, the predominantly academic atmosphere of the camps obviously offered an unequaled opportunity to young and old to widen their intellectual horizons.

Technical education was also provided in one of the camps. In 1940 an Organization for Rehabilitation through Training (ORT) school was built by the Canadian branch of the organization. As refugees could be released to do skilled labor, many gratefully embarked upon retraining under the tutelage of the few professional technicians who remained in the camp. Once they were free, these men became a boon to Canada's war industry.

The third form of formal education was religious. There were approximately sixty rabbinical students, who were closely knit and preoccupied themselves with prayer and study. Some had academic ambitions and studied in the camp school as well, but most limited themselves to the less structured yeshiva setting. The yeshiva students encountered many of the same problems that confronted the academic students. Not only were they woefully short of study materials, but these young refugees also lacked rabbinical guidance; there were no teachers among them, and they were therefore dependent upon one another for direction. The yeshiva students were released as a group in the spring of 1942. For most of them, internment had meant years of perseverance and study. Their studies were no different from what they would have been outside the barbed wire, just more difficult.

Organized schooling provided academic, spiritual, and technical training to the interned refugees. But there was also a great deal to be learned from internment life itself. The diversity of people and interests, the physical labor, the humor that overcame despair—this was the curriculum of internment. Art and music occupied a special place in camp life. Classical and popular music combined with the artistic endeavors of internees to provide varied entertainments. In just one camp there were as many as nineteen pianists. A former conductor and coach of the Vienna State Opera was among the refugees as well. These musicians and artists were later to become mainstays of Canada's creative arts. Oscar Cahen's paintings hang in the National Gallery of Canada. Franz Kramer is chief of the Music Division of the Canada Council. Helmut Kallman heads the Music Section of the Public Archives of Canada. Walter Homburger directs the Toronto Symphony Orchestra, and other ex-internees teach art and music at Canadian universities. The camps afforded these men room for expression. Once they were finally released, Canada provided them with a very willing audience.

Release for most of these young refugees came about through their being sponsored as students. The government accepted a scheme whereby bona fide students could be sent to Canadian schools and universities as long as their maintenance was guaranteed by Canadian citizens. Those with money available to them found nominal sponsors. Others looked for help from relatives, acquaintances of their families, and even complete strangers. The Refugee Committee did its best to find people to act as sponsors, in both the Jewish and non-Jewish communities. Many prominent members of both groups took on the responsibility for refugee students. But sponsors could not be found for every refugee who wanted to complete his education. There were also problems of anti-Semitic quotas in various university faculties, especially pharmacy, medicine, and engineering. Some refugees had to find jobs and slowly work their way through university. One of these men, Josef Kates, eventually became chairman of the Science Council of Canada and then chancellor of Waterloo University. In all, about two hundred refugees were released as students. If they had returned to England, such opportunities probably would not have been offered to them. Invited into wealthy homes, they soon made connections in the upper echelons of Canadian society and were able to excel in their careers, with a large proportion reaching prominence in the academic, cultural, and professional fields. These were the war years; classrooms were not crowded, and competition for jobs was limited. The refugee students had all the advantages.

For many years the future of the released internees in Canada remained uncertain. They had to wait until the war was over to be given immigrant status. The Canadian government, through its Immigration Branch, had always made it clear that their presence in the country was not particularly welcome. These refugees had slipped in through the back door, and any one of them who wished to return to Europe was encouraged to do so. A few did. Others, frustrated by 279 the hostility of their reception, or attracted to the varied educational opportunities in the United States, chose to settle south of the border. The refugees who did stay on to become Canadian citizens tended to be youthful; the older men, less adaptable to a new country and culture, were more likely to return to familiar surroundings. As a result, it was not the instructors from the camp schools who became part of a blossoming Canadian culture but their students. This was not, therefore, an immigration of intellectuals who transferred European culture and thought to Canada. Rather, it was an influx of potential intellectuals, whose attitudes and needs were shaped by a European past, yet whose contributions to Canadian life would be influenced by the education they received, both in internment and in Canadian educational institutions. Characteristic of the paths these potential intellectuals and artists would take are the stories of those four men whom the *Toronto Star* lauded in the early post-internment years. The two academics, Ulrich Goldschmidt and Johanns Holtfreter, became professors—but at American universities. Gerhard Kander, the promising violinist, is now a stockbroker in Toronto. And the pianist, Helmut Blume, became dean of the faculty of music at McGill University.

Those who persevered in their pursuits, and stayed in Canada, became an integral part of the cultural and intellectual landscape of the country. Had the environment been more welcoming, possibly more refugees would have remained. As it is, ex-internees populate universities and scientific and cultural institutions, both north and south of the border. There are prominent ex-internees in almost every field of endeavor. Whether they derived their impetus primarily from their backgrounds or from the internment experience is open to debate. There can be no doubt, however, that the camps left a lasting impression on them. One of these ex-internees is Henry Kreisel. In 1948, when he was still in his twenties, his first novel, *The Rich Man*, was published to widespread critical acclaim. Now professor of comparative literature at the University of Alberta, Kreisel assesses what the internment experience meant to him. He writes:

Intellectual and creative activity was greatly encouraged in the camps, in spite of the very limited opportunities and resources available. What was available in the long, long evenings was time. There were endless discussions and debates on art and music, on politics and religion. The great *Kulturkampf* of late 19th century Germany was fought out every day between the theologians and the secularists. The great political struggles of the left were fought out, and the struggles between liberal capitalism and socialism. I am sorry that I did not record my impressions of these debates, always lively, often passionate, sometimes violent. I suppose I took them for granted. But I learned and absorbed a lot. It was not until many years later that I finally realized that I had had a liberal education in many ways more remarkable than the article available in universities.[15]

Notes

1. *Toronto Star*, June 3, 1942.

2. *Toronto Star*, May 26, 1944.

3. *Toronto Star*, no date, in "Internees Files," Johanns Holtfreter, National Archives, Canadian Jewish Congress, Montreal (cited as (CJC).

4. For details on the internment of refugees in Great Britain and in Canada, see Paula Jean Draper, "The Accidental Immigrants: Canada and the Interned Refugees," *Canadian Jewish Historical Society Journal* 2, pts. 1 and 2 (1978).

5. In Camp "R" at Red Rock Ontario, 174 refugees, many of them Jews, spent June to December 1940 in close quarters with 1,000 Nazi civilians.

6. Francois Lafitte, *The Internment of Aliens* (London, 1940), p. 46.

7. Memo for File, Oct. 29, 1940, Central Registry Files, 621-B pt. 1, Department of External Affairs, Canada (cited as DEA).

8. Col. Stethem to Dr. Skelton, Nov. 2, 1940, Central Registry Files, 621-B pt. 1, DEA.

9. Office of the Attorney General, Decision in the Matter of Hermann Bondi, Feb. 5, 1941, General Files, CJC.

10. Memo to Travers, Feb. 14, 1944, Visa Division, Department of State, Record Group 55, FW842.111/445, [U.S.] National Archives, Washington, D.C.

11. See Henry L. Feingold, *The Politics of Rescue: The Roosevelt Administration and the Holocaust, 1938–1945* (New Brunswick, N.J., 1970), pp. 159ff.; Saul S. Friedman, *No Haven for the Oppressed: United States Policy toward Jewish Refugees, 1938–1945* (Detroit, 1973), pp. 121ff.; David S. Wyman, *Paper Walls: America and the Refugee Crisis, 1938–1941* (Boston, 1968), pp. 191ff.

12. Internees Matriculation Results, 1941, Acc. Nos. 391/1–2, McGill University Archives, Montreal.

13. Until 1942, Jews needed a 65 percent average to enter McGill University, while non-Jews were admitted with averages of 50 percent.

14. Visit to Camp "L," Sep. 8, 1940, General Files, CJC.

15. Henry Kreisel, "Diary of an Internment," *White Pelican*, Summer 1974, p. 10.   281

Shanghai Chronicle: Nazi Refugees in China

RENATA BERG-PAN

This presentation is dedicated to Raymond and William Pan—both refugees from Shanghai.

With the help of a transit visa from Germany through France or Italy and approximately $540 for a ticket, a refugee from Nazi Germany could board a ship (usually on the Lloyd-Tristino Line) sailing from Trieste to Shanghai—via Alexandria, through the Suez Canal (or occasionally around the Cape of Good Hope), from there to Bombay, Singapore, Hong Kong, and finally, after a voyage of about four weeks, into the muddy waters of Shanghai Harbor. This route, however, was open only before Italy entered the war—that is, until June 10, 1940. Thereafter, a refugee had to use the land route, beginning in Moscow, traveling on the Trans-Siberian railroad to Manchuria (Manchouli), journeying to Harbin, and arriving in Dairen, whence a boat took him to Shanghai.

Although Nazi refugees found a haven in other Chinese cities—such as Harbin, Tientsin, Tsingtao, Peking—for all practical purposes Shanghai became synonymous with refugee life in China. (It was there that the Jewish relief organizations began to open their offices in the mid-1930s.)

Why would anyone from central Europe wish to travel more than seven thousand miles to a country whose culture and language are among the most difficult for most Westerners to grasp? Why would anyone wish to come to a city that promised little chance for economic success to a penniless foreigner (a *yang-kueitze*)? Shanghai, moreover, had a reputation for harboring pestilence and being wracked by wars. The answer is that Shanghai—that is to say, the International Settlement—required neither visas nor police certificates. It did not ask for affidavits of health, nor did it call for proof of financial independence. There were no quotas, and no one demanded that an immigrant be of unblemished moral character or of Nobel Prize stature. It did not matter to which political party a new arrival belonged. The city was essentially color-blind and tolerant toward all religions and political persuasions. Shanghai was a place to which any refugee could go.

Immigration to Shanghai of refugees fleeing Hitler's Europe occurred in three phases. The first began in 1933, when numerous professionals, mostly academics and physicians, left Germany. The second phase of immigration began immediately after the so-called *Kristallnacht*, November 10–11, 1938, unleashed by far the largest stream of German and Austrian refugees (seventeen thousand) to enter Shanghai. It reached its peak in early 1939, by which time most other countries had closed their doors to European émigrés. In August of that year, severe restrictions were also imposed upon immigration to Shanghai, because by that time the burden of absorbing the refugees had become too heavy for the local population, including the local resident Jewish communities. After November 1, 1939, immigration was so restricted for refugees from Europe that it almost ceased completely. Nevertheless, a third group of Polish refugees, leaving shortly after Hitler's invasion of Poland and numbering about one thousand persons, traveled eastward across the USSR, and after a stay in Kobe, Japan, where they were treated with great hospitality, finally arrived in Shanghai in the fall of 1941.

The earliest group of refugees was received with some degree of cordiality, since its members usually had managed to bring along money and valuable possessions that allowed them to remain financially independent. Moreover, during the early phase of immigration, professionals, in this case mostly physicians, had a good chance to enter the job market and earn respectable livings. It was not necessary for doctors, for example, to submit to new medical examinations; proof of licensing in the country of origin was usually sufficient for opening a practice or for gaining permission to work in a hospital. The later arrivals had a much more difficult time. For one thing, the already existing Shanghai Jewish communities, the Ashkenazi and the Sephardi, who had established themselves dec-

284

ades before and who in general were very wealthy, did not welcome the large contingent of new arrivals with open arms, although they did not shut them out entirely either. How did the refugees manage to survive, and how did they honor the muses?

With a population of four million Chinese plus one hundred thousand foreigners (including 29,000 Japanese, 15,000 Russians, 9,000 British, 5,000 non-Jewish Germans and Austrians and 4,000 Americans), Shanghai in 1939 was a city of contradictions. A city with five universities, several first-rate hotels, a considerable number of scientific and scholarly institutions, a good symphony orchestra, and one English-language theater, it also contained many hidden opium dens, prostitutes, beggars, crooks, and starved ricksha coolies. Health conditions were so out of control that the Municipal Council in one year (1935) picked up 20,746 dead bodies, most of which were Chinese, from the streets. In one winter night, hundreds of people froze to death.

In many ways Shanghai resembled the city of Mahagonny, where the greatest crime was not to have any money. From the opera *The Rise and Fall of the City of Mahagonny*, written and composed by two refugees of this era, Bertolt Brecht and Kurt Weill, we remember the following words: "If you make your bed, you must lie there, and nobody cares what you do, and if somebody kicks, it is I, dear, and if someone gets kicked, it is you." Those who were kicked during the late 1930s were mostly the masses of poor Chinese. Exploited by the foreign interests controlling that Far Eastern city, harassed by their own civil war as well as by their Japanese masters, their struggle for survival was harder and more fierce than that of the refugees. Many refugees at one time or another could afford a maid, always a Chinese. Yet, so far, I have not come across a single case of a European refugee in Shanghai having to clean house and cook dinner for a Chinese master. The standard of living of the Chinese was so far below that of the refugees that the latter were frequently robbed, often by their servants but even more frequently on the open streets.

Up to the time of the Sino-Japanese hostilities, Shanghai was a comparatively wealthy city. Consumer goods were shipped in from the fertile Chinese hinterland, and there was always sufficient demand for them. In addition, no import tax was levied on foreign goods. By the early 1930s, textiles, food, and cotton had replaced the former trade of tea, silk, and opium. Cheap labor and inland water transportation compensated for the lack of energy and raw materials. 285

Industrial goods were frequently produced in shops operated from private homes, and electricity was inexpensive. The economy, in short, flourished, for a certain segment of the population if not for everyone. Conditions changed drastically with the onset of the conflict with Japan, when the city was cut off from the hinterland and when foreign investors began to look elsewhere. By 1939 Shanghai was no longer an economically thriving city.

Refugees arriving in 1933 or shortly thereafter could live in any one of three foreign settlements—the International Settlement, the French Concession (also called Frenchtown), and the Japanese-controlled Hongkew district (Little Tokyo). The second and largest group of immigrants generally settled in Hongkew, the desolate northeastern suburb of Shanghai, bordered on the west by the Hongkew Creek, the south by the Whangpoo River, and the east by the Yangtzepoo River. It had been bombed by the Japanese in 1937 and had also been practically reduced to rubble by the Chinese armies, as they carried out a scorched-earth policy during their retreat into the interior of the country. One of my interviewees compared the general blight of Hongkew to that prevailing in the Bronx, in New York City, at the present time. Nobody really wanted to live in Hongkew, yet rents there were about 75 percent lower than anywhere else, and food was much cheaper as well. (Of the eighteen thousand European refugees in Shanghai, approximately fifty-five hundred lived in either Frenchtown or the International Settlement, where at most they could afford a room or two.) Most refugees lived in the so-called lane houses, typical structures in the Hongkew district. These were buildings lined up in rows, surrounded by a wall with a gate, and sometimes watched by Sikhs. One out of ten refugees lived in refugee camps.

The Chinese who lived in the district frequently had to learn German, Yiddish, or English in order to themselves survive—as waiters, for example, or as small shopkeepers. With very few exceptions, even among the children, the refugees did not know and did not bother to learn the Chinese language because of a sense of cultural superiority.

It is generally agreed that the years 1939 to 1941 were the best in the entire seven- to eight-year time span during which most refugees lived in Shanghai. Those three years were characterized by a spirit of hope, optimism, and a sense of community that translated itself into creative activities leading to a wholesale importation of European-Jewish values into the Far East. Thus the refugees rebuilt much

286

of the dreary, burnt-out Hongkew district, creating a "Little Vienna" on Chusan Road. They established schools and kindergartens, founded soccer clubs and Boy Scout groups, and established several newspapers (there were five German-language newspapers), of which the *Shanghai Jewish Chronicle* was probably the most prestigious, although it paid rock-bottom salaries to its journalists. The Hongkew community, moreover, built synagogues and had the Sabbath observed even by the non-Jewish population. There was an adult education center, offering courses in Jewish history, Chinese poetry, the influence of Greek culture upon Europe, and other intellectual subjects, although the courses were generally attended by at most a dozen students.

It was during this period that the muses that had fled Hitler flourished most vigorously, with Euterpe decidedly the most popular. The refugee population had a disproportionate number of professional and amateur musicians among them; there were numerous concerts and other musical events, and Hongkew prided itself on having its own chamber orchestra. The amateur musicians were doctors of medicine, including, for example, Erich Marcuse, who was an outstanding conductor, and Arthur Wolf, whose compositions had previously been well-received in Germany.

At least sixty German-language theatrical productions were offered in Hongkew from 1939 to 1947, including works by Hugo von Hofmannsthal, Bertolt Brecht and Kurt Weill (*The Threepenny Opera*), Klabund, Theodore Lessing, August Strindberg, Sophocles, George Bernard Shaw, John Galsworthy, and Noel Coward. Most, though, were light operas and operettas such as the *Merry Widow, The Count of Luxemburg*, and *The Bat*—a cultural fare that caused considerable chagrin among the more serious-minded members of the refugee community. There was a good deal of cultural snobbery among the audience in Hongkew because a very large number of its residents had come from Berlin and Vienna, which had been rival cities in Europe in the 1930s. This led to disputes, even quarrels, among the Berlin and Vienna refugees in Shanghai.

There also were several local playwrights whose works were performed in Hongkew. Conditions for the performance of plays were often primitive, and there were no financial rewards. A Yiddish theater survived in Hongkew for approximately two years, but since the potential audience was much smaller for Yiddish than for German, its success was not spectacular. The fine arts were represented, too. Hongkew was proud to have housed, at one time or another,

287

271 artists.

In general, as far as the muses were concerned, it has to be said that the Europeans occupying the Hongkew district created their own artistic world and did not interact much with the local cultural scene. An exception was Hans Jacoby, who recently completed his memoirs about his Shanghai years. He mingled with the Chinese population and had access to the more wealthy members of Chinese society. He painted several portraits of Chinese citizens. He also tried initially to live in an area not inhabited by foreigners, but since such areas were crime-ridden in Shanghai at the time, he later moved back into one of the settlements. Few Chinese-inspired themes are reflected in the artistic works of the refugees. Several writers have claimed that the Hongkew community left its impact upon Chinese music. This may very well be the case; anyone listening to the new music coming out of the People's Republic of China will detect unmistakable Western influences, and one of the most famous Chinese folk songs, "Nan-gu sheng, Nan-gu sheng, gu-sheng, san-ke-ei," was inspired by Dvořák's *New World* Symphony.

The muses fell almost silent with the beginning of the Pacific war. Plays and concerts could no longer be produced without severe strain. As a result of mounting inflation and reduced funds from the relief agencies, there was no money for lighting a stage, for paper, for nails, for the simplest costumes, even for heat in the rehearsal rooms. Moreover, the Pacific war—compounded by the Sino-Japanese war and the civil war in China itself—made survival difficult for the refugees. Shanghai was bombed several times, and at least 130 refugees (not to mention countless Chinese) lost their lives during these air raids.

In 1943 the Japanese, who since 1941 had complete control of Hongkew, declared one section of the district a restricted area. All persons of foreign origin who had arrived after 1937 were asked to move into what came to be called the "ghetto" within Hongkew, an area comprising less than one square mile, into which sixteen thousand refugees were added to the one hundred thousand Chinese who already lived there. In order for inhabitants to leave the ghetto, they needed a pass, which could be obtained only when they had a job requiring travel out of the ghetto. These three years, 1943–45, were genuinely years of hardship for the refugees as well as for the Chinese. The problems of survival assumed gigantic proportions, and, in general, there was little time, money, or spirit for cultural and artistic production. Yet, Alfred Dreyfuss, a communist who lives

288

in East Germany, and who for a while taught at a Shanghai University, recalled playing a house concert (Brahms's String Quartet no. 51 in C Minor), when suddenly an air raid struck Shanghai. While his group of players continued with their music, a bomb hit the top floor of the building in which they were performing and tore off the leg of a young boy sleeping there.

The Hongkew ghetto was reopened in 1945, and its inhabitants were allowed to leave. But, until Hongkew was drained of its artistic talent, the muses were honored as much as they had been earlier. In 1954, when all but a dozen refugees had departed Shanghai, the Joint Distribution Committee closed its offices. The new Communist Chinese government had been eager to expel all foreigners, including the refugees in its territories. Most members of the Jewish community immigrated to Israel or the United States. By April 1981 only one member of the refugee community remained in Shanghai, Max Leibowitz—a man totally disabled by Parkinson's disease. Among the refugees who settled in Shanghai, former Secretary of the Treasury Michael Blumenthal became perhaps the most illustrious. The muses who fled Hitler left Shanghai and were, for a while at least, replaced by the "one hundred flowers." But that is another chapter in the history of the city and in the history of cultural adaptation.

Acknowledgments

I am especially indebted to those persons who provided me with information necessary for this presentation: Dr. Sybil Milton of the Leo Baeck Institute, who called my attention to the most recent memoirs written about Shanghai refugee life; Mr. Adolph Glassgold, formerly director of the Joint Distribution Committee in Shanghai; Mr. David Chien, a Chinese lawyer who worked on refugee problems in Shanghai; and Dr. David Kranzler, whose book on the subject has been of great help to me and who was very generous in providing me with additional information I requested.

289

The Reception of the Muses in the Circum-Caribbean

JUDITH LAIKIN ELKIN

Because Caribbean societies are distinctively if erratically Catholic, and because they have never embraced the ideal of cultural pluralism, it is necessary when discussing the admission and acculturation of immigrants to distinguish between those who profess the dominant faith and those who do not. In this paper, I consider Jews exclusively.

Some Jewish intellectuals and artists fleeing Germany and Austria found refuge in the republics of the circum-Caribbean, but their reception was, in the fullest sense of the word, restrained. Few were admitted, fewer were able to convert temporary havens into permanent homes, and fewer still were able to make meaningful contributions to the arts and sciences while living in these countries. Generalizations for so large an area, so scattered a population, must always allow for exceptions, but it is nevertheless apparent that the circum-Caribbean benefited little from the flight of the muses.

Given this negative finding, the question becomes, why not? Why should the Caribbean area not have gained elements vital to the development of the arts and sciences in the same measure as the United States, its immediate neighbor, did? What does the failure of German Jewish muses to acculturate to the Caribbean tell us about this migration? What does it tell us about Caribbean societies? The answer cannot lie in the nature of the immigrant stream, since in the darkling years leading down into the Holocaust Kingdom, an entire population—women, children, men; painters, technicians, cobblers, professors—was on the move in search of refuge. They entered where they were admitted, according to rules of admissibility established not by themselves but by their hosts. Instead, the reason must be sought in the nature of the circum-Caribbean societies: in their attitudes toward immigrants, their immigration law, their acquiescence in United States policy, and, last, the immigrants' reaction to all these factors.

The sources for a study of these questions are diffuse, and generalizations perilous. The trajectories of the Caribbean nations, linked by conquest in the sixteenth century, have diverged at an accelerating rate. Each nation has generated its own society and follows a distinct national policy, although during the 1930s these were still confined within boundaries marked out by the U.S. Department of State. In the scholarly world, although Latin American studies has a permanent place, and Jewish studies has recently gained academic acceptance, Latin American Jewish studies is a newly emerging discipline that has not yet generated the data needed for a global formulation of issues. Only a start has been made.[1]

Data concerning legal immigration are on the public record, but statistics for Jews are difficult to separate from general population figures. Many of the figures offered in this paper can only be informed estimates, while the variety of situations into which the refugees came makes it impossible to present information for directly comparable groups. Files can be found for some immigrants in the archives of Jewish immigration agencies such as the American Joint Distribution Committee (AJDC) or the Hebrew Immigrant Aid Society (HIAS)—but only for persons who migrated with their aid (by no means all did). Undoubtedly, numbers of immigrants entered Latin America illegally, by bribing consular and port officials. An unknown number of Jews converted to Catholicism in order to gain entry to Colombia and Venezuela, which demanded certificates of baptism. Also among the refugees were persons defined as Jews under the Nuremberg laws, but who did not regard themselves as Jews. No attempt has been made here to trace clandestine immigration.

For all these reasons and more, the evidence concerning immigration and acculturation of German-speaking Jewish intellectuals and artists to the circum-Caribbean is fragmentary. But it is also highly suggestive. Of the twelve Spanish-speaking republics that might be included in the circum-Caribbean, seven are examined briefly to determine their receptivity to Jewish immigration. Within these restricted parameters, the question is asked: what was there about these societies that discouraged the acceptance of Jewish "muses"?

Venezuela was not a country of immigration during the first half of this century. In the generation 1900–35, only thirty thousand immigrants were admitted; consequently, in 1941, foreigners comprised barely 1.2 percent of the Venezuelan population.[2] Immigration figures for the crucial years are extremely low: 2,914 immigrants of all origins entered the country in 1939–40, and 597 entered between 1941–44. These numbers may have included six hundred overt Jews.[3] The entry of even this small cohort caused government officials to speculate publicly as to whether or not Jews were assimilable, and much concern was expressed for the need to maintain the country's "demographic equilibrium."

Nor was immigration an outstanding concern of Colombia, despite the election of Liberal administrations in 1934 and again in 1938. The Colombian government collaborated with the United States by permitting the latter to conduct a counterespionage operation from its embassy and by nationalizing the German airlines so that German pilots could be replaced by Americans.[4] However, these acts stemmed from Colombia's relationship to the United States, not from sympathy for the victims of Nazism. In 1938 the Colombian government ordered its consuls in Europe not to issue visas to any person who had lost his nationality or who had no guarantee of being able to return to his country of origin. The following year, all legal immigration was halted. As a result of restrictive policies, only 3,695 Jews entered Colombia during the decade 1933–43; of these, 2,347 were German-speaking.[5] A majority of them appear to have been businessmen and their families—people with sufficient funds to pay the fees that were extracted from them along the way.

Mexico was one of the few republics of the circum-Caribbean with a pre-existing Jewish population, but Mexican Jews had no influence on government immigration policy. Beginning in 1930 Mexican immigration law favored immigrants of Latin and Catholic culture, on the ground that it would be easier to assimilate them. Six years later severe limitations were placed on the types of workers who could be admitted, with preference given to agricultural and industrial workers. In 1938 a full-fledged quota system was instituted; the limit for Germans was set at five thousand per year.[6] The Evian Conference of 1938 had no impact on Mexican priorities. In 1940 immigration law was further tightened so that only Spanish citizens and nationals of Western Hemisphere countries could be admitted. Thus no more than seven hundred German-speaking Jewish refugees may have entered Mexico during the peak migration years. (A small number were admitted on parole in 1942 on condition they leave Mexico at war's end.)

A 1940 occupational census among Ashkenazic Jews of Mexico City showed only 2½ percent of adult males working in the liberal professions.[7] This proportion had risen to 10 percent a decade later. However, not many of these could have been refugees from Nazism, since a 1957 census found that just 7 percent of Mexican Jews originated in Germany or Austria, and many of these stemmed from earlier migrations.

At Evian, as is well known, the Dominican Republic dictator Rafael Trujillo was the only head of state to offer a haven to Jewish refugees, promising to admit one hundred thousand Jewish refugees from Nazism on the condition that they dedicate themselves to agriculture. Accordingly, a corporation (Dominican Republic Settlement Association, or DORSA) was formed, an agreement reached between it and the Dominican government that extended religious toleration to settlers, and a colony established at Sosua on land donated by El Benefactor. A total of about eight hundred Jewish refugees lived at Sosua at some time during the war, working as farmers.[8]

Characteristic of the way in which refugees arrived at Sosua is the story told by one of its settlers. As a youth he had studied piano and harmony with Alban Berg, while also obtaining a diploma in architecture. Fleeing Austria, his family spent two years in a Swiss refugee camp where they heard about Sosua, which was presented to them as an experiment in determining whether Europeans could live and work in a subtropical climate. They took the chance. The young man utilized his architectural training to design and construct homes and furniture for the colonists; later, he taught art and music at the local public school. Although free to work as he pleased, he had no contact with Dominicans in the same profession. In 1946 he immigrated to the United States, becoming a professor of art and music at a small college.

There are known to have been quite a few intellectuals, artists, and professionals in this group. Refugee doctors, nurses, and physiotherapists established a hospital in Sosua from which they mounted a mosquito control program that reduced the incidence of malaria in the province of Puerto Plata. But all the professional persons who can be traced left the island at the end of the war. A dentist now living in the United States avows that he experienced no problem practicing his profession in Santo Domingo, but he left. Lothar Deutsch, painter and sculptor, lived and worked in the Dominican Republic throughout the war, but he, too, immigrated to the United States when it ended. One of those who relocated to the United States explained his motivation to the writer in private:

> Though I was at the Dominican Republic for six years and enjoyed being there, I did not consider making it my permanent home. My reason is that the cultural vacuum at that time made me aware that I was living there only for the duration.

A Jewish population remains in the Dominican Republic today. It is engaged in the occupations preferred by the government: dairy farming and sausage making.

Ecuador was the last country in the world to continue admitting German Jewish refugees, maintaining a liberal admissions policy to the beginning of 1939. However, from 1938 on, immigrant visas were issued only to persons who committed themselves to agriculture or industry exclusively. Once inside the country it was possible to buy permits to change one's occupation, but these were difficult to come by and were often revoked due to the desire of local merchants to limit competition. As a result, although there are still families living in Quito today that can be traced to this migration, there are few professionals among them. Two lawyers originating in the German Jewish refugee stream could be identified; both worked for Jewish communal institutions. Jewish dental surgeons practiced illegally in Quito for a time but were closed down by the government. The difficulty of moving into a profession, even one for which a person had trained and one in which there was a shortage of skilled manpower, is illustrated by the case of two young Jewish women who opened a kindergarten in Quito. Although they had been educated in Ecuadorian schools and at the Universidad de Quito, the government closed their school on the ground the women had violated the terms of their admission to the country (when they were children) as agricultural workers.[9]

Some German-speaking Jews succeeded as entrepreneurs and took part in Ecuador's modernization. But intellectuals have found the cultural *ambiente* impermeable, and there is continuing emigration from that country of Jewish college-bound youth.

Panama benefited directly from the expulsion of Jewish professors from their posts at German universities. In 1935, when the Universidad Interamericana was founded with 175 students in rented premises, the nuclear faculty included no fewer than eleven German professors. These were Richard Behrendt (sociology, political economy), Werner Bohnstedt (geography), Franz Borkenau (sociology), Erich Graetz (biology, chemistry), Paul Honigsheim (sociology, anthropology), Siegfried Mallowan (chemistry), Carlos Mertz (statistics, public finance), and four others named Wolf (Roman law), Hart (Roman law), Luban (commercial law), and Fischer (psychiatry).[10] As a group these men helped shape the new institution (later, the Universidad Nacional), teaching a generation of students who went on to occupy important positions in Panamanian life. All but Mertz were Jews.

Although these men succeeded in their professional lives—Behrendt became dean of social and economic sciences; Graetz, dean of the faculty of science—all but two left Panama after the war. Borkenau became an adviser on Soviet affairs to the government of the Federal Republic of Germany; Behrendt taught Latin American studies at the Free University of Berlin; Honigsheim went to Michigan State University, where he completed his book *On Max Weber.*

Why did they leave? Personal motivations must have varied, but a questionnaire circulated among students of these professors forty years after their graduation revealed some interesting clues. The former students credited the German professors with having had a profound influence on the university and on Panamanian life. However, they sensed that they felt themselves to be transients. Many expressed unease that, in teaching current social and economic theories, they were exposing themselves to accusations of antireligious attitudes in the popular press. It is suggestive that the two professors who stayed on in the country were both chemists and thus far less likely than the sociologists or political economists to run into social barriers to the free exercise of intellect.

Cuba was far and away the greatest recipient of German Jewish refugees during this period. Between twelve and twenty thousand Jewish immigrants landed on the island between 1933 and 1944. The majority had been issued tourist or transit visas, and they reimmigrated quickly to the United States or Mexico. While Washington closed its consulates in Germany, Italy, and Nazi-occupied territories in June 1941, Cuban consulates remained open another year. During that time Cuban consular officials legally issued or sold large num-

296

bers of travel documents, many of which were later repudiated. In April 1942 the Cuban government announced it would accept no more transmigrants born in Axis-controlled countries.

AJDC records for some eight thousand immigrants who entered Cuba with their assistance in the years 1937–44 show that 49 percent of them came from Germany and Austria. Reflecting high levels of education among German Jews, almost one-quarter of this cohort practiced an intellectual profession; 2.6 percent described themselves as artists.[11]

Jewish immigration tapered off following the notorious *St. Louis* incident of 1939, when 930 passengers aboard a German vessel, all of them holding landing certificates issued by the Cuban director general of immigration and 734 also in possession of valid visas for entry into the United States, were denied permission to land and were shipped back to European ports. Exclusion of the *St. Louis* refugees, combined with an intense barrage of Nazi propaganda coming from Gestapo and Hapag agents on the island and considerable anti-Semitism emanating from official sources and the press, caused those refugees who had been admitted to view Cuba as a temporary haven. Moreover, labor legislation favoring the native-born made it extremely difficult for an immigrant to earn a living; consequently, most recent immigrants had to depend on U.S. Jewish philanthropic organizations. Under the circumstances, these organizations themselves were eager to move their charges off the island and into an economy where they would be able to support themselves.

Yet several did succeed in integrating themselves temporarily into Cuban national life. Three became university professors: Heinrich Friedland (education), Desiderio Weiss (language), and Boris Goldenberg (sociology). There were also several practicing Jewish lawyers and quite a few artists and writers. Physicians, however, were not allowed to practice: a Dr. Kaganoff, unable to obtain a license, worked as a hospital interpreter, dispensing medical opinions to those who relied on him for translation. At the end of the war, he, along with many others, left the island.

Goldenberg's biography, published in the preface to his book, *The Cuban Revolution and Latin America*, is instructive.[12] Born in Russia, he was schooled in Germany (for which reason he is included in the present sample). Having been a member of the Communist party—he was expelled from it in 1929—he was arrested by the Nazis but succeeded in escaping to France. When that country fell to the Nazis, he escaped once more, this time to Cuba. There he joined

297

various Marxist revolutionary groups and was an early supporter of Fidel Castro. However, he broke with the revolutionary regime one year after its victory and in 1960 returned to Europe.

Those who did not leave Cuba immediately after World War II left in the aftermath of the Cuban revolution, either because fidelista economic policies undercut the basis for their existence or because, like Goldenberg, they became disenchanted with the revolution. Sender Kaplan, former editor of the respected *Havaner Lebn*, now resident in Miami, summarizes succinctly the impact of the German Jewish immigrants: "They all left."

No political development in the Caribbean can be studied without reference to the role of the United States. Although the American government at first encouraged Latin Americans to open their doors to immigrants,

by June 1940 the Latin American division [of the Department of State] was actually discouraging the acceptance of refugees in the Caribbean and Central America on the ground that spies had infiltrated the refugee stream.[13]

In 1944 an FBI report on Sosua, based on a Cuban police report, alleged active espionage within the colony, replete with shore-to-ship signals (presumably, the flashlights of the settlers). Throughout this period the State Department informally discouraged the Caribbean republics from accepting refugees because of alleged danger to the Panama Canal.

The established community of Panamanian Jews, who were Sephardim, accepted the policy in good faith. To them one German was like another. Although they lodged and fed a number of Jewish refugees in 1941, the community cooperated willingly with security measures initiated by their government.

The National Government took steps, upon the request of the United States, to protect the Panama Canal against acts of sabotage. The fact was that little was known of the Germans, and there could have been spies among them. All male refugees were detained; the women and children stayed for some time under the protection of the ladies of Kol Shearith Israel.[14]

The end of the war brought no evidence of spies among Jewish refugees.

Intermittently, when the United States security psychosis let up, the issuance of travel documents resumed, motivated in no small part by simple greed—large sums of money could be extracted from desperate refugees or from the Jewish organizations trying to help them. Many survived the middle passage because of the venality of individual officials, although sometimes, as in the *St. Louis* debacle, someone overplayed his hand, with disastrous consequences for the refugees.

When it came to buying and selling travel documents, those with ready cash were in an advantageous position. Intellectuals and artists were seldom among this number unless they could be ransomed by family or colleagues; here, the small size of established communities in the Caribbean area, and their disengagement from Jewish life elsewhere, made ransom most improbable.

While there was no strong indigenous Jewish population to bargain for the entry of Jews, there were well-entrenched Spanish communities inclined toward fascism and highly organized German groups carrying on Nazi propaganda, particularly in Cuba. They were not entirely successful in closing off Jewish immigration, but neither did they create a welcoming environment for refugees.

The evidence is that the nations of the circum-Caribbean were not interested in enticing Jewish muses to their shores. Governments either closed off immigration entirely, established quotas on the U.S. model, or designed a system of preferences that did not fit the refugees' demographic profile: that they be Latin, of Catholic culture, and engage in farming. These preferences, rooted in social norms, were often legislated in a spirit of idealism that did not reflect existing realities. The vision of the contented farmer and happy proletarian comported ill with the reality of landless campesinos and an underdeveloped industrial sector that offered neither land nor jobs to newcomers. The technical, scientific, and creative skills that these refugees had to offer, and that might have been put to use generating jobs and restructuring agriculture, were neither sought nor, when they entered accidentally, nurtured. Being an intellectual or an artist was no recommendation under Caribbean immigration laws at this time.

The most exclusionary policies were followed by the largest of the Caribbean republics, those with the greatest economic potential (Colombia, Venezuela, Mexico). Thus, the immigrant pool from which intellectual or artistic initiative could emerge remained very small. The smaller, less developed republics (Ecuador, the Dominican Republic, Panama, Cuba) followed more generous policies but placed severe economic and intellectual limitations on the immigrants' activities. The lack of fit between the host societies' expectations of the immigrants and the immigrants' norms and levels of education limited the degree to which the immigrants could integrate themselves socially and economically (we do not speak of political integration, since that is permitted to few Latin Americans). There were few factory workers or farmers among German and Austrian Jews of the period, and those who fancied themselves cast in the mold of the pioneer were more likely to be attracted to Palestine than to (in the words of one Sosua veteran) "some far-off tropical island."

The volatility of Caribbean politics was another factor in the transience of this group. In none of the Caribbean republics were there constitutional guarantees of equality before the law. In predominantly Catholic societies Jews could not acquire the degree of social integration necessary to protect their human rights in the absence of such guarantees. A benevolent dictator was a shaky pillar to lean on: no one could foresee the consequences of his assassination. A violent change in government could totally alter the conditions for their existence. The relative underdevelopment of intellectual life did not create a milieu conducive to achievement; intellectuals in public life were particularly vulnerable since the conformist atmosphere nurtured by the Catholic church made dissent appear to be subversive of the established order. (This is probably another reason that immigration legislation tended to favor farmers and factory workers.) Aware of the broadening of opportunity that greeted equally impoverished and disoriented immigrants to the United States, even those refugees who lived quite happily in the Caribbean area during the war left when it was over.

It should be kept in mind that many immigrants whose occupations would not qualify them for "muse" status remained intellectuals in their own terms. Although constrained to turn to farming, trade, or cottage industry to earn their livelihood, they nevertheless sustained an active internal Jewish life. But cultural activities that do not derive from the Hispanic and Catholic tradition are not often acknowledged in these societies, leaving specifically Jewish muses invisible to non-Jewish observers.

Despite gaps in the data, this overview suggests that the attitude toward immigration expressed in the legislation of the circum-Caribbean republics limited the number and type of immigrants who would be admitted and, once they were admitted, limited the activities in which they could engage. Preference for farmers and factory workers resulted in the creation of small classes of these persons in all the countries surveyed, but it did not create the conditions for growth of an intelligentsia. Though here and there a vagrant muse may be sighted on a university campus or in a radio station, nowhere in the circum-Caribbean did a muse of international stature emerge. These republics spurned the opportunity to import and naturalize the creative talent Nazism cast loose in the world, affirming instead a commitment to the status quo and a reaffirmation of values imposed upon them four centuries earlier by the Spanish conquest.

Notes

1. A basic bibliography for this subject is available in Judith Laikin Elkin, *Latin American Jewish Studies* (Cincinnati, 1980).

2. J.L. Salcedo Bastardo, *Historia fundamental de Venezuela* (Caracas, 1977), p. 543.

3. Jacob Shatzky, *Comunidades judías en Latinoamérica* (Buenos Aires, 1952), p. 60.

4. Vernon Lee Fluharty, *Dance of the Millions: Military Rule and the Social Revolution in Colombia, 1930–1956* (Pittsburgh, 1957), p. 60.

5. Shatzky, *Comunidades judías*, p. 92.

6. The history of Mexican immigration policy is summarized in Harriet Sara Lesser, "A History of the Jewish Community of Mexico City, 1912–1970" (Ph.D. diss., Jewish Theological Seminary and Columbia University, 1972).

7. Tovye Meisel, "Yidn in Meksike," *Algemeine Entsiclopedia* 5 (1957): 410.

8. The island's limited absorptive capacity, the use of inappropriate recruiting methods, the almost total lack of farmers among German Jews, and disbelief in the approach of the final solution kept enrollment down. The Sosua story is told in Brookings Institution, *Refugee Settlement in the Dominican Republic* (Washington, D.C., 1942), and in DORSA's *Sosua, Haven for Refugees in the Dominican Republic*, Pamphlet no. 4 (New York, 1941). A documentary film on the colony is being prepared by Harriet Taub of Sosua-Sol Productions.

9. American Joint Distribution Committee Archives: Ecuador.

10. Nestor G. Porcell, "Imagen e influencia de los docentes alemanes en la naciente universidad y en la cultura nacional," *Revista Loteria no. 261*, Noviembre 1977, pp. 1–29.

301

11. Leizer Ran, ed., *Hemshej oif kubaner erd* [Dual title: *Continuidad hebrea en tierra Cubana*, Almanaque conmemorativo del 25 aniversario del Central Israelita de Cuba, 1925–50] (Havana, 1951), p. 80.

12. Boris Goldenberg, *The Cuban Revolution and Latin America* (New York, 1965).

13. Henry L. Feingold, *The Politics of Rescue: The Roosevelt Administration and the Holocaust 1938–1945* (New Brunswick, N.J., 1970), p. 129.

14. E. Alvin Fidanque et al, *Kol Shearith Israel: Cien años de vida judía en Panamá, 1876–1976* (Panama, 1977), p. 231.

JUDITH LAIKIN ELKIN

Das andere Deutschland: The Anti-Fascist Exile Network in Southern South America

RONALD C. NEWTON

As this symposium is being held under the genial, elfin sign of Albert Einstein, I would like to begin with an Einstein story. In 1925 Einstein visited Argentina to lecture at the National University of Buenos Aires and to raise money for Zionism from "wealthy Jews." According to the socialist *Deutsche Zeitung* of Buenos Aires, the great physicist was the object of an anti-Semitic whispering campaign within the capital's German colony; he was snubbed by the German Scientific Society and other important German-speaking circles. Einstein himself, however, felt that it was not really so bad. He wrote in his diary that he was embarrassed by the fulsome welcome of the German community: "Strange people, these Germans," he mused after meeting the German minister. "I am a foul-smelling flower to them yet they keep tucking me into their buttonholes."[1] In Argentine circles Einstein the scientist seems to have made little impact, but the image of Einstein the humanitarian remained.

Let me sketch in some background for my larger themes.

1. Argentina remained neutral during World War I, a fact of great importance to German industrialists and policy planners. German capital holdings in Argentina actually increased during the war years, and they were augmented again in the early 1920s by major invest-

ments, particularly in dependencies of the great German chemical, pharmaceutical, metallurgical, electrical, and heavy-construction combines. In the 1930s this establishment profited handsomely from German economic revival under Nazi rule and the regime's trade offensive toward Latin America. Nevertheless, most of its leaders were careful to avoid any ideological commitment to Nazism. They were aware that in the last analysis their properties were hostage to British and American sea power—any illusions on this score were scuttled with *Graf Spee* in December 1939—and on occasion they acted to short-circuit adventures proposed by Nazi agents-on-mission, adventures that might have pushed Argentina's Fascists into an open break with the Allies and hence invited the latter's overwhelming retaliation.[2]

2. In the 1920s Argentina, then believed to be a "land of the future," exerted a great pull on the German imagination: from 1918 to the Depression, perhaps 130,000 to 140,000 German-speaking immigrants entered the country. Success eluded most of them; one-third to one-half left again. Still, by the late 1930s the ethnic minority had grown to about a quarter of a million persons, the greatest number of whom were peasants of Russian or East European origin. In addition, there were two to three hundred thousand Jews in Argentina. The economic elite of the Jewish collectivity was of western European origin and was a significant element of the cosmopolitan international community that dominated the country's economic life. The majority, however, were *Ostjuden*; between them and the "top-hat Jews" was an enormous socioeconomic and cultural abyss that would only slowly and imperfectly be bridged after 1933. There were thirteen million Argentines altogether in 1931, sixteen million in 1947.[3]

3. Shock waves from the founding struggles of the Weimar Republic had done much to politicize the German-speakers. Both the left and the right were well represented, but because of its wealth derived from land, trade, banking, and branch-plant industry, the right was dominant. Its influence was strong in the elaborate network of churches, schools, welfare agencies, clubs, and other voluntary associations that serviced the immigrant communities. The German right also had extensive contacts with its Argentine compeers, the most important of which had developed as a result of German military trainers who had been working with the Argentine Army since the first cadre arrived in 1900.

304

4. By the 1930s there existed in Argentina a thriving tradition of German scientific and technical work. German academics were influential in a number of university science faculties, notably those at Buenos Aires, La Plata, and Córdoba. Prussian educationists had founded a seminar for the training of the elite of secondary-school teachers before World War I; German engineers had played a large role in the construction of Buenos Aires's port works and subways and in the administration of the railroads; other technicians dominated certain branches of federal and provincial bureaucracy such as meteorology, hydrology, mining, cartography, and the state petroleum corporation. Such scientific and technical collaboration evolved almost entirely under governmental auspices: academic or technical personnel were nominated by German education ministries or professional associations and were brought to Argentina under public contract. The giant German firms recruited through the professional associations at home, not in Argentina. There were few opportunities for free-lancers, much less for nonconformists.

5. In any case the heyday of the foreign expert was passing in the 1930s, as a function of the rise of a creole middle class that typically looked for fulfillment not in entrepreneurship but in the professions and bureaucracy. Joseph Goebbels's Propaganda Ministry in Berlin capitalized skillfully on the yearning of this new class for recognition of its credentials and status by organizing, usually through the Argentine-German Cultural Institute, lavishly funded "cultural exchanges." By September 1939 several hundred creole professionals, academics, journalists, and politicians had made subsidized trips to Hitler's Reich or had otherwise benefited from German cultivation. The Nazis had thereby created nuclei of Fascist sympathizers in precisely those professional and academic circles that might otherwise have been of great help to qualified professionals then in desperate flight from the Nazi terror. Worth pondering are the benefits that were thereby denied Argentine scientific, academic, and cultural life.[4]

6. From the military coup of September 1930 until the beginning of 1938, Argentina's government was authoritarian, unrepresentative, and tolerant of Fascist agitators and movements. Then, however, through a slip-up in the system of electoral fraud, the nation gained a democratically inclined president, Roberto Ortiz, who remained in office until failing health forced him to resign in mid-

Das andere Deutschland

1940. Ortiz was followed by a regime headed by his vice-president, Ramón Castillo, that was conservative, nationalistic, and unaccommodating to U.S. demands for "hemispheric solidarity"—including a declaration of war upon the Axis—in the aftermath of Pearl Harbor. Castillo was deposed in turn by a military conspiracy in June 1943. The principal figures of the subsequent governing junta proved also to be authoritarian, nationalistic, and resistant to United States blandishments. Colonel Juan Perón gained national prominence through skillful and energetic exploitation of his position as secretary of labor; he would be elected president in his own right early in 1946. Persistent rumors that members of the wartime junta were subsidized by the Germans have never been confirmed, but there is little reason to doubt them.

7. More than six million Europeans migrated to Argentina between the mid-nineteenth century and the Great Depression. In 1931, however, the age of virtually unrestricted immigration came to an end. The price of visas was raised sharply; only persons in possession of capital or skilled trades, or those who had close relatives already domiciled in Argentina, were permitted to purchase them. And beginning in August 1938 entry was granted only to persons who had specialized training (especially in agriculture) or a "call from relatives" (llamada de parientes).

In April 1933 an Aid Committee of German-speaking Jews (Hilfsverein Deutschsprechender Juden) was founded in Buenos Aires to assist refugees by arranging lodging and employment for newcomers and organizing job-retraining courses in the manual arts. It worked closely with similar organizations in western Europe, particularly the Hicem in France. The prominent banker Adolfo Hirsch was its leader and financial mainstay. The committee raised funds also among the local Jewish community and, beginning in 1937, received money from two organizations in New York, the Refugee Economic Corporation and the GOINT Corporation. Years later, the committee's first president, Alberto Klein, told me of the hardships suffered by the refugees and of his regrets that more could not be saved. "But," he added, "those who made it to Argentina were those who possessed capital, talent, initiative. It was a process of natural selection. We got the best."[5]

RONALD C. NEWTON

The aid committee also worked closely with the Jewish Colonization Association (JCA), a British-registered philanthropy that had been active since the 1890s in creating Jewish agricultural settlements on its extensive landholdings in the provinces of Buenos Aires and Entre Rios and in Brazil. Argentine immigration officials, although eager in principle to attract agricultural settlers, were unwilling to permit the JCA much latitude because of their concern that European Jews of the urban business and professional classes would not remain long on the land.[6] The JCA therefore moved slowly, settling fewer than one hundred families per year on its holdings. Usually an urban family in Europe was obliged to send a young male member ahead as a "pioneer" to undergo training and apprenticeship; if all went well he would be able to "call" his family to Argentina within a year or so. By 1939 the JCA had some twenty-five thousand Jewish settlers under its control, most of them in the newer settlements in Entre Rios. It had placed 205 German-Jewish families in the preceding two years and could take another 140 into Argentina and 50 into Brazil immediately. In the first years the colonies grew and prospered with the wartime boom in agricultural commodities. With the advent of the military regime in mid-1943, however, the settlers were increasingly subjected to anti-Semitic harassment and various persecutions at the hands of local officials; it was here that the status of the JCA as a British corporation served it well, for the British Embassy could be called upon to use its considerable influence to help. The cityward drift of young people, already a matter of concern, accelerated. Under both the junta and Perón, anti-Semitic outbreaks continued, making the situation of the Jewish communities uncertain. After 1945 many young agriculturists moved to Palestine, and by the 1960s the agricultural settlements appeared moribund.[7]

It has been estimated that altogether in the twelve years of the Third Reich between forty and forty-five thousand Jewish refugees entered Argentina. No exact figure can be arrived at because the majority of entries were illegal and unrecorded. In the last years of the 1930s, the European-based consuls of the Latin American states— notably Chile, Paraguay, Bolivia, and Cuba—had done a brisk business in the sale of visas (many of which would not be honored by home governments) to persons desperate to escape the oncoming catastrophe. Argentina was then an incomparably more prosperous and "civilized" nation than its neighbors were and, moreover, had a large Jewish community from whom some help might be expected.   307

Many who succeeded in escaping to any part of South America were able, in time, to make their way by clandestine mountain, jungle, and river routes to Buenos Aires—indeed, they were still doing so after 1945, when many earlier arrivals were already on the move to the United States or Israel. On a per capita basis Argentina received more Jewish refugees in this period than any other country *in the world* except Palestine.[8]

In the same period there were in Argentina several thousand anti-Nazi German and Austrian refugees who were not Jews. It is impossible to be more precise about their numbers, for, like the Jews, many entered the country illegally from neighboring republics. The official immigration figures, too, do not discriminate between "German" supporters and opponents of the Hitler regime. Elements of the anti-Nazi opposition were able to collaborate in a number of areas. In 1934, for example, the nazification of the German-language schools (which would finally emerge as a public scandal in 1938) caused a coalition of refugee Jews, socialists (whose rallying-point was the old Vorwärts club), and anti-Fascist republicans associated with the *Argentinisches Tageblatt* to create the Pestalozzi School in a suburb of Buenos Aires. As the first rector of the school, they summoned Alfred Dang, a socialist journalist already in exile in Geneva. His work with the school and in local journalism was so successful that he gained the distinction of being one of the first two Germans in South America to be stripped of citizenship by the Nazis. Dang remained in Buenos Aires after the war and died there in 1956.[9]

The day-to-day existence of the anti-Fascists was extremely precarious.[10] The statutes of Jewish charitable organizations prevented them from aiding non-Jews. The latter had difficulty learning Spanish and obtaining revalidation of professional degrees, and beginning in late 1936 they faced the competition of professional and academic refugees from war-torn Spain. The following year the need to provide for German veterans of the International Brigades brought about the creation of the Das andere Deutschland (DAD), a multipurpose organization central to the refugee experience in Argentina and southern South America until its closure in 1948. The driving force in its founding, and its leader throughout the war years, was August Siemsen. Born in 1884 in Westphalia, the son of a Protestant minister, Siemsen was a journalist and teacher who had been elected to the Reichstag as a socialist in 1930. He went into exile in Switzerland in April 1933 and was called to the Pestalozzi School faculty in

January 1936. Many other teachers at the school were also members of DAD's *Vorstand* (executive committee), among them Walter Damus, Heinrich Groenewald, and Hans Lehmann. The *Vorstand* also included the socialists Rolf Ladendorff, Ernst Lakenbacher, and Rudolf Levy. A third group active in DAD was the Freie Deutsche Bühne (Free German Theater) under the leadership of P. Walter Jacob; its political cabarets were widely popular and an important source of funds for DAD's work.[11]

As the Argentine authorities would not permit the founding of a political organization, Das andere Deutschland consisted in effect of the several thousand subscribers to the journal of the same name, which also continued until 1948. DAD served as an aid society for anti-Fascist exiles, a liaison with Spanish and Italian anti-Fascists, a local propaganda force through its Pestalozzi School contacts and the columns of the *Argentinisches Tageblatt* and the *Semana Israelita*, and a sustainer of the morale of refugees unable to extricate themselves from remote primitive towns in the Argentine interior or in Bolivia or Paraguay. These links with refugees in the interior of the continent were extremely important: the latter gathered political intelligence, which the DAD network passed along to the Allied missions; they also distributed summaries of war news prepared by DAD to small and financially strapped Spanish- and Portuguese-language newspapers, journals that hitherto had been receptive to the boiler-plate propaganda sent to them gratis (or for a small gratuity) by the German and Italian news agencies.

Siemsen and his co-workers were harassed periodically by the Argentine police at the behest of the German Embassy, and for a time in 1943 and 1944 they were forced to move their operations to Montevideo in democratic Uruguay. To their right, they confronted in Argentina the local organization of the Black Front under the vocal and corrupt leadership of Bruno Fricke, Otto Strasser's deputy for South America. To their left, Siemsen maintained good relations with the German and Austrian communists until 1942, when the latter joined the network being organized throughout the Americas by Freies Deutschland, whose headquarters were in the large exile community in Mexico City. Early in 1943 Siemsen called an anti-Fascist congress in Montevideo in an attempt to unify the increasingly contentious fragments of the German-speaking diaspora; however, it was sabotaged by the representatives of Freies Deutschland. Thereafter, the latter, subsidized by the Soviet Embassy and apparently looked upon benignly by the Americans, claimed to speak for all the German anti-Fascists in the Americas. In fact, however, most of DAD's adherents in southern South America appear to have remained loyal through the remainder of the war.

Siemsen never entertained the thought of remaining in Argentina once the war was over. He wrote endlessly of the need to construct a just and peaceable socialist society in postwar Germany; his most mature thinking was summed up in his *Germany's Tragedy and the Future of the World*, published in Buenos Aires in 1945. He finally returned to Germany in 1952 and, shocked at the Nazi survivals and impending militarization of West Germany, promptly moved to East Berlin. There he died in 1958.[12]

In addition to Siemsen, the most distinguished German-speaking refugees to live out the war in Argentina were probably Fritz Busch, P. Walter Jacob, and Paul Zech. Concerning their Argentine experience, the least is known about that of Busch, the Wagnerian musical director. He had grown concerned by the Nazification of the Wagnerians' shrine, Bayreuth, early in the 1920s and ceased to conduct there after 1924, resisting many Nazi inducements to do so. Although "Aryan" and "politically uncompromised," he chose to go into exile once the war began. He was fearful, however, of being seen as an Allied quisling and therefore refused to take public stands. He allowed himself to be interviewed once by Siemsen but otherwise held himself aloof from the wrangling and activism of exile politics. He returned to Germany after the war.[13]

Jacob, a Jew, left Germany in April 1933 and followed the trail of exile through Holland, France, Luxembourg, and Czechoslovakia until he arrived in Buenos Aires in 1938. In April 1940 the Free German Theater, which he had created from the raggle-taggle of theater people among the refugees, opened its doors in Buenos Aires; it remained in existence for ten years. It did not shy away from political theater, such as a highly praised production of Lillian Hellman's *Watch on the Rhine*, but Jacob was aware that its survival depended upon both the tastes of the local German-speaking public and the good will of the Argentine censor; it was necessary, therefore, to keep didacticism at a low key. Jacob defended this policy by maintaining that he was working toward revolutionary ends through conservative means: it appears, that is, that Jacob took very seriously his duty to the theater itself, to the preservation of the classic German tradition as well as the great technical innovations of the Weimar period. Outside the theater he worked actively for DAD; he made extensive friendships in the Argentine political and theatrical

310

worlds and in ten years wrote some two hundred articles in the *Tageblatt* and the *Semana Israelita* as well as longer essays and books on theatrical subjects. In 1950 he returned to Germany to resume his career there in theater and television; in 1967 he became professor of dramatic arts at the University of Cologne. It is likely that Jacob and members of the Freie Deutsche Bühne were among the refugees who left the deepest imprint on their Argentine hosts, for the theatrical world of Buenos Aires in the postwar decades made major advances in sophistication.[14]

The proletarian poet, novelist, and dramatist Paul Zech gained much of his reputation in Germany during the 1920s. He was fifty-two years old in April 1933 when he was fired from the Berlin City Library because of his membership in the Social Democratic party. He went into exile in August and before the year was out had arrived in Buenos Aires. There he was supported by a brother until 1937, when they quarreled. Zech was bitterly unhappy in exile; he never reconciled himself to the fact that his wife had chosen to remain in Germany, nor did he make the least accommodation to Argentine life. He did much journalistic writing and translation from the Spanish but had difficulties getting his work published in the anti-Fascist publishing houses of Europe. Beginning in 1938 he received forty dollars a month from the American Guild for German Cultural Freedom. The following year his poetry collection *Neue Welt: Verse der Emigration* sold eleven copies in Buenos Aires; this threw him into a fit of impenetrable gloom. Politically Zech was closer to the Communist party than to the Social Democrats of the DAD circle. In 1941 he became publisher of the Buenos Aires *Volksblatt,* which followed the communist line. He became increasingly quarrelsome and bitter toward both Argentine Germans and creoles as the war years passed; isolated, he could think only of leaving Buenos Aires, which he detested, and returning home to Germany. He had made plans to do so, when he collapsed and died on a Buenos Aires street on September 7, 1946.[15]

At war's end most non-Jewish anti-Fascists returned to Europe; most Jews, except those who moved on to the United States or Palestine, remained. The Perón regime's attitude toward Jews was equivocal, but the wartime refugees had little choice; Europe had to be put behind them, and there was every reason to consolidate the hard-won economic advances of the past decade in Argentina. Among non-Jewish refugees part of the reluctance to remain stemmed from repugnance at the increasingly fascist character of the Perón

311

regime; in part, also, their motives were economic and occupational. Argentina had had little room for intellectuals and members of the free professions; by the 1930s the native-born had begun to inflate these occupational strata—particularly in some specialties such as law and medicine. In so far as makers of immigration policy in the 1930s had been able to affect events, they excluded Jews from the professions; most of the latter had consequently gravitated to private business. There by dint of great enterprise many had prospered in the interstices of an export-dominated economy—in furs, garments, mass retailing, mass journalism. Their children would take advantage of Argentina's public education system in the 1940s, 1950s, and 1960s to enter technological careers, economics, and the natural and social sciences. They would also bear the brunt of revived anti-Semitism in the aftermath of the collapse of the second Perón government in 1976.

A final ironic note: even if Argentina made small use of the talents of the anti-Fascist refugees of the 1930s and 1940s, it *did* gain technical expertise of a sort from exiles of a more dubious character. In 1945 and 1946 the U.S. government insisted that Argentina expel the *Graf Spee* sailors, the crews of two U-boats that surrendered there, and hundreds of other Germans whom it considered "spies" or "undesirables." The Argentine government complied after a fashion: it met the quotas set by the Americans by rounding up Germans without friends or influence, while numbers of individuals deeply implicated in the secret war of 1939–45 were able to escape molestation. Many of those deported, of course, simply turned around after reaching Europe and picked up their Argentine lives as soon as possible. Simultaneously underway was the famous movement of war criminals and political irreconcilables *to* Argentina. Hans Ulrich Rudel, Kurt Tank, Adolf Galland, Johann von Leers, Otto Skorzeny, and many others gave technical assistance to the Argentine police and helped to build up the armaments and aerospace industry. In 1951 a refugee Austrian physicist claimed to have produced an atomic reaction using only materials available in Argentina; the Perón regime's crows of triumph turned soon to embarrassed silence when it became clear that the man and his work were frauds. In 1949 Enrique Prebisch of the University of Tucumán began openly to recruit German engineers and applied scientists with the support of the government in Buenos Aires.

But let us allow the shrieks of righteous indignation—such as those emitted periodically by the U.S. State Department—to die away. For

312

it must be pointed out that by this time the United States, the USSR, and to some extent Britain had scooped up all the luminaries of German weapons technology and research; France had filled out the battalions of the Foreign Legion with thousands of ex-SS men under new identities and was expending their blood generously in Indochina. What Argentina got were the opprobrium and the leavings.

Notes

1. Ronald W. Clark, *Einstein: The Life and Times* (New York, 1971), p. 403.

2. The most remarkable affair of this sort involved one Osmar Hellmuth, an Argentine-born German who in late 1943 undertook a clandestine mission to Germany to seek armaments for the military junta that had seized power in June of that year. Hellmuth's trip was arranged by the local *Abwehr/SD* representatives; it was betrayed to the British, almost certainly by a group within the German Embassy that included the big businessman Ludwig Freude. The Allies, by threatening to reveal the junta's complicity, forced a break in relations between Argentina and Germany in January 1944.

3. On the 1920s immigration, see Ronald C. Newton, *German Buenos Aires, 1900–1933: Social Change and Cultural Crisis* (Austin, 1977).

4. "Nazi-Umtriebe in Argentinien" (ca. 1937), pp. 43–100, in Wiener Library, London.

5. Interview, Buenos Aires, October 1968.

6. The German ambassador, Edmund Freiherr von Thermann, reported to Berlin in 1937 that the government was resistant to mass Jewish immigration, but for political reasons imposed administrative rather than legal hindrances. Thermann to Auswärtige Amt. May 3, 1937; Inland II A/B 83-76 Sdh 1, Politisches Archiv des Auswärtigen Amtes, Bonn.

7. Morton D. Winsburg, "Jewish Agricultural Colonization in Entre Rios, Argentina: Some Social and Economic Aspects of a Venture in Resettlement," *American Journal of Economics and Sociology* 27 (July 1968):285–95; 27 (October 1968):423–28; 28 (April 1969):179–91.

8. On Jewish refugee immigration generally, see Winifred Hunter, American clerk, Consulate Buenos Aires, Voluntary Report No. 188, April 16, 1938, "The Jewish Refugee and the Argentine Immigration Problem," Record Group 59 (1930–39), 840.48 Refugees/186, National Archives, Washington, D.C.; Robert Weisbrot, *The Jews of Argentina: From the Inquisition to Perón* (Philadelphia, 1979); Delegación de Asociaciones Israelitas Argentinas, *Diez años de obra constructiva en la América del Sur* (Buenos Aires, 1943) report of the Aid Committee of German-speaking Jews and other Jewish rescue organizations; comparative data in Bernard Wasserstein, *Britain and the Jews of Europe* (New York, 1979), p. 7. Wasserstein unaccountably ignores Argentina.

313

9. *Biog. Handbuch der Deutschsprachigen Emigranten nach 1933*, vol. 1 (New York, 1980), p. 122. See also Inland II A/B, 83–76 27/10:3, Ausbürgerungsliste, Pol. Archiv des Aus. Amtes, which included such names as Hans Beimler, Alfred Kantorowicz, Klaus Mann, Erwin Piscator, Gustav Regler, Otto Strasser, and a remarkable old anti-Fascist battler from Porto Alegre, Brazil, named Friedrich Kniestedt.

10. The Social Democratic Party Archive at the Friedrich Ebert Stiftung, Bad Godesberg, holds the correspondence between the SPD *Vorstand* in exile and socialists of the diaspora. The Alfred Rinner—Dang correspondence is a mine of information on the day-to-day life of refugees in Argentina, as are the letters to Franz Stampfer of Oda Lerda-Olberg. She was the black-sheep offspring of a naval family of Bremerhaven, and the widow of an Italian socialist. Although invalided she was still going strong as a journalist and activist at the age of seventy. *Das andere Deutschland* (Buenos Aires) 5, no. 54 (September 1942):19.

11. Winifred Seelisch, "Das Andere Deutschland: eine politische Vereinigung deutscher Emigranten in Südamerika," Diplomarbeit für das Otto Suhr Institut, Berlin, ca. 1969; files of *Das andere Deutschland*, 1937–48, in Hoover Institution, Stanford, Calif., and Library of Congress, Washington, D.C.; also biographical entries in *Biog. Handbuch der Deutschsprachigen Emigration nach 1933*, vol. 1.

12. U.S. Ambassador Norman Armour strongly endorsed DAD and its works in 1942. He was much impressed by Ernst Damereau, whom he credited with beginning the anti-Fascist movement in Buenos Aires in 1934, and with Ernst Alemann, publisher of the *Tageblatt*; and observed that DAD had more active members in Argentina (2,000) than the Nazi party had, despite the latter's resources for coercion. Armour to Secretary of State Cordell Hull, Jan. 2, 1942, no. 3780, Record Group 59, 862.20235/715, National Archives, Washington, D.C. The FBI's "legal attachés," however, were apparently more comfortable with the Black Front, whose members were more active in the manufacture and sale of anti-Fascist intelligence.

13. *Das andere Deutschland* 7, no. 89 (December 1944).

14. P. Walter Jacob, *Theater: Sieben Jahre Freie Deutsche Bühne in Buenos Aires* (Buenos Aires, 1946); Seelisch, "Das andere Deutschland," p. 46.

15. Arnold Spitta, *Paul Zech im südamerikanischen Exil, 1933–1946* (Berlin, 1978). A good general study of the period.

Appendix

THE MUSES FLEE HITLER: Cultural Transfer and Adaptation in the
United States, 1930–1945
Smithsonian Institution, February 7–9, 1980

PROGRAM

Thursday, February 7

Session 1

Introduction: S. Dillon Ripley, Secretary, Smithsonian Institution

BACKGROUND TO THE MIGRATION

Chairman: Charles Blitzer, Assistant Secretary for History and Art, Smithsonian Institution

"The Intellectual Decapitation of Germany under the Nazis"
    Alan Beyerchen, Associate Professor of History, Ohio State Uni-
    versity

"The Movement of Peoples in a Time of Crisis"
    Herbert A. Strauss, Professor of History, City College, City Uni-
    versity of New York

FREE PUBLIC FILM SHOWING of *Hans Richter: Artist and Filmmaker*   315

Session 2

THE GREAT FLIGHT OF CULTURE

Chairman: Daniel J. Boorstin, Librarian of Congress

"American Refugee Policy in Historical Perspective"
Roger Daniels, Chairman, Department of History, University of Cincinnati

"'Wanted by the GESTAPO, Saved by America': Varian Fry and the Emergency Rescue Committee"
Cynthia Jaffee McCabe, Curator for Exhibitions, Hirshhorn Museum and Sculpture Garden

"The Bauhaus and Its Further Development in America"
Wolf von Eckardt, Architecture Critic, *Washington Post*

Session 3

THE INTERACTION OF CULTURES: TRANSPLANTING THE ARTS, PART 1

Chairman: Joseph D. Duffey, Chairman, National Endowment for the Humanities

"European Writers in Exile"
Alfred Kazin, Critic, Distinguished Professor of English, City University of New York Graduate Center and Hunter College

"The Music World in Migration"
Boris Schwarz, Professor Emeritus of Music, Queens College, City University of New York

Friday, February 8

Session 4

THE INTERACTION OF CULTURES: ADAPTATION AND INFLUENCE

Chairman: Abram Lerner, Director, Hirshhorn Museum and Sculpture Garden

"The Linguistic Adaptation of the Refugees to the American Milieu"
Helmut F. Pfanner, Professor of German, Purdue University

"German Intellectuals in Southern California in the 1930s and 1940s"
  Jarrell C. Jackman, Historian, Santa Barbara Trust for Historic Preservation

"Social Theory in a New Context"
  H. Stuart Hughes, Professor of History, University of California, San Diego

Session 5

THE INTERACTION OF CULTURES: TRANSPLANTING THE ARTS, PART 2

Chairman: John Beardsley, Adjunct Curator, Corcoran Gallery of Art

"American Skyscrapers and Weimar Modern—Transactions between Fact and Idea"
  Christian F. Otto, Associate Professor of Architecture, Cornell University

"Hans Hofmann's Role in the Transmission of Modernist Aesthetics to America"
  Cynthia Goodman, Adjunct Curator, Fine Arts Museum of Long Island

"German Hollywood Presence and Parnassus: Central European Exiles and American Filmmaking"
  Hans-Bernhard Moeller, Professor of Literature and Film, University of Texas, Austin

AN EVENING OF MUSIC BY ÉMIGRÉ COMPOSERS
Performed by the 20th Century Consort

Saturday, February 9

Session 6

THE INTERACTION OF CULTURES: THE SCIENCES

Chairman: Robert Kargon, Willis K. Shepard Professor of the History of Science, Johns Hopkins University

"The American Environment for Immigrant Chemists"
  P. Thomas Carroll, Ph.D. candidate in the History of Science, University of Pennsylvania

317

"The Migration of Mathematics"
>Nathan Reingold, Editor, Joseph Henry Papers, Smithsonian Institution

"The Gestalt Psychologists in Behaviorist America"
>Michael M. Sokal, Associate Professor of History, Worcester Polytechnic Institute

Session 7

THE MUSES FLEE HITLER: SOME UNANSWERED QUESTIONS
(Panel Discussion)

Chairman: Gerald Holton, Mallinckrodt Professor of Physics and Professor of the History of Science, Harvard University
>Preliminary remarks on Einstein and his epoch.

Panelists: Fritz K. Ringer, Professor of History, Boston University
>Susan Jacoby, Writer

THE MUSES FLEE HITLER II: Cultural Adaptation in Worldwide Perspective
Smithsonian Institution, December 27–28, 1980

PROGRAM

Saturday, December 27

Session 1

WESTERN EUROPE

Chairman: Mack Walker, Professor and Chairman, Department of History, Johns Hopkins University

"Intellectual Émigrés in Britain, 1933–1939"
>Bernard Wasserstein, Associate Professor of History and Director, The Tauber Institute, Brandeis University

"The Emergency Rescue Committee: Alternate Routes of Escape"
>Cynthia Jaffee McCabe, Curator for Exhibitions, Hirshhorn Museum and Sculpture Garden

"The Role of Switzerland for German-Language Refugees"
>Helmut F. Pfanner, Professor of German, Purdue University

319

"A Turkish Winter: The Experience of Refugees from Nazi Germany in Turkey"
Mark A. Epstein, Research Associate, Institute for Near East History, University of Munich

"Shanghai Chronicle: Nazi Refugees in China"
Renata Berg-Pan, Associate, Department of Media Studies, New School for Social Research

Session 5

LATIN AMERICA

Chairman: Eugene Sofer, U.S. House of Representatives Staff

"European Immigration to Brazil in the 1930s: Obstacles to Assimilation"
Robert M. Levine, Professor of History, State University of New York at Stony Brook

"The Reception of the Muses in the Circum-Caribbean"
Judith Laikin Elkin, Great Lakes Colleges Association

"Das andere Deutschland: The Anti-Fascist Exile Network in Southern South America"
Ronald C. Newton, Associate Professor of History, Simon Fraser University

"The Two Destinies of Stefan Zweig and Georges Bernanos in Brazil during World War II"
Jean-Jacques Lafaye, Editor, *L'Attitude*

Select Bibliography

Abella, Irving, and Troper, Harold. *None Is Too Many: Canada and the Jews of Europe, 1933–1948.* Toronto, 1982.

Arendt, Hannah. *The Origins of Totalitarianism.* New York, 1951.

Bentwich, Norman. *The Rescue and Achievement of Refugee Scholars: The Story of Displaced Scholars, 1933–1952.* The Hague, 1953.

Boyers, Robert. *The Legacy of the German Refugee Intellectuals.* New York, 1972.

Bracher, Karl Dietrich. *The German Dictatorship: The Origins, Structure and Effects of National Socialism.* Translated by Jean Steinberg. New York and Washington, D.C., 1970.

Cazden, Robert E. *German Exile Literature in America, 1933–1955: A History of the German Press and Book Trade.* Chicago, 1970.

Clark, Ronald W. *Einstein: The Life and Times.* New York, 1971.

Davie, Maurice R. *Refugees in America. Report of the Committee for the Study of Recent Immigration from Europe.* New York, 1947.

Dittrich, Kathinka, and Würzner, Hans, eds. *Die Niederlande und das deutsche Exil, 1933–1940.* Königstein, West Germany, 1982.

Duberman, Martin B. *Black Mountain: An Exploration in Community.* New York, 1972.

Fermi, Laura. *Illustrious Immigrants: The Intellectual Migration from Europe, 1930–1941.* Chicago, 1968; 2d ed., 1971.

Fleming, Donald, and Bailyn, Bernard, eds. *The Intellectual Migration: Europe and America, 1930–1960.* Cambridge, Mass., 1969.

Friedman, Saul S. *No Haven for the Oppressed: United States Policy toward Jewish Refugees, 1938–1945.* Detroit, 1973.

Fry, Varian. *Surrender on Demand.* New York, 1945. Abr., rev. ed.: *Assignment Rescue.* New York, 1968.

Gay, Peter. *Weimar Culture: The Outsider as Insider.* New York and Evanston, 1968.

Gold, Mary Jayne. *Crossroads Marseilles, 1940.* Garden City, N.Y., 1980.

Grossmann, Kurt R. *Emigration: Geschichte der Hitler–Flüchtlinge 1933–1945.* Frankfurt am Main, 1969.

Häsler, Alfred A. *The Lifeboat Is Full: Switzerland and the Refugees 1933–1945.* New York, 1969.

Hughes, H. Stuart. *The Sea Change: The Migration of Social Thought 1930–1963.* New York, 1975.

Johnson, Philip C. *Mies van der Rohe.* 3rd rev. ed. New York, 1978.

Kranzler, David. *Japanese, Nazis and Jews: The Jewish Refugee Community of Shanghai, 1938–1945.* New York, 1976.

Krispyn, Egbert. *Anti-Nazi Writers in Exile.* Athens, Ga., 1978.

Laqueur, Walter. *Weimar: A Cultural History, 1918–1933.* New York, 1976.

McCabe, Cynthia Jaffee. *The Golden Door: Artist-Immigrants of America, 1876–1976.* Washington, D.C., 1976.

Mann, Erika and Klaus. *Escape to Life.* Boston, 1939.

Mann, Golo. *The History of Germany since 1789.* Translated by Marion Jackson. New York, 1968.

Mann, Klaus. *The Turning Point: Thirty-five Years in This Century.* New York, 1942.

Mann, Thomas. *Doctor Faustus.* Translated by H. T. Lowe-Porter. New York, 1948.

———. *The Story of a Novel: The Genesis of Doctor Faustus.* Translated by Richard and Clara Winston. New York, 1961.

Marcuse, Ludwig. *Mein zwanzigstes Jahrhundert: Auf dem Weg zu einer Autobiographie.* Munich, 1960.

Mosse, George. *The Crisis of German Ideology: Intellectual Origins of the Third Reich.* New York, 1964.

Nabokov, Vladimir. *Pnin.* New York, 1953.

Neumann, Franz, et al. *The Cultural Migration: The European Scholar in America.* Philadelphia, 1953.

Neumark, Fritz. *Zuflucht am Bosporus: Deutsche Gelehrte, Politiker, und Künstler in der Emigration 1933–1953.* Frankfurt am Main, 1973.

Paris-Paris 1937–1957. Paris, 1981.

Pfanner, Helmut F. *Exile in New York: German and Austrian Émigré Writing, 1933–1945.* Detroit, 1983.

Pike, David. *German Writers in Soviet Exile, 1933–1945.* Chapel Hill, N.C., 1982.

Pross, Helge. *Die deutsche akademische Emigration nach den Vereinigten Staaten.* Berlin, 1955.

Ramati, Alexander. *Barbed Wire on the Isle of Man: The British Internment of Jews.* New York, 1980.

Remarque, Erich Maria. *Shadows in Paradise.* New York, 1972.

Ringer, Fritz K. *The Decline of the German Mandarins: The German Academic Community, 1890–1933.* Cambridge, Mass., 1969.

Roeder, Werner, and Strauss, Herbert A. *International Biographical Dictionary of Central-European Émigrés, 1933–1945.* Vol. 1: *Politik, Wirtschaft, Gesellschaft.* New York, 1980. Vol. 2: *The Sciences and the Arts.* New York, 1982.

Rubin, William S. *Dada and Surrealism.* New York, 1968.

Sherman, A. J. *Island Refuge: Britain and Refugees from the Third Reich, 1933–1939.* Berkeley and Los Angeles, 1973.

Spalek, John M. *Guide to the Archival Materials of the German-speaking Emigration to the United States after 1933.* In collaboration with Adrienne Ash and Sandra H. Hawrylchak. Charlottesville, Va., 1978.

Spalek, John M., and Strelke, Joseph, eds. *Deutsche Exilliteratur seit 1933.* Part 2. Vol. 1: *Kalifornien.* Bern, 1976.

Stern, Fritz. *The Politics of Cultural Despair: A Study in the Rise of the Germanic Ideology.* Berkeley and Los Angeles, 1961.

Strauss, Herbert A., ed. *Jewish Immigrants of the Nazi Period in the U.S.A.* New York, 1978.

Tabori, Paul. *The Anatomy of Exile: A Semantic and Historical Study.* London, 1972.

Thomas, Gordon. *Voyage of the Damned.* New York, 1974.

Wasserstein, Bernard. *Britain and the Jews of Europe, 1939–1945.* Oxford, 1979.

Widmann, Horst. *Exil und Bildungshilfe: Die deutschsprachige Akademische Emigration in die Turkei nach 1933.* Frankfurt am Main, 1973.

Wingler, Hans. *Bauhaus: Weimar, Dessau, Berlin, Chicago.* Cambridge, Mass., 1969.

Wolfe, Tom. *From Bauhaus to Our House.* New York, 1981.

Wyman, David S. *Paper Walls: America and the Refugee Crisis, 1938–1941.* Amherst, Mass., 1968.

Zuckmayer, Carl. *A Part of Myself.* Translated by Richard and Clara Winston. New York, 1970.

Notes on Contributors

IRVING ABELLA is professor of history at Glendon College, York University, Toronto. He is the author and editor of various publications including *Nationalism, Communism and Canadian Labour* (1973), *On Strike* (1974), and *The Canadian Worker in the Twentieth Century* (1978). He is also the co-author of *None Is Too Many: Canada and the Jews of Europe, 1933–1948* (1982).

RENATA BERG-PAN studied English and comparative literature at the University of Washington and earned a doctorate at Harvard University in 1971. As a member of the teaching staffs at the Massachusetts Institute of Technology, Harvard University, Queens College of the City University of New York, and Indiana University, she has lectured on a variety of subjects, including film theory, history, literature, philosophy, English, German, and French. Her most recent publications are *Bertolt Brecht and China* (1979) and *Leni Riefenstahl* (1980).

ALAN BEYERCHEN attended the University of California, Santa Barbara, where he received his B.A. in German (1967) and M.A. (1968) and Ph.D. (1973) in European history and history of science. He has authored *Scientists under Hitler: Politics and the Physics Community in the Third Reich* (1977) and is associate professor of history at Ohio State University.

CARLA M. BORDEN studied at Barnard College (B.A. 1970) and Columbia University (M.A. 1974), where she concentrated in comparative sociology. She also has a considerable interest in folklife and ethnicity and has done research in those fields in the United States and in Eastern Europe. At the Smithsonian since 1973, she is associate director of the Office of Smithsonian Symposia and Seminars, coordinating a variety of interdisciplinary education programs.

P. THOMAS CARROLL is a doctoral candidate in the Department of History and Sociology of Science, University of Pennsylvania, and assistant professor of history, Rensselaer Polytechnic Institute. Between 1973 and 1975 he was a Mellon Fellow at the American Philosophical Society Library, where he edited a guide to the library's collection of Darwin letters. With Robert F. Bud, Jeffrey L. Sturchio, and Arnold Thackray, he is preparing an extensive quantitative analysis of American chemistry since 1876.

ROGER DANIELS, professor of history, University of Cincinnati, is a specialist in modern United States history. His books include *The Politics of Prejudice* (1962; rev. ed., 1978), *The Bonus March* (1970), *The Decision to Relocate the Japanese Americans* (1975), and *Concentration Camps, North America* (1981). He is currently finishing a volume comparing the history of Chinese Americans and Japanese Americans.

PAULA JEAN DRAPER holds an M.A. in history from the University of Toronto and is currently completing her Ph.D. at the Ontario Institute for Studies in Education. Her dissertation deals with the German and Austrian Jewish refugees interned in Canada and their treatment by the Canadian Jewish community and the Federal Government of Canada. She has published articles on this subject in the *Canadian Jewish Historical Society Journal* (1978).

JUDITH LAIKIN ELKIN is author of *Jews of the Latin American Republics* and acts as president of the Latin American Jewish Studies Association. A former U.S. Foreign Service Officer, she has taught Latin American history at Wayne State University and Albion College; she is presently assistant to the president, Great Lakes Colleges Association.

GERALD HOLTON is Mallinckrodt Professor of Physics and professor of history of science at Harvard University and, concurrently, visiting professor at the Massachusetts Institute of Technology. Among his books are *The Scientific Imagination: Case Studies* and *Thematic Origins of Scientific Thought: Kepler to Einstein*.

H. STUART HUGHES taught at Stanford University and Harvard University before becoming professor of history at the University of California, San Diego, in 1975. He is the author of nine books, including a trilogy on European intellectual history in the twentieth century—*Consciousness and Society, The Obstructed Path*, and *The Sea Change*, the last of which deals with the emigration from central Europe.

JARRELL C. JACKMAN majored in German at the University of California, Los Angeles, and holds an M.A. in American studies from California State

University, Los Angeles, and a Ph.D. in history from the University of California, Santa Barbara. His dissertation, a chapter of which has been published by the *Southern California Quarterly*, was on German émigrés in southern California. He spent four years in Germany, one on a German Academic Exchange fellowship and three as a lecturer in history for the University of Maryland. At present, he is projects administrator for the Santa Barbara Trust for Historic Preservation.

ALFRED KAZIN, educated at the College of the City of New York and Columbia University, is distinguished professor of English at the City University of New York Graduate Center and Hunter College. His books include *On Native Grounds* (1942), *A Walker in the City* (1951), *The Inmost Leaf* (1955), *Contemporaries* (1962), *Starting Out in the Thirties* (1965), *Bright Book of Life* (1973), and *New York Jew* (1978). He is now working on *The Gathering of the Forces*, a historical and critical study of nineteenth-century American writers.

CYNTHIA JAFFEE McCABE is curator for exhibitions of the Hirshhorn Museum and Sculpture Garden. She studied at Cornell University (B.A. 1963) and Columbia University (M.A. 1967). She is the author of *The Golden Door: Artist-Immigrants of America, 1876–1976*, the publication accompanying the Hirshhorn's Bicentennial exhibition. She has served as assistant professorial lecturer at George Washington University and as adjunct assistant professor at the University of Maryland, College Park. In 1982 she received the John J. McCloy Fellowship from the Metropolitan Museum of Art for further research on the Emergency Rescue Committee, and she is currently planning a major exhibition on the subject.

RONALD C. NEWTON is professor of Latin American history, Simon Fraser University, Burnaby, British Columbia. His principal research interest is European ethnic minorities in the Americas. He is the author of *German Buenos Aires, 1900–1930* (1977) and is completing a book on Great Power rivalry in Argentina and the secret war there between 1933 and 1945.

CHRISTIAN F. OTTO is an associate professor at Cornell University. A member of the Department of Architecture, he is also head of the graduate field of History of Architecture and Urban Development. His research interests focus on Europe in the eighteenth and twentieth centuries. In the last years, he has published *Space into Light: The Churches of Balthasar Neumann* and several shorter pieces of criticism and biography; he has recently completed a major study on the architectural and urban history of the Modern Movement in the Weimar Republic. From 1975 to 1981, he served as editor of the *Journal of the Society of Architectural Historians*.

HELMUT F. PFANNER was born in Austria in 1933, where he started his career as a public school teacher. In 1957 he came to the United States to study at the University of Kansas. After receiving his Ph.D. at Stanford University, he taught at the Universities of Washington and Virginia and at Purdue University. He is presently at the University of New Hampshire. Publications include books on Hanns Johst, Oskar Maria Graf, and the German and Austrian exile in New York.

NATHAN REINGOLD has been editor of the Joseph Henry Papers at the Smithsonian since 1966. Author of *Science in Nineteenth Century America: A Documentary History* (1964), he prepared a twentieth-century sequel (with Ida H. Reingold), *Science in America: A Documentary History, 1900–1939* (1981). He received his B.A. (1947) and M.A. (1948) from New York University and a Ph.D. in American civilization from the University of Pennsylvania (1951). Currently, he is on the Governing Council of the Rockefeller Archives Center (serving as a member of its Executive Committee on Grants and on Access) and on the Planning Committee for the American Academy of Arts and Sciences's program on knowledge in American society.

BORIS SCHWARZ, born in St. Petersburg, Russia, in 1906, moved as a child to Berlin, where he studied the violin and made his debut as a concert violinist at age fourteen. In 1936 he settled in the United States. He was concertmaster of the Indianapolis Symphony and first violinist with the Toscanini-NBC Orchestra. In 1941 he was appointed to the faculty of Queens College, City University of New York, and was named professor emeritus in 1976. He received his Ph.D. in musicology from Columbia University in 1950. In 1972 he published *Music and Musical Life in Soviet Russia*, and another book, *The Great Violinists*, is in press.

HERBERT A. STRAUSS was graduated from the Oberschule der Jüdischen Gemeinde in Berlin in 1942, after having been excluded by racial law from his home-town *gymnasium*. From 1940 to 1942, he was auxiliary rabbi of the Berlin Jewish Community. He then spent nearly a year in hiding in Berlin before enrolling in the University of Bern, where he received a Ph.D. (1946). He immigrated to the United States in 1946. He is a professor in the Department of History, City College, City University of New York; secretary of the Research Foundation for Jewish Immigration, New York; and director, Zentrum für Antisemitismusforschung, Technische Universität Berlin. His publications include works on the Jewish emigration during the Nazi period.

HAROLD TROPER is associate professor of history, Ontario Institute for Studies in Education, University of Toronto. He has written widely on immigration and ethnicity; his books include *Immigrants: A Portrait of the Urban Experience, Issues in Cultural Diversity*, and the recently completed *None Is Too Many: Canada and the Jews of Europe, 1933–1948* with Irving Abella.

BERNARD WASSERSTEIN was born in London and educated at Balliol and Nuffield colleges, Oxford, and at the Hebrew University of Jerusalem. He is the author of *The British in Palestine* and *Britain and the Jews of Europe, 1939–1945*. He is currently director of the Tauber Institute at Brandeis University.

Index

337

London University, 251
Long, Breckinridge, 80
Long Island University, 146
Loomis, F. Wheeler, 175
Lorant, Stefan, 255
Lorentz, Hendrik A., 175, 180
Los Angeles, Calif., 19, 25, 98, 99, 107, 140, 141, 144, 156. *See also* California, southern; Hollywood, Calif.
Lost in the Stars (Kurt Weill and Maxwell Anderson), 148
Lost Weekend (film), 102
Lowinsky, Edward, 148
Ludwig, Carl, 235
Ludwig, Emil, 245
Lustig, Bernard, 199
Luxembourg, 310
Lyman, Theodore, 172

M
McCabe, Cynthia Jaffee, 15, 18
McCarran, Pat, 72
McGill University, 272, 276, 277, 280
McGraw-Hill Building (New York, N.Y.), 159
Mächler, Martin, 154
McKinley, William, 63
MacLane, Saunders, 221
McLuhan, Marshall, 257
Madrid, Spain, 86
Maeterlinck, Maurice, 123
Mahler, Gustav, 139
Maillol, Aristide, 89
Malaquais, Jean, 90
Malkin, Joseph, 140
Mallowan, Sigfried, 296
Manchester Guardian, 252
Manchuria, China, 283
Mann, Erika, 105, 244
Mann, Golo, 82, 84, 85, 242
Mann, Heinrich, 31, 36, 82, 84, 85–86, 96, 243
Mann, Klaus, 105, 236, 314n.9
Mann, Nelly, 84, 85
Mann, Thomas, 20, 31, 81, 82, 85, 86, 102–3, 108, 123, 124, 126, 127–31, 132, 241, 242
Mann ohne Eigenschaften, Der (Robert Musil), 243
Marchwitza, Hans, 242
Marcu, Valerie, 82
Marcuse, Erich, 287

Marcuse, Herbert, 26, 116, 117, 123, 126
Marcuse, Ludwig, 19
Maritain, Jacques, 123, 124
Marseilles, France, 18, 79, 82, 83, 84, 87, 89, 90
Martinů, Bohuslav, 140
Marx, Julius, 242
Marx, Karl, 31, 112, 116, 118, 126, 131
Massachusetts Institute of Technology, 173, 178, 193, 211, 221, 224
Massey, Vincent, 265, 266
Mass und Wert (Thomas Mann and Konrad Falke), 242
Mason, Max, 206
Masson, André, 79, 87, 88
Mathematical Association of America (MAA), 208, 218, 227n.12
Mathematical Reviews, 217, 225
Matisse, Henri, 79, 89
Matisse, Pierre, Gallery (New York, N.Y.), 79
Maugham, W. Somerset, 86
Maurer, Julius, 172
Maurois, André, 123
Mayer, Hans, 245
Mees, C.E. Kenneth, 193
Meffert-Moreau, Carl, 245
Mehring, Walter, 81, 83, 84, 245
Memoirs of a Revolutionary (Victor Serge), 82
Mencken, H.L., 257
Mengelberg, Willem, 139
Menger, Karl, 222
Menuhin, Yehudi, 143
Merck and Company, Inc., 199
Merry Widow, The (Franz Lehar), 287
Mertz, Carlos, 296
Metro-Goldwyn-Mayer Studios, 141
Metropolis of Tomorrow (Hugh Ferriss), 160
Metropolitan Opera (New York, N.Y.), 139, 146, 147
Mexico, 24, 259, 293–94, 296, 298
Mexico City, Mexico, 294, 309
Meyer, Karl, 197
Meyer, Michael A., 67
Meyerhof, Otto, 196, 199
Miami, Fla., 156
Michaelis, Leonor, 195
Michelson, Albert, 172, 181
Michigan State University, 296
Midsummer Night's Dream, A (William Shakespeare), 105

339

Mies van der Rohe, Ludwig, 21, 151, 152–56, 162–63
Migration and Refugee Assistance Act, 73
Mihaly, Jo, 243
Milhaud, Darius, 140, 143, 144–45
Millikan, R.A., 171, 172, 179–83 passim
Mills College, 144, 145
Milne, E.A., 175
Mimesis (Erich Auerbach), 124
Minneapolis, Minn., 139, 156
Miracle of German Economics, The (Hans Priester), 277
MIT. See Massachusetts Institute of Technology
Mitropoulos, Dimitri, 139
Modern Architecture: Romanticism and Reintegration (Henry-Russell Hitchcock), 159
Modern Building (Walter Curt Behrendt), 159
Modern Movement (in architecture), 158, 159, 160
Modigliani, Amedeo, 89
Modigliani, Giuseppe, 89
Moeller, Hans-Bernhard, 20
Moeller van den Bruck, Arthur, 33
Moholy-Nagy, László, 21, 151
Möhring, Bruno, 154
Moldenhauer, Hans, 149
Moley, Raymond, 67
Mommsen, Theodore, 134
Mondale, Walter, 61
Montesquieu, 132
Monteux, Pierre, 139
Montevideo, Uruguay, 309
Morgenstern, Julian, 68
Morse, Arthur, 61
Morse, Marston, 212
Moser, Karl, 159
Moses and Monotheism (Sigmund Freud), 125
Moscow, Soviet Union, 244
Mosse, George, 33
Mount Wilson Observatory (California), 172, 180
Movement for the Care of Children from Germany, 273
Muck, Karl, 139
Mueller, Hans, 176
Mühsam, Erich, 123
Müller, Adam, 31
Mumford, Lewis, 160

Munich Agreement, 265
Murrow, Edward R., 206
Museum of Modern Art (New York, N.Y.), 81, 158, 162
Musik im Dritten Reich (Joseph Wulf), 136
Musil, Robert, 123, 243
Mussolini, Benito, 139, 265
Mutter Courage (Bertolt Brecht), 244
"My First Impression of the U.S.A." (Albert Einstein), 173–74

N
Nabokov, Vladimir, 123, 124, 125, 127, 130
Nachmansohn, David, 196
Namier, Lewis, 251
Namuth, Hans, 84
Napoleon, 33, 36
Nash, Ogden, 148
Nathan, Hans, 149
National Endowment for the Humanities (Washington, D.C.), 53
National Gallery (London), 254
National Gallery of Canada (Ottawa), 279
National Research Council (Washington, D.C.), 175, 176, 177; Fellowships, 177, 180
National Socialists. See Nazis and Nazism
National University of Buenos Aires, 303
Natonek, Hans, 82, 83
Nazi Germany. See Nazis and Nazism, Third Reich
Nazis and Nazism, 9, 17, 18, 19, 29, 36, 38–41, 46, 47, 49, 70, 82, 89, 125, 126, 136, 142, 182, 183, 196, 200, 201, 205, 206, 213, 216, 217, 223, 235–39 passim, 242, 244, 255, 261, 273, 293, 297, 304, 305, 310; anti-intellectualism of, 16; anti-Semitism of, 34, 36, 48; depicted in films, 105–6; racial attitudes of, 16, 219
NBC Orchestra, 136
Nef, John Ulric, 194
Neilson, William A., 80
Netherlands, The, 30, 50, 51, 56, 69, 237, 310
Nettl, Paul, 148
Neuberg, Carl, 196

A Note on the Typefaces Used in This Book

The text of this book, as well as the chapter headings, is set in Trump Medieval, designed in Germany by Georg Trump and issued nine years after the end of the Nazi period by the Weber Type Foundry.

The main title, set in Albertus Bold, is the work of Berthold Wolpe. It is of interest to observe that Wolpe left Germany at the advent of the Nazi regime, taking up residence in England, where to this day he continues a distinguished career in the printing arts. He is thus both a contributor to and a legitimate subject of this book.